Chicken Soup for the Soul®

THE WISDOM OF DADS

Our
101
BEST
STORIES

Chicken Soup for the Soul® Our 101 Best Stories:
The Wisdom of Dads; Loving Stories about Fathers and Being a Father
by Jack Canfield, Mark Victor Hansen & Amy Newmark

Published by Chicken Soup for the Soul Publishing, LLC   www.chickensoup.com

Cover photo courtesy of Corbis, © Peter Beck. Interior photos courtesy of Photos.com

Cover and Interior Design & Layout by Pneuma Books, LLC
For more info on Pneuma Books, visit www.pneumabooks.com

Distributed to the booktrade by Simon & Schuster. SAN: 200-2442

Publisher's Cataloging-in-Publication Data
(Prepared by The Donohue Group)

Chicken soup for the soul. Selections.
   Chicken soup for the soul : the wisdom of dads : loving stories about fathers and
being a father / [compiled by] Jack Canfield [and] Mark Victor Hansen ;
[edited by] Amy Newmark.

   p. ; cm. -- (Our 101 best stories)

ISBN-13: 978-1-935096-18-4
ISBN-10: 1-935096-18-4

1. Fathers--Literary collections. 2. Fatherhood--Literary collections. 3. Fathers--
Conduct of life--Anecdotes. 4. Father and child--Literary collections. I. Canfield, Jack,
1944- II. Hansen, Mark Victor. III. Newmark, Amy. IV. Title.

PN6071.F3 C485 2008
810.8/03520431   2008932010

PRINTED IN THE UNITED STATES OF AMERICA
on acid∞free paper
16 15 14 13 12 11 10 09   03 04 05 06 07 08

Chicken Soup for the Soul®
for the Soul

Our
101
BEST
STORIES

THE WISDOM OF DADS

Loving Stories
about Fathers
and Being a Father

Jack Canfield
Mark Victor Hansen
Amy Newmark

CSS

Chicken Soup for the Soul Publishing, LLC
Cos Cob, CT

Chicken Soup for the Soul

Contents

❶
~The Power of a Father's Love~

❷
~Supportive Dads~

❸
~Taking Dad's Advice~

❹
~Single Fatherhood~

❺
~Treasured Moments~

❻
~Learning from the Kids~

❼
~Father Knows Best~

❽
~The Lighter Side~

❾
~Fun and Games~

❿

~Gifts and Gratitude~

Chicken Soup for the Soul

A Special Foreword

by Jack and Mark

For us, 101 has always been a magical number. It was the number of stories in the first *Chicken Soup for the Soul* book, and it is the number of stories and poems we have always aimed for in our books. We love the number 101 because it signifies a beginning, not an end. After 100, we start anew with 101.

We hope that when you finish reading one of our books, it is only a beginning for you too -- a new outlook on life, a renewed sense of purpose, a strengthened resolve to deal with an issue that has been bothering you. Perhaps you will pick up the phone and share one of the stories with a friend or a loved one. Perhaps you will turn to your keyboard and express yourself by writing a Chicken Soup story of your own, to share with other readers who are just like you.

This volume contains our 101 best stories and poems about fathers and their wisdom. We share this with you at a very special time for us, the fifteenth anniversary of our *Chicken Soup for the Soul* series. When we published our first book in 1993, we never dreamed that we had started what became a publishing phenomenon, one of the best-selling series of books in history.

We did not set out to sell more than one hundred million books, or to publish more than 150 titles. We set out to touch the heart of one person at a time, hoping that person would in turn touch another person, and so on down the line. Fifteen years later, we know that it has worked. Your letters and stories have poured in by the hundreds of thousands, affirming our life's work, and inspiring us to continue to make a difference in your lives.

On our fifteenth anniversary, we have new energy, new resolve, and new dreams. We have recommitted to our goal of 101 stories or poems per book, we have refreshed our cover designs and our interior layouts, and we have grown the Chicken Soup for the Soul team, with new friends and partners across the country in New England.

In this new volume, we have selected our 101 best stories and poems about fathers and their wisdom from our rich fifteen-year history. The stories that we have chosen were written by fathers and by their children. Some of them made us laugh, some made us cry. They all made us appreciate the special bond between fathers and children and the special reverence that children hold for their wise old dads.

We hope that you will enjoy reading these stories as much as we enjoyed selecting them for you, and that you will share them with your families and friends. We have identified the 35 *Chicken Soup for the Soul* books in which the stories originally appeared, in case you would like to continue reading about parenting and families among our other titles. We hope you will also enjoy the additional titles about parenting, sports, and life in general in "Our 101 Best Stories" series.

With our love, our thanks, and our respect,
~*Jack Canfield and Mark Victor Hansen*

THE WISDOM OF DADS

The Power of a Father's Love

The best thing to hold onto is each other.
~Anonymous

LEARNING TO LOVE

*Often the deepest relationships can be developed during
the simplest activities.*
~Gary Smalley

Trissa came up to me a few minutes before math class. "Hey,
Richie, you know about cars," she said. "Mine's making a
funny noise. Could you take a look at it?"

"Sure," I said, and then another girl named Arielle spoke up.

"Can I come watch?" she asked. "I want to learn how to fix cars,
too."

A year ago I didn't even know what a distributor cap was. But
nowadays my friends come to me with their car problems. They
think I'm some kind of expert, but my new dad, Roger—he's the real
expert. He taught me everything I know about engines and transmissions. But Roger also taught me more important stuff—about life
and love, and what it truly means to become a man.

My real dad left when I was just a baby, and for fifteen years
it was just my mom and me. When the other guys played football
with their dads, I could only watch. And it was a little embarrassing
going on fishing trips when my mom was the only woman there. But
I convinced myself it didn't really matter. After all, how could I miss
having a dad when I'd never had a dad to lose?

I was happy when we moved from Brooklyn to Nyack, New
York, where my mom works for Sears. There was a lot more room
to ride bikes and play ball, and at school there were coaches who

taught me how to swing a bat and catch a pass—you know, the sort of things your dad's supposed to teach you.

I made a lot of new friends in Nyack, and my mom even started dating. Some of the guys were okay; others I thought were total jerks. But the night Mom and I met Roger at a New Year's Eve party, I didn't know what to think.

Roger was six feet, three inches tall and 250 pounds, with long hair and a beard. He was loud and a little hard of hearing, and his forearms were as big around as my thighs.

"Nice to meet you," Roger boomed when somebody introduced us. When he shook my hand, it disappeared inside his huge paw, callused and scarred from years of construction work and working in the boiler room of a Navy ship during the Vietnam War.

I thought Roger was one scary dude, but on the drive home when we talked about him, Mom got sort of dreamy. "He's actually very gentle," she said, and told me how sensitive Roger had seemed when he talked about his two sons who had drowned seventeen years before in a canoeing accident.

I still thought Roger was a little freaky, but a few nights later when he called I tried not to make a face as I handed Mom the phone. They talked for hours, and a few nights after that Roger took Mom to dinner. I didn't know whether to feel happy for her or worried she'd maybe flipped her lid.

Then one night Roger was sitting in our living room waiting for Mom to get ready while I was talking to my grandparents on the phone. I told my grandma I loved her when I finished talking to her, but to my grandfather I just said goodbye.

Hanging up, I was surprised when Roger cleared his throat to speak—and even more surprised by what he said. "I know why you didn't tell your grandfather you love him," he began. "It's because he's a guy, and you were embarrassed to tell him how you feel."

Roger talked some about his sons who had drowned. "Not a day passes when I don't wish I'd said 'I love you' to them even more than I did. 'I love you' isn't just something you say to women," he said. Now

I was really confused because here was this giant tough guy with tears rolling down his cheeks.

I still remember the first time Mom and I visited Roger's house. The place overflowed with old newspapers and magazines, and everywhere you turned there were broken toasters and televisions Roger had always meant to fix. Then we went out to the garage—and wow!

Ever since I was little I've loved taking things apart to see how they work. Radios, my Ghostbusters game—I could take them apart fine, but there were always parts left over when I tried to put them back together. And the only tools I ever had were the screwdrivers and pliers from the kitchen drawer.

But Roger's garage was one big workshop full of tools I'd never even seen before.

For the next hour, Roger showed me reciprocating saws, ratchets and about a thousand other tools. "Maybe one day we can work on a project together," he said, and I forced myself not to smile because what if he never did? What if Roger was just pretending to like me to impress my mom?

I guess you could say Roger swept my mom off her feet, because it wasn't long before we were packing our things to move into his house. Roger and I spent days hauling junk to the dump in his pickup. We also refinished the floors.

A few weeks later, Roger taught me how to work a stick shift driving back and forth in the driveway. Then we went to the Department of Motor Vehicles to get my learner's permit.

Another day Roger brought home an old Ford Escort that barely ran. "We'll fix her up together, and then you'll have something to drive," he said. This time I didn't even try to hide my smile.

When we discovered the Escort's transmission was shot, Roger bought a used transmission from the junkyard, and we jacked up the car and swapped it out with the old one. It was hard work, especially for a tall, skinny kid like me. But one night Mom gripped my forearm and smiled. "You're putting on muscle," she said.

"I know," I said proudly, and I owed it all to Roger.

Even after we got it running, Roger and I spent hours tinkering with my car, and we did a lot of talking while we worked. Roger told me about when he was my age and he and his dog Silus used to sit beside the tracks for hours watching the trains roll by, and how he'd worked at a gas station for free just so he could learn to fix cars.

Roger also talked about some of the many kids he'd taken into his home over the years—abused kids, kids strung out on drugs, even a few who had spent time in jail. Roger helped these guys through some pretty tough times, and many of them have grown up to become successful businessmen, policemen and firemen. They still come by with their wives and families to thank him.

These days our house is full of tiny parts from a piano Roger and I are rebuilding because we both want to know what makes it work. We also love going for long drives through the country, stopping at farms to check out the animals while we talk about life. Sometimes we talk about girls and sex and stuff like that, but after hearing stories about the kids Roger helped, he didn't have to warn me about abusing drugs and alcohol. I don't want to screw up my life or wind up in prison. I want to grow up to be hard-working, honest and caring—just like Roger.

Besides my mom, Roger is the only person I know who will always be there for me, no matter what. Thanks to Roger I've grown tougher on the outside, but inside I know it's okay to care about people and tell them so.

Last Father's Day, I wrote Roger a letter telling him how much he'd changed my life. "I never had a dad until I was a teenager, but now I have the greatest dad in the world," I wrote. "You've taken me places I never would have gone, both out in the world and inside myself, and your 'I love yous' are the most reassuring and wonderful words I've ever heard in my life."

~Bernard "Richie" Thomassen as told to Heather Black
Chicken Soup for the Christian Teenage Soul

PRAY FOR KYLE

We are made to persist. That is how we find out who we are.
~Tobias Wolff

I remember sitting in the middle of my hometown baseball diamond one hot summer day when I was a kid, head between my knees, glove over my head and tears of frustration at my inability to hit a curveball streaming down my dirty cheeks.

Nothing anyone could have said right then could possibly have suppressed my anger. I didn't care if Dale Murphy himself appeared to tell me that he couldn't hit a curveball when he was a kid. I was furious, and there was no changing it.

Then I smelled my dad's cologne.

He crouched down beside me, snow cone in one hand, glove in the other, and sat on second base. He assured me my lack of prowess at hitting the "old number 2" hadn't marked the demise of my young career, and that we'd work on it until I ripped every last one of them.

We spent hours working on it, so much that my old man is probably incapable of throwing a baseball anymore. But you know what? I learned how to knock the crap out of a curveball that day, and seeing him beam with pride every time I did so made it obvious to me that a mutilated rotator cuff was totally worth it to him.

That's a lot like Kyle Petty. Most of his NASCAR Winston Cup dreams having already been fulfilled, he sacrificed any remaining glory to help his son achieve his high-speed hopes and dreams.

Kyle tossed his own career aside to assure that Adam's would prosper. He was perfectly content with that. It was obvious in the way he carried himself, how he tripped over himself with glee at how well his son was performing in a race car.

Then the unthinkable happened.

As the NASCAR Winston Cup Series steered to Loudon, New Hampshire, for Sunday's New England 300, Petty faced the stiffest test of his lengthy career. For the first time, he returned to the race-track that claimed his eldest son's life and, sadly enough, a significant part of his own.

Kyle is a wonderful man, arguably the most giving, caring, thoughtful man ever to grace the racetrack. When his son was so tragically taken from him, a part of him died as well. Still, he gives far more to others than he gives to himself.

He doesn't want to give to himself. He doesn't want to feel whole. He'll never get over Adam's death, doesn't want to. He feels that the day he wakes up and doesn't hurt, that Adam isn't as close to him as he once was.

That is so, so sad.

July 7 was one of the greatest father/son days in NASCAR history. Ricky Hendrick won the inaugural NASCAR Craftsman Truck Series race at Kansas City with his father on hand to celebrate.

Jon Wood finished fourth in that same race, his father Eddie calling countless times from Daytona to check in on his son's progress. In one of the most poignant moments in NASCAR history, Dale Earnhardt Jr. won the Pepsi 400 that night. You know his daddy was smiling.

After the 400, I remember being so happy for all three of those kids. I remember thinking how awesome it must have been for those fathers to experience such a triumphant day with their sons. I called my father to discuss it with him, and during our conversation I remember thinking about Kyle.

He wanted moments like that with Adam so badly.

Sometimes life has its own curveballs.

~Marty Smith
Chicken Soup for the NASCAR Soul

THE PRICE OF A CHILD

"Daddy, how much did I cost?"

Perched on my parents' cedar chest in the bedroom, I listened to their casual talk about budgets and paychecks—talk as relevant back in 1967 as it is today. My then-six-year-old mind concluded, wrongly, that my family was poor.

Dad stood at his dresser, looking at bills. He wore faded jeans, an undershirt and white canvas shoes stained grass-green from mowing our lawn. Mom folded laundry on the bed, making even towers of sun-dried clothes. I spotted my new shorts sets and thought about day camp.

Their money talk continued, and Dad joined me on the cedar chest. I plunked the springy metal watchband on Dad's tan wrist, thinking that the white skin underneath reminded me of a fish belly. Just as I started to ask him to "make a muscle" so I could try pushing his flexed biceps down, a thought hit me like icy water from a garden hose: Dad had to pay for me.

While the story of my birth ranked as a bedtime favorite, I had never considered hospital bills, or the countless meals I'd eaten, or the price of summer clothes.

"Daddy," I interrupted again, "how much did I cost?"

"Oh, let's see." He sighed in distraction and placed his watch on the safety of his dresser. "About a million dollars."

A light went out inside me. A million dollars. Because of me, Dad worked two jobs. Because of me, he drove an old car, ate lunch at home and had his dress shoes resoled—again.

With my eyes and chin down, I inched off the cedar chest and shuffled into the kitchen. From a shelf, I took my granny-shaped bank, which held every penny I owned—seven dollars even. And not seven dollars in assorted change, but seven cool, shiny silver dollars, one for every birthday and one for the day I was born.

The bank's rubber plug surrendered, and the coins poured into my hands. I had often played with these coins in secret, jostling them in a small drawstring bag in my roles as gypsy or runaway princess. They had always been put back in the bank, though, and I felt secure pleasure in just knowing they were there. But that day, the "clink" of returning each coin sounded hollow.

If the topic had changed when I returned to my parents' bedroom, I didn't notice. Tugging on Dad's shirt, I held out my first payment on a million dollars.

"Here," I sniffed. "Maybe this will help pay for me."

"What?" Dad's confused look matched my own. Didn't he remember what he'd said? Didn't the sight of me remind him of how much I cost?

My tear-filled eyes, which I couldn't seem to take off the bank, finally made sense to him.

Dad knelt down and pulled me close. "You didn't cost a million dollars, but you're worth a million-million dollars. And if that's what I'd have to pay for you, I'd do it. Now dry those eyes and put your bank away."

Today, I often pull this memory out, turn it over and feel the warm satisfied weight of it in my heart. Back then, no price could be put on my worth to my dad. No price can be put on his worth to me now.

~Debi Stack
Chicken Soup for the Father & Daughter Soul

PLAY CATCH WITH ME, DAD

Kids spell love T-I-M-E.
~John Crudele

"Play catch with me, Dad?"
I hope you don't forget
about the small kid
with the baseball and the mitt.
I know that you are busy
with important things all day,
but it makes me feel so special
when you take some time to play.
Things like winning and losing
don't mean that much to me.
It's just being with you
that makes us family.
So, even if you are tired
from the day you've just had,
please don't forget
to play catch with me, Dad.

~Tom Krause
Chicken Soup for the Sports Fan's Soul

THE PROMISE

I looked up from our base camp on Mt. Shasta and saw that the heavens were almost white, so filled with stars. Our party was alone except for a single tent perched on the snow nearby. Its occupant was a young man about twenty-two years old.

Occasionally, I glanced over and saw him packing his daypack for the next morning's climb. First he put in a small box, then two bottles and a lunch. He saw me staring and waved. I returned the greeting and got busy with my own preparations.

The next morning, the sun greeted the crisp dawn. After breakfast, my companions and I eagerly started our ascent. I went into my slow, steady trudge, trailing the others.

After a little while, the young man from base camp drew beside me and asked if it was okay to hike along. I hesitated. I really didn't want any company. Besides, I noticed that he limped; and I wasn't certain whether he could reach the top. I didn't want to abort my attempt at the summit to aid him.

"I'm glad for the company," I replied, in spite of my misgivings.

His name was Walt, and he told me that it was his third attempt to reach the top.

"When I was about twelve," he explained, "my father brought me here and we started up, but the weather got bad, and we were forced to turn back."

Pausing, he smiled proudly. "Dad was a great outdoorsman and a wonderful climber."

We traversed for a short way in silence before Walt continued.

"I was born with a problem with my left leg, so I've always had trouble walking and running. But Dad refused to let that keep me back. When I was just a tiny kid, he used to take me into the Sierra to teach me to fish. I remember the first time I baited my own hook and hauled in a trout. He insisted that I clean it myself. It was the best fish I ever tasted."

We stopped by the side of the trail to put on our crampons. As we moved higher, he carried on with his story.

"When I got to be about nine, Dad started taking me into the mountains. Gradually, my leg became stronger, and eventually I could keep up with him. Last summer he called and asked if I would like to try for the summit again. We hadn't seen much of each other since my parents' divorce, and I jumped at the chance to be with him."

Walt looked down toward our base camp.

"We camped where you saw my tent. Neither of us was really in a hurry to climb. We just wanted to be together and catch up on the years we had missed. He told me that all he ever wanted was to live with his family and grow old among his children and grandchildren. Dad had long silent spells, and there was a sad aura about him."

I spoke little. I was trying to save my breath for the steeper incline. As we climbed higher, Walt kicked the steps, making my work easier. We came to a steep chute, narrow and icy, and it seemed to me that his limp was hardly noticeable.

"Why don't you lead?" he asked. "I remember that rocks tend to break away here, and I'd hate to knock one loose and have it hit you."

Ten minutes later, we stopped for a rest. By then I knew he was all of twenty-one, married and had a three-month-old son.

"My father and I got this far last time when I became ill from the altitude and my leg buckled under me. The pain got so bad, I couldn't go on. Dad hoisted me onto his back and, somehow, he brought us both into camp before getting help. The search and rescue team carried me to the hospital. Dad and I promised each other that we would try again."

Then Walt looked down and squeezed back a tear. "But we never got to do it. He died last month."

After a solemn moment, we trekked onward, and just below the summit, we rested again on a small rock outcropping. The sky blazed blue, and I could see at least 180 degrees to eternity. The sun was high, and its rays warmed me as I ate some trail food.

A few feet away, Walt sat on a boulder holding in both hands the box he had packed the night before. He whispered, "We're going to make it this time. You carried me last time, and now it's my turn to carry you."

At that point, Walt rose abruptly, and with no further word he headed to the peak. I stared into his face as he strode past me. He seemed to be in a trance with an almost beatific smile lighting his face. I followed.

Finally, we reached the top. I was only a few steps behind.

Carefully, Walt knelt on the snow, reached into his pack and reverently removed the box. Then, after digging a hole about fifteen inches deep and attentively pouring some of his father's ashes into it, he covered the hole and built a small stone cairn over it.

When he stood up, he faced north, then east, south and west. Turning his body toward each direction once again, he reached into the box and gently sprinkled some ashes to each compass point.

Walt's face was painted with joy and triumph behind a rush of tears. He flung the last of the remains into the wind and shouted, "We made it, Dad, we made it! Rest on our mountaintop. I promise I'll be back when your grandson can meet you here."

~Mel Lees
Chicken Soup for the Nature Lover's Soul

6

TAKE MY HAND

The guardian angels of life fly so high
as to be beyond our sight, but they are always looking down upon us.
~Jean Paul Richter

The car crept slowly up the dark mountain road as February winds dusted the slick pavement with new-fallen snow. From the front seat, my two college friends navigated the old car over the icy road. I sat behind them with a broken seat belt.

The back end of the car fishtailed. "No problem, Mary," Brad reassured me, gripping the steering wheel. "Sam's house is just over the next ridge. We'll make it there safely."

I heaved a sigh. "I'm glad Sam's having a party. It'll be so good to see everyone again after Christmas break." I hoped my cheerful friends could bring me up from one of the lowest points of my life. Even Christmas at home in Hawaii had been disappointing, leaving my heart empty and hollow. Nothing had been the same since Dad died two years ago.

Sensing my despair, Dad's sisters had taken me aside after Christmas dinner. "Pray to the heavens, honey," they coaxed. "Your daddy is there. He can hear you and help you."

Pray? Bah, humbug, I thought, as I left the family gathering. I've given up on God.

Moonlight glistened off the icy pavement. Our car approached the bridge traversing the canal waters feeding the nearby lake. As we crossed the bridge, the car began swerving out of control. "Hang on!" Brad screamed. We spun 360 degrees before careening off the road. The car rolled over, slammed onto its top, and my body crashed through the rear window and onto the frozen earth. As I groaned, only half-conscious, I noticed no sounds from the front seat. I started crawling, hoping to find the road, and help. Digging my elbows into the ground, I dragged my battered body across the rough terrain. With the next pull, I slid over a knoll and somersaulted down the other side and into the freezing canal water.

The pain and cold left me limp. Then I heard a voice scream, "Swim!"

I began to stroke with my arms.

"Swim!" the voice called. It sounded like Dad. "Swim harder, Mary Ann!"

He was the only one who called me Mary Ann. "Daddy!" I cried, as the current pulled me under. I thrust myself through the surface of the water when I heard him scream again, "Swim harder!"

"Daddy, where are you? I can't see you!" I yelled, as the frigid waters pulled me under again.

Too frozen and weak to fight, I felt myself sinking deeper into the darkness. My head swayed back, and I gazed up through the surface of the water where a bright golden light glowed. Then I heard Daddy holler again, "Swim, Mary Ann! Take my hand!"

With all my might, I hurled my body upward, through the water and into the light. There, my daddy's hand extended. I recognized his touch, his grip as he pulled me up.

Then the light, the hand—the moment—vanished. I was clutching a chain extended across the canal.

"Daddy!" I cried. "Come back! Help me. Help me, Daddy!"

"Over here!" another voice yelled. "She's over here!" A stranger leaned toward the water's edge. "Hold on to the chain and pull yourself to shore!"

Hand over hand, I yanked my frozen torso within the stranger's reach, and he lifted me to the bank. My body and my mind were numb.

"Let's get you to the hospital," the man said, wrapping me in a blanket. He sniffed near my face. "Have you been drinking?"

"No," I mumbled.

As I drifted into a merciful state of unconsciousness, I heard him say, "You were calling for your daddy."

I came to in the emergency room, where I was treated for hypothermia. My friends had sustained only cuts and bruises.

"You're all lucky," the highway patrolman said. "Especially you, young lady. Those chains are strung across canals to keep animals and debris from flowing into the lake. I can't believe you knew to grab it when you did, or had the strength to in that freezing water."

"I had help," I muttered.

"You must have had help, Mary," the patrolman said. "You were deathly close to being sucked into the underground siphon that pumps water into the lake. Another ten feet, and we'd never have found your body." He patted my shoulder. "Somebody up there is looking after you."

Not just somebody, I thought. My Daddy.

That afternoon in the canal was the last time in my life I've been afraid. Even years later, when our infant daughter had open-heart surgery, I had a faith-filled peace no one could understand. I can feel that, with Dad's help, the hand of God is over me. I need only to reach out and grasp it.

~Mary Ann Hagen
A Second Chicken Soup for the Woman's Soul

7

MY FATHER'S SON

Children have more need of models than of critics.
~Carolyn Coats,
Things Your Dad Always Told You, but You Didn't Want to Hear

It was one of those excruciatingly cold New England mornings in 1964. A four-day-old snow had turned to ice as it pressed against my bedroom window. In my twelve-year-old sleepiness, I staggered through the dark hallway into the bathroom, hearing the truck's engine idling audibly outside.

Peering out, I saw his figure—a dark shadow moving against the white background, his breath clouding the air when he exhaled. I heard his work boots crunching the hard snow with his giant steps. I saw his dark face hidden beneath a knit cap, the upturned coat collar, the woolen scarf wrapped around his neck and chin. One gloved hand guided the ice scraper across the truck's windshield; the other brushed the shavings like a crystal beard from the truck's old weathered face.

Daddy. Moving with a quick purpose, driven by a commitment and a responsibility taught him thirty-five years earlier in Depression-era Georgia. Daddy. A silent gladiator who was stepping once more into the hostile arena of the day's battle. Daddy. Awake while the rest of the world slept. And as he slid behind the steering wheel, driving carefully from the driveway onto the street, the truck was swallowed up by dawn's dimness. As I returned to the warmth of my blankets—in my own bed, in my own room—I knew I could go back to sleep, to dream, because Daddy was outside facing the cold.

Throughout the many junior- and senior-high mornings I watched my father go to work, I never told him how that vision affected me. I simply wondered at his ability to do what he did: keeping the kitchen filled with food, making the payments on my music lessons, covering the car insurance so I could drive during my senior year, piling the Christmas gifts beneath the tree, taking me to Boston to buy new clothes, dragging me to church on Sundays, driving me to visit college campuses on his day off, kissing and teasing my mother in the living room, and nodding off in his easy chair in the middle of a sentence. Perhaps it was because these scenes seemed so ordinary that I never spoke of them, never weighed them beyond my own selfish adolescent needs.

And then at college, away from him — when his presence became merely the voice over the phone during weekend calls or the name scribbled at the bottom of the weekly letter stuffed with a ten-dollar bill — I thought other men were more significant than Daddy. Those men who taught my classes in polysyllabic words, wrote articles in journals and explained complex theorems and philosophies. Daddy never did any of that — he couldn't with only a high school education. My hero worship made me a disciple to Ivy League scholars who ignited my dormant ideas and dead men whose names were printed on book covers, buildings and the currency I hungered to possess.

Then, as I traveled to Europe in my later college years, I realized I had seen more, had traveled farther and had achieved greater distinctions than Daddy ever had. I was filled with a sense of self-importance, puffed up with grad-school grants, deluded with degrees and accolades assigned to my name.

Then, I entered the formidable arena — the job, the relationships, the creditors, the pressures and the indignities of racial politics. As I reached my late twenties, I looked forward to returning home, talking with Daddy, sharing a ball game, watching an old Western on television, drinking a beer, listening to a story about his childhood days in Georgia and hearing his warm, fulfilling laughter. I rediscovered Daddy again — not as a boy in awe, but with respect as a man. And I realized a truth that I could not articulate as a child — Daddy was always there for me. Unlike the professors, the books, the celebrity heroes, the mentors, he was always there. He was my father, a man who committed himself to a thankless job in a society that had written him off with statistics and stereotypes.

When I reached my early thirties, when I became a father myself, I saw my own father with greater clarity. As I awoke in the early morning hours, compromised my wants, dealt with insults and worked overtime in order to give my son his own room—with his own bed and his own dreams—I realized I was able to do those things because my father had done them for me.

And now, at age forty-seven, when I spend precious moments with my own thirteen-year-old son, when we spend fleeting moments together at a movie, on a basketball court, in church or on the highway, I wonder what he thinks of me. At what point will I slip away from his world of important men, and will there be a point when he'll return to me with a nod of understanding? How will he measure my weaknesses and strengths, my flaws and distinctions, my nightmares and dreams? Will he claim me in the name of love and respect?

Sometimes the simple lessons are the most difficult to teach. Sometimes the most essential truths are the most difficult to learn. I hope my son will one day cherish all the lessons and truths that have flowed to him, through me, from his grandfather. And as my son grows older, I believe that he, too, will measure his steps by the strides I have made for him, just as I have achieved my goals because of the strides my father has made for me. When my son does this, perhaps he will feel the same pride and fulfillment that I do when I say, "I am my father's son."

~Mel Donalson
Chicken Soup for the African American Soul

8

APOLOGY TO A CHILD

By the time that you can read this
You may not know me well
But then again, we may be close
You can never really tell.
You used to call me "Daddy"
I used to hold you tight
I used to bathe you every day
And tuck you in at night.
I should have held your Mommy more
We should have sat and talked
The love grew cold, the words got hot
And then one day I walked.
I cried the night I left you all
I cried again today
It seems sometimes that's all I've done
Since that night I went away.
I hope you know I love you
Though I wasn't always there
I think about you constantly
And you're always in my prayers.
I hope someday you'll understand
That this thing hurt me, too
I hope you'll know, I always have
And always will love you.
Last night I drove to where you live
I saw your bedroom light

I sat and watched and thought of you
Until the sky grew bright.
I'm not the man I used to be
I've learned a lot since then
I wish that I could turn back time
And live with you again.
But I can't change the things I've done
Or take back things I've said
All I can do is write these words
While lying here in bed.
I hope that when you read this
You will know this one thing's true
That no one else in this whole world
Means more to me than you.

~Ron Wutka
Chicken Soup for the Father & Daughter Soul

CAN'T LET GO

Let your tears come.
Let them water your soul.
~Eileen Mayhew

I had said goodbye to my husband, Joe, so often, but this time was different.

We now had our first child. After nights of soul-searching and what-ifs, we made the difficult decision that Joe would go by himself to Alabama for the six-month training course, and I would stay behind with our new son. It was important that I hold on to my teaching position near our home at Fort Hood, plus we were part of a strong network of friends whom I could count on to see me through the rough spots.

On Joe's last evening at home — always a melancholy time — I bathed little Joey, got him into his sleeper and was heading to the bedroom when Joe gently touched me on the shoulder. Lifting the baby from my arms, he said he wanted to tuck Joey in tonight.

They headed down the hall, and I busied myself with meaningless tasks, expecting Joe to emerge from the bedroom within a few minutes. A half hour went by, and still he had not come back. Figuring he was having trouble getting our son to fall asleep, I tiptoed to the baby's room and peeked into the dimly lit room.

Sitting in the rocking chair, moving slowly back and forth, was my husband, stifling quiet sobs. He was holding our sleeping infant in his arms as though he would never let go.

I whispered, "Honey, what can I do?"

His pained eyes met mine, and after a moment he mumbled, "I just can't put him down."

That night, we stood over Joey's crib, holding each other, consoling ourselves and saying over and over that we would make it through this separation and be together again soon.

Joey is six now, and he has a four-year-old brother named Jack. There have been many farewells since that night, yet my military hero still fights back tears when it's time to leave once again in service to his country and give his boys that last, long hug goodbye.

~Julie Angelo
Chicken Soup for the Military Wife's Soul

FATHER'S SECRET

I am frequently the brunt of family jokes because I have no sense of direction. Once, when we were discussing death and the here-after, my son jokingly remarked, "Well, I certainly hope there are heavenly guides, Mother, otherwise, you will never find the way."

I smiled and assured him that I wasn't worried. "I'll just watch for the hill with the privet hedge," I said. When his eyebrows came together in a questioning frown, I hastened to tell him a story about my father.

Pop was raised in a fatherless home at a time when government assistance was unheard of. The family of five struggled mightily to survive. That Spartan upbringing caused my father to be extremely tightfisted.

When we children—two older brothers and myself—became aware that other children got spending money from their parents, we made the mistake of asking Pop for some. His face turned stone cold. "If you're old enough to ask, you're old enough to earn," he rumbled. And so, when the need arose, we scurried about the neighborhood seeking odd jobs or peddling produce from the garden.

His attitude didn't soften as we grew into adulthood and drifted away to jobs or college. There was a period of time when none of us had a car, so we had to ride the bus whenever we came home. Though the bus stopped about two miles from home, Pop never met us, even in inclement weather. If someone grumbled (and my broth-ers grumbled a lot), he'd say in his loudest father-voice, "That's what your legs are for!"

So when I went away to college, I knew I was in for a long walk whenever I came home. The walk didn't bother me as much as the fear of walking alone along the highway and country roads. I also felt less than valued that my father didn't seem concerned about my safety. That feeling was canceled one spring evening.

It had been a particularly difficult week at college. Tests and long hours in labs had left me exhausted. I longed for home and a soft bed. As other students were met at their stops, I gazed wistfully out the window. Finally, the bus shuddered to a stop at my destination point, and I stepped off, lugging my suitcase to begin the long trek home.

A row of privet hedge edged the driveway that climbed the hill to our house. Once I had turned off the highway to start the last lap of my journey, I was always relieved to see the hedge because it meant that I was almost home.

On that particular evening, the hedge had just come into view when a gentle rain began to fall. I stopped to put a book in my suit-case and when I stood up, I saw something gray skimming along the top of the hedge, moving toward the house. Upon closer observation, I realized it was the top of my father's head. Then I knew — each time I'd come home, he had stood behind the hedge, watching, until he knew I had arrived safely. I swallowed hard against the threatening tears. He did care, after all.

On subsequent visits, that spot of gray became my beacon. I could hardly wait until I was close enough to watch for its covert movement above the greenery. Upon reaching home, I would find my father sitting innocently in his chair. "So! It's you!" he'd say, his face lengthening into mock surprise.

"So you see," I told my son, "I'm not worried about finding my way to heaven when I die." There may be light at the end of a tunnel, as many who have cheated death have reported, but beyond that, I think I'll see a row of privet hedge climbing a hill, and my father will be waiting at the top. "So! It's you!" he'll say.

And I'll reply as I did then, "Yes, Pop, it's me. I'm home."

~Betty Stanley
Chicken Soup for the Father & Daughter Soul

SOME SNOWBALLS DON'T MELT

Snowball came into our lives during the winter of 1974. I was four years old. From the moment my daddy brought the plump puppy home, he and the dog formed a close bond. Though snow is scarce in Central Texas, Daddy looked at the bumbling white German Shepherd puppy and dubbed him Snowball. Picking him up, my father gazed into his soulful brown eyes. "This dog is going to make something of himself," Daddy said as he stroked the pup's soft, fluffy head. Soon the two were inseparable.

While Snowball was still very young, my father began training him to prove that the dog could earn his keep. A good herding dog is essential for a working cattle ranch, so Daddy began preparing him for his role as a cow dog. Snowball's determination to please my father was amazing. To watch Daddy and Snowball herd cattle together was to watch poetry in motion. Daddy would point at a cow and Snowball would become a white blur as he zigzagged through the herd and chased the selected cow into the corral.

During the day, Daddy worked for the highway department. Every morning, Snowball would mournfully watch as my father left for work in the truck. Even though it was apparent that the dog wished to go, he made no move toward the truck. Snowball knew that a pat on the head and a raised tailgate meant that he was not to go; however, a smile, a lowered tailgate and the command to "get in" were an invitation to go with my father. In that case, Snowball bounded toward the truck as if there were no limits to his joy.

At the same time every weekday afternoon, Snowball would casually stroll to the end of the driveway, lie down under a redbud tree and patiently gaze down the long gravel road, looking for my daddy's truck. Mama and I did not have to look at the clock to know that it was time for Daddy to come home: Snowball's body language clearly announced my father's imminent arrival. First, the dog would raise his head, his ears erect, and every muscle in his body would become tense. Then, slowly, Snowball would stand, his gaze never wavering from the direction of the gravel road. At that point, we could see a cloud of dust in the distance and hear the familiar whine of my daddy's diesel truck coming down the road. As my father got out of the truck, Snowball would run to him, voicing his joyful delight. Despite the dog's great bulk, he danced around my father with the grace of a ballerina.

One Saturday morning when Snowball was six, Daddy took him and Tiger—our other cow dog, an Australian Shepherd—to work cattle at my granddaddy's house, while my mother and I went to visit my mother's mother, Nana, who also lived nearby. While we were there, the phone rang. From my perch on a stool near the phone, I could hear the panic-stricken voice of my father's mother on the other end of the line. The blood drained from Nana's face as she motioned to Mama to take the phone receiver. Granny told Mama that, while Daddy was working Granddaddy's cattle, a Hereford bull had trampled him. Although the extent of his injuries was unknown, it was obvious that Daddy needed medical attention. It was decided that I was to remain at Nana's house while Mama took Daddy to the emergency room. Tearfully, I sat huddled in a corner of an ancient sofa while Nana tried, unsuccessfully, to console me.

A short time later Granddaddy called Nana's house and asked her to bring me over to see if I could do something with that "darn dog." As Nana and I drove to Granddaddy's, I sat on the edge of the seat and pushed against the dashboard, willing the car to go faster. As Nana drove her wheezing Nova up the sand driveway, I could see my daddy's battered blue truck parked underneath a lone pine tree close to my grandparents' house. When I got out of the car, I heard a mournful wail. It pierced the stillness of the afternoon, causing the hair on the back of my neck to stand on end. In the back of the truck stood Snowball, howling his heartbreak and misery to the world. Granddaddy had hoped that the sight of me would calm Snowball, but Snowball and I had never been that close. I did everything I could to comfort him, but nothing worked.

As I tried in vain to soothe the dog, Granddaddy pointed a gnarled finger at Snowball and said, "That dog is a wonder. He probably saved your daddy's life."

Granddaddy told us that all the cattle, except a Hereford bull, were herded into the corral. The stubborn beast refused to go in, despite Snowball and the rest of the dogs doing their best to herd him. Granddaddy guessed that the extreme heat of the day had enraged the bull. His patience tested to the limit, the bull turned and charged at my father, who was standing nearby. Catching Daddy off guard, the bull knocked him to the ground and ran over him. As the bull pawed the ground in preparation to charge again, a blur of white streaked between the bull and my father. Snarling at the enraged bull, Snowball stood firmly planted in front of my father. Then, with a heart-stopping growl, Snowball hurled himself at the bull, and began to drive the Hereford away. According to Granddaddy, Snowball's action gave my father enough time to crawl under a nearby truck. Trotting to the truck that my daddy lay underneath, Snowball took a wolflike stance and bravely turned away each one of the determined bull's attacks. Working as a team, Snowball, Tiger and my uncle's dog Bear kept the bull away from the truck until my granddaddy and uncle could reach Daddy.

Later that afternoon Mama returned home with my father, and everyone in the family was greatly relieved to learn that Daddy had no life-threatening injuries. Snowball, on the other hand, remained inconsolable until Mama let him into the house to see my father. On silent feet, Snowball padded into the bedroom and quietly placed his head on my parents' bed. Daddy petted him and thanked Snowball for saving his life. Satisfied, the shepherd padded outside, a "doggy grin" on his face.

Unfortunately, Snowball wasn't able to save my father six years later when Daddy was killed on the job. On that terrible day, the faithful dog went to his place at the end of the driveway to wait for his master. There was confusion on his old face as he watched car after car turn into our driveway. I could read his thoughts: So many cars, so many people, but where is my master? Undeterred, Snowball kept his vigil far into the night, his gaze never leaving the road. Something happened to Snowball after Daddy died—he grew old. It appeared that it was his love and devotion for my father that had kept him young and had given him the will to live. Day after day, for two years following my father's death, the dog staggered to his spot at the end of the driveway to wait for a master who would never return. No amount of coaxing or pleading could convince Snowball to quit his vigil, even when the weather turned rough.

It soon became very obvious to Mama and me that it was getting harder for Snowball to get around. The weight that he gained over the years was hard on his hip joints. Just the effort of lying down or getting up was a chore, and his once-powerful strides were now limited to a halting limp. Still, every day he returned to his spot at the end of the driveway. The day finally came when Snowball was unable to stand by himself. He whined his frustration and pain as Mama and I helped him to stand. After getting his balance, the old dog, his gaze never wavering from his destination, made his way out to his daily lookout post.

After two months of helping Snowball to stand, my mother and I tearfully agreed that it was time to do the humane thing for the fourteen-year-old cow dog. Our neighbor's son was a vet, and we arranged for him to come to the house and give Snowball the injection. Snowball lay down on the ground and placed his head in my mother's lap, his eyes filled with love and understanding. We all felt he knew what was about to happen.

After the vet gave him the injection, Snowball smiled his "doggy grin" for the first time since my father died, then slipped away quietly in my mother's arms.

Our throats choked with tears, we wrapped the body of the gallant dog in an old blanket and buried him beneath the spot at the end of the drive that he had occupied for so many years. The group huddled around the dog's grave all agreed that Snowball had "smiled" because he knew that, once again, he would be with the person he loved the most. If there is a heaven for animals, which I hope and believe there is, I can picture Daddy and his beloved dog together there, once again sharing the joy of each other's company—this time for eternity.

~Debbie Roppolo
Chicken Soup for the Dog Lover's Soul

PEELA

That's the way things come clear. All of a sudden.
And then you realize how obvious they've been all along.
~Madeleine L'Engle

U p until she was five years old, my sister Peela (that's what I called her and still do) had my mom all to herself. Then Mom remarried, and Peela felt a little left out. Mom's new husband, my dad, adopted Peela shortly after, and she took his last name. When she was eight years old, I came along, and when she was ten, my little sister, Barbara, was born.

For her whole life, Peela felt like she was an outsider in our family. She got in trouble a few times as a teenager. She never felt like she belonged and thought that Dad never really cared for her. Even though her birth father had another family with several kids, and her visits with him were few and far between, she adored him in her own little fantasy.

Over the years, Peela always remembered our dad on Father's Day and his birthday with cards or letters. She began this as a young girl, with drawings and handmade cards, and continued into adulthood, never forgetting a special occasion. Still, she felt certain that he was untouched by her gifts.

Peela was fifty years old when Dad passed away. She couldn't bring herself to visit him in the hospital. She feared sarcasm or even rejection. But she came to support Mom the minute we called and informed her of his passing. She had no tears for Dad, only concern for Mom. Peela had lost her own husband a few years earlier, and so she was very helpful in guiding Mom through making funeral arrangements.

Mom and I decided that Peela could help us go through some of Dad's belongings during her stay. He had a big gun cabinet with several drawers on one side. As we went through drawer-by-drawer, paper-by-paper, we found out he was quite the pack rat. Then we saw it—a bundle of cards, pictures and letters all kept together—every single thing Peela had given him over the years. I'll never forget her looking at me with tears welling up in her eyes, then crying, "He really did care."

We should have known.

~Donna J. Gudaitis
Chicken Soup for the Father & Daughter Soul

THE WISDOM OF DADS

Supportive Dads

You know, fathers just have a way of putting everything together.
~Erika Cosby

MY DAD

*In every person's life there needs to be a counselor
or a caring, nurturing, encouraging friend. They give people guidance.
They give people hope. They help them accept themselves for who they are.
They help them set goals. They help them find their purpose.
It is truly the work of angels.*
~Tom Krause

The earliest memory I have of my father is one of me as a young boy grabbing his hand and him guiding me along as we walked together. I'll always remember that. As I grew older, I remember my dad and I listening to the high school basketball games together on our transistor radio. I would write the names of the players on a piece of paper and keep track of each player's points as the game went on. I never could stay awake for the whole game because I was still young and I always fell asleep before the game was over. When I would wake up in the morning, I would be in my bed and the score sheet would be lying next to me. The score sheet would be filled out with the final score on it completed by my father before he carried me to bed. I'll always remember that.

I remember the times when my father would bring his bread truck by the house early in the morning on those cold days when I was home from school over Christmas break. I used to ride on the floor of that bread truck as he delivered the bread to the stores. The smell and the warmth from the bread made my mouth water and kept me warm both at the same time. I'll always remember that.

In high school, I became very interested in athletics. My father would attend all my games. My senior year, our football team qualified to play in the state championship game. It was the first time in the history of our school. The night before the game my father came to me and sadly told me that he would not be able to attend the game. He had to deliver the bread to the stores and the game was a three hour drive from his route. He said he would listen to the game on the transistor radio. I said that I understood. The next day, as game time approached, I thought about my dad. As I lined up for the opening kick-off I happened to look across the field into the parking lot. There I saw his bread truck pulling into the stadium. He made the game and we won that state championship. I'll always remember that.

Years later, I had become a teacher and coach. Early one morning my wife and I were awakened by the sound of the telephone ringing at 5:30 A.M. As I struggled to answer the phone I'll never forget the sound of the sheriff's voice on the other end telling me Dad had just been killed in an automobile accident on his way to work. Cattle from a nearby farm had broken through their fence and wandered onto the highway. Being a dark, rainy morning my father had not seen them as he came over a ridge. The impact spun the car sideways in the highway before a semi-trailer collided with it. I was devastated. I could hear my heart beat in my ears. I hung up the phone and walked back into the bedroom and sat on the edge of the bed. My wife kept asking me who was on the phone but I couldn't speak. The hardest thing I've ever done in my life was say the words, "my dad is gone." I'll never forget that.

After that things didn't really matter to me. I went about my life but I really didn't care. It was as if someone had taken my heart from my body and I was just a robot. I went to work. I still taught school but I was just going through the motions.

One day I was on the playground at school supervising a first grade recess when something happened that I couldn't foresee. A little boy walked up to me and grabbed my hand. His hand held mine by the last two fingers, the same way I used to hold my father's when I was his age.

In that instant, my father came back to me. In that instant I found my purpose again. You see, even though my father was gone he had left something with me. He left me his smile. He left me his compassion. He left me his touch. My purpose was to use those gifts as he did. From that day forward I started. I'll always remember that!

~Tom Krause
A 6th Bowl of Chicken Soup for the Soul

THERE IS AN OZ

Once you choose hope,
anything's possible.
~Christopher Reeve

They arrive exactly at 8:00 A.M. to take her home, but she has been ready since before seven. She has taken a shower—not an easy task lying down on a shower stretcher. She isn't allowed to sit up yet without her body brace, but regardless, here she is, clean and freshly scrubbed and ever so anxious to go home. It has been two-and-a-half months since she has seen her home—two-and-a-half months since the car accident. It doesn't matter that she is going home in a wheelchair or that her legs don't work. All she knows is that she is going home, and home will make everything okay. Even Dorothy says so: "Oh, Auntie Em, there's no place like home!" It's her favorite movie.

As they put her in the car, she thinks now of how much her father reminds her of the scarecrow in The Wizard of Oz. Like the scarecrow, he is built in pieces of many different things—strength, courage and love. Especially love.

He isn't an elegant man. Her father is tall and lanky and has dirt under his fingernails from working outside. He is strictly blue collar—a laborer. He never went to college, didn't even go to high school. By the world's standards he isn't "educated." An awful lot like the scarecrow—but she knows differently. He doesn't speak much, but when he does, she knows it is worth remembering. Even worth writing down. But she never has to write down anything that her father says because she knows she'll never forget.

It is hard for her to sit comfortably while wearing the body brace and so she sits, stiff and unnatural, staring out the window. Her face is tense and tired and older somehow, much older than her seventeen years. She doesn't even remember the world of a seventeen-year-old girl—it's as if that world never was. And she thinks she knows what Dorothy must have meant when she said, "Oh, Toto, I don't think we're in Kansas anymore." It is more than an issue of geography, she is quite certain.

They pull out onto the road to begin their journey and approach the stop sign at the corner. The stop sign is just a formality; no one ever stops here. Today, however, is different. As he goes to coast through the intersection, she is instantly alert, the face alive and the eyes flashing. She grips the sides of the seat. "Stop! That's a stop sign! You could get us killed! Don't you know that?" And then, more quietly and with even more intensity, "You don't know what it's like—you have never been there." He looks at her and says nothing. The scarecrow and Dorothy journey onward.

As they continue to drive, her mind is constantly at work. She still hasn't loosened her grip on the seat. She thinks of the eyes, the eyes that once belonged to her—big, brown, soulful eyes that would sparkle with laughter at the slightest thought of happiness. Only the happiness is gone now and she doesn't know where she left it or how to get it back. She only knows that it is gone and, in its absence, the sparkle has gone as well.

The eyes are not the same. They no longer reflect the soul of the person because that person no longer exists. The eyes now are deep and cold and empty—pools of color that have been filled with something reaching far beyond the happiness that once was there. Like the yellow brick road, it stretches endlessly, maddeningly, winding through valleys and woodlands, obscuring her vision until she has somehow lost sight of the Emerald City.

She lightly touches the tiny gold bracelet that she wears. It was a present from her mother and father, and she refuses to remove it from her wrist. It is engraved with her name on the side that is visible to others, but as in everything there are two sides, and only she knows the other is there. It is a single word engraved on the side of the bracelet that touches her skin and touches her heart: "Hope." One small word that says so much about her life and what is now missing from it. She vaguely remembers hope — what it felt like to hope for a college basketball scholarship or maybe a chance to dance professionally. Only now, she's not sure she remembers hope as it was then — a driving force, a fundamental part of her life. Now, hope is something that haunts her.

The dreams come nightly. Dreams of turning cartwheels in the yard or hitting a tennis ball against a brick wall. But there is one, the most vivid and recurring, and the most haunting of all.... There is a lake and trees, a soft breeze and a perfect sky. It is a scene so beautiful it is almost beyond imagining. And in the midst of it all, she is walking. She has never felt more at peace.

But then she awakens and remembers. And remembering, she knows. She instinctively fingers the bracelet, the word. And the fear is almost overwhelming — the fear of not knowing how to hope.

She thinks of her father's God and how she now feels that God abandoned her. All at once, a single tear makes a trail down her thin, drawn face. Then another and another, and she is crying. "Oh Daddy, they say I'll never walk again! They're the best and they say I'll never walk. Daddy, what will I do?"

He looks at her now and he stops the car. This is the man who has been with her down every road, every trail and every path — so very like the scarecrow. And he speaks. "I know that they can put you back together. They can put steel rods in your back and sew you up. But look around you. Not one of your doctors can make a blade of grass."

Suddenly she knows. He has taught her the most valuable lesson in her life and in all her journey: that she is never alone. There is an Oz; there is a wizard; there is a God. And there... is... hope. She releases her grip on the seat, looks out the window and smiles. And in that instant she loves her father more than she has ever loved him before.

~Terri Cecil
Chicken Soup for the Teenage Soul II

15

SAFE HARBORS AND SAILING SHIPS

I had been a registered nurse for about a year when I decided to move from my home in Milwaukee, Wisconsin, to take a job at a veteran's hospital in Prescott, Arizona. It was a lonely time — my first venture away from home.

I spent many evenings alone in my small apartment worrying about how I would achieve my goals and wondering if the move had been the right decision for me. I often thought it might have been better if I had stayed in Milwaukee.

As I sat on my secondhand sofa, eating my dinner from a burger bag, I thought about home. I pictured myself in the kitchen with my mom, making delicious strawberry jams and grape jellies. Later, I imagined myself sitting at the table with my mom and dad, and my brothers and sister, eating warm apple cobbler topped with dairy-fresh whipped cream. I missed the warmth of home and its love and security.

One day, I was feeling particularly blue. Although I loved my job, my heart ached for my loved ones. Perhaps it would be better if I moved back home, I reasoned.

That morning at work I was surprised to receive a package in the mail from my father. He hardly ever shops. What would have inspired him to send me a gift? I tore away the brown wrapper, opened the package and pulled out a poster silhouetting a large ship, sailing into a blushing sunset. The words emblazoned across the gentle reflective waves touched me to the core. "Sailing ships are safe in their harbor, but that's not what sailing ships were built for."

I could see my father's face smiling in approval. For the first time, my decision to leave home and set out on my own felt right. I knew my father, even though he was not a demonstrative, affectionate man, was trying to tell me he missed me but supported my decision to go. He wanted me to be where I felt called to be; and he wanted me to do what I felt called to do.

Mark Twain once said, "Twenty years from now you will be more disappointed by the things that you didn't do than by the things you did do. So throw off the bowlines. Sail away from the safe harbor. Catch the trade winds in your sails. Explore. Dream. Discover."

I knew I would sail farther still, because my quest was championed by my father's love.

~Cynthia Fonk with Linda Evans Shepherd
Chicken Soup for the Father & Daughter Soul

A SACRED PART OF FATHERHOOD

There are very few monsters who warrant the fear we have of them.
~Andre Gide

N o one ever told me that when I became a father I would have to touch fish.

"Hurry, Dad, it's gonna get away," my eight-year-old son complained.

We'd gotten up way too early for being on vacation, but Brandon wanted to catch his first fish. He'd been talking about it nonstop for weeks. My head was foggy, and I had a sharp pain in my sternum. We'd been hunched over the railing of the local pier for two hours, and the top rail had etched a permanent mark in my chest. The smell from the sardine scales on my hands, coupled with the sight of the seagull droppings all over the pier, was making me a little nauseated.

I've already touched the sardines, isn't that enough? I screamed inside.

Imagine my surprise when the weather-beaten old man who ran the pier sold me the bait. "Those are dead fish!" I protested.

"They're sardines," he instructed. "Best darn thing for catching mackerel." After receiving a complete lesson in how to cut up the sardines and bait the hook, I was sent off to the chopping station.

I had been anxious all morning about what I was going to do if we caught a fish. How was I going to get it off the hook? Ever since

I was a boy, I'd been afraid of fish. The first fish I ever caught was a sunny, and when I tried to take it off the hook I got spined. I had never gotten over the fear.

I must have baited our hooks more than thirty times. If we stood on the bottom rail, and leaned out far enough, we could see the fish nibbling at our bait. Suddenly one latched on. I reeled in the fish, and we both stood frozen, staring at it.

"Hurry, Dad, it's gonna get away. Get it off!"

I just stood there, frozen, holding the fishing pole. I looked like one of those posed suits of armor in a museum, except that I had a flailing mackerel on the end of my lance. People were beginning to stare.

In the softest, most soothing voice I could muster, I said, "Okay Brandon, I want you to grab the fish around its middle, and then carefully take the hook out of its mouth."

He took a step back. "I can't. I'm afraid."

I was stunned. It was as if I was looking at myself thirty years ago. My throat tightened. My son had thirty years of fear ahead of him. Thirty years of struggling with loving to fish, but not being able to take his catch off the hook. Thirty years of snickers over his innovative ways of removing a fish from a hook without having to actually touch it. Thirty years of shame.

The prospect of it was more than I could bear. In disbelief, I heard myself saying, "It's okay, son, there's nothing to be afraid of."

Brandon watched in awe as I firmly gripped the six-inch mackerel around its middle. He took a step closer. The mackerel's eyes bulged slightly from the pressure, and its mouth opened wide. It was as if the fish were helping me. It felt natural. I removed the hook from the fish's lip with ease and rested the pole against the rail.

"Dad, can I hold it?"

It was tricky, but I handed off the prize to my eager son. When he was through admiring his first catch, Brandon agreed that we should throw it back. We leaned over the rail and watched it swim away.

As we packed up our gear, Brandon asked, "Dad? When you were my age, were you afraid of fish?"

"A little. But I got over it, just like you."

~Peter Balsino
Chicken Soup for the Fisherman's Soul

ACROSS THE POND

Fill your paper with the breathings of your heart.
~William Wordsworth

A blue-collar worker with a young family to support in the 1950s and '60s in England, Eddie Knight was very much the breadwinner, while his wife, Alice, took care of the home and the children. While Eddie worked, the day-to-day dealings with his two daughters and his son were mainly Alice's domain.

As the children grew up and left the nest, it was Alice who wrote the letters to keep in touch. Imagine then how delighted his elder daughter, now living 200 miles away in London, was, when on her twenty-first birthday she received a letter from her dad. He finished the wonderful letter by writing, "And don't expect a letter every twenty-one years!"

As time passed, Alice did sterling work, writing letters and staying in touch with the children. In 1983, the news came that the elder daughter, now married with two small children, was leaving England with her family to move to the United States, to Rochester, New York. Alice's letters became even more important and were like a lifeline as the little family struggled to settle in a new land and a new culture. Hearing about familiar things quelled the homesickness they all felt at first.

Three months after they had moved, the unthinkable happened. Alice had a fatal asthma attack. Family on both sides of the Atlantic were devastated at the shocking loss. Struggling with his grief after losing his beloved wife of forty years, Eddie made a decision. The way he could honor Alice's memory would be to continue her writing tradition. So he picked up his pen, and a remarkable correspondence began that would span fifteen years and thousands of miles across the Atlantic.

Every week, letters between father and daughter would wing their way between England and the U.S. Each contained as many pages as the weight limit for a regular airmail stamp would allow, and every bit of white space on the paper—both front and back—was completely covered with writing. The writing was never a chore but became an important part of the lives of both father and daughter. Imparting as well as receiving news became an eagerly anticipated activity each week.

At first their letters were full of feelings of their sad loss, but soon the daughter was giving much-needed advice, as Eddie learned how to keep house like Alice had. He wrote of some laundry disasters and asked how to get once-white underwear, now pink, white again. He courted advice about how to iron shirts, what cleaned the bathtub best, how to clean windows without streaks, and he asked for recipe tips. He always kept his sense of humor, and the letters were a joy to read.

That first Christmas, Eddie decided to make "Alice's Shortbread," a family tradition. His letters caused great merriment in Rochester as he related tales of the dough falling apart, or of it sticking to the pan, or any other malady that can befall shortbread. Finally, he triumphantly wrote of his success, a perfect shortbread, and enclosed the winning recipe. His daughter immediately sent a Hallmark card to congratulate him.

For Eddie it became a ritual each evening to sit down and write about his day. It didn't matter how uneventful it had seemed, he always found something of interest to impart: a lovely bird he had seen at his bird feeder, a neighbor he had bumped into on his grocery shopping expedition, news of his English grandchildren or a wonderful sunset. His letters were always interesting; he always found life a joy.

Across the pond, his eldest set aside each Sunday afternoon so she could fill her six sides of paper telling Eddie all about her family's new life. She wrote of the adventures they were having in their adopted country and of her husband's new job, of an unfamiliar school system, of different customs, strange food and great adventures. She described their exploration of the local beauty spots, as well as taking him on their journeys to Florida and the sunny Caribbean. She sent photographs of the children so he could see them grow. She showed him the beauty of a New York fall when Mother Nature dons her most beautiful colors, and of the huge snows of winter, courtesy of Lake Ontario. Through her letters, he experienced their new lives and learned so much about a different land.

Eddie cut articles and photographs out of the local and national newspapers to keep the family in touch with their homeland. He wrote of his trips to Ireland, and of a fortnight spent cruising along the Danube River. He told her about his choir concerts and the thrill of performing. When Torvill and Dean turned the ice dancing world on its head at the Olympics with "Bolero," father and daughter watched on both sides of the Atlantic, and afterward each rushed to write to share the thrill of it all. They talked of politics and the ups and downs of family life. He kept her in touch with home; she showed him a whole new world. And they knew that despite being apart geographically, very few dads and daughters had the opportunity to "talk" as they did. He once wrote that he felt that he knew his American grandchildren far better than his English ones who lived only a few streets away.

In 1996, the blue envelopes from England stopped. Eddie fell down the stairs at home and moved into a nursing home. The weekly correspondence from America continued to arrive each week, and the nurses delighted in reading the letters to him. Eddie was no longer able to write, but he still eagerly awaited the arrival of the familiar blue airmail envelope. In Rochester, the absence of the envelopes signaled the passing of time and the inevitable aging of a beloved father.

Two years later, Eddie died peacefully in his sleep. When his son went through his things after his death, he discovered boxes and boxes of letters. Eddie had lovingly kept them all. Across the Atlantic, in Rochester, there were more boxes of letters, for she had kept all of Eddie's letters, too. They had amassed a fifteen-year history of a family and a father, both struggling with new lives, but with this loving lifeline between them.

I am the daughter, and Eddie was my father. Even now when something exciting or interesting happens to us, I have a strong urge to pick up my pen and tell Dad all about it.

For someone who once wrote not to expect a letter every twenty-one years, my dad certainly stepped up to the plate after Mum's death and achieved his aim of keeping the whole family together. His letters — his legacy of love — will connect generations.

~Linda Bryant
Chicken Soup for the Father & Daughter Soul

18

WHEN THE WORLD STOPPED TURNING

A sking your father about dating is always difficult, especially if you are the son of a strict, religious Filipino immigrant. In fact, bringing up any subject always seemed to be arduous for me. However, dating the opposite sex was not only a topic that was rarely mentioned in my homestead, but it almost appeared strictly taboo. Thus, dating while in high school was not allowed for any of my siblings, and I was certain that my father would not change the rule for me. Even though he had no qualms about grounding his children for disobedience, it was the sheer disappointment from him that we feared the most.

Although any child would normally be deterred by punishment from a stern father, something made me pick up the telephone. With two weeks left in my senior year of high school, that something made me ask out the most beautiful girl in my school.

My father was raised with a strong moral code. Determined to raise his children with the same values, he pushed us to academically achieve as well as respect his rules. He always felt that romantic relationships were strictly adult in nature, and children were not mature enough to cope with or understand them. Moreover, he felt that children who prematurely participated in romance got nothing in return but distraction from their education, precocious mental stress and, most important, unplanned pregnancies.

We respected that opinion. Well, at least we respected it outwardly.

Inwardly, we thought he was ruining our adolescent years. Like all other teenagers, we felt the urge to pursue the opposite sex. However, due to my father's quiet sternness and seemingly immobile moral code, none of us children ever had the audacity to ask otherwise.

It was his quiet stance on the matter, as well as my squeamish nature that brought me to the tough current situation. Here I was, on the phone, asking out the most beautiful girl in the school. Not only was I not sure that my father would even let me go, but I wasn't sure how I'd manage borrowing his car for the occasion. With the exception of my older sisters going to an occasional dance or hanging out with a male friend, my situation would be wholly different. To remedy this awkward scenario, my only hope was that this girl would turn me down!

Unfortunately, she accepted my offer. I couldn't believe it! While celebrating my unimaginable joy at having a date with the prettiest girl in the entire school, a sudden eruption of reality caused it to skid to a halting stop. Through my elation, I had completely forgotten about my parent's restrictions. How was I to tell my father about a date? How was I to tell my father I needed his car?

I went to my mother with a cry for help. Being the more sympathetic of my two parents, she was actually proud of my accomplishment. For her, the problem seemed simple to solve: we would not tell my father. In my house, the world appeared to turn regardless of my father's participation or foreknowledge. Being a devoted physician, he was constantly consumed by work and study. He was often quiet and reserved. Going out on a date and merely not mentioning it would be an easy task to pull off. Although this idea was a little immoral, it certainly wasn't unconventional. My mother had occasionally concealed a bad grade or a speeding ticket from my father. I knew for a fact that the secrecy of my "date" was safe with my mother. Problem solved.

Despite being excited about the plan, I was very concerned about the car situation. My mother drove a minivan, the most uncool vehicle a teenager could drive. My father, however, drove a Toyota Camry. Now mind you, it wasn't a Corvette, but it certainly didn't have a sliding door. The only problem was sneaking the Camry out of the garage. My mother had a solution for that as well. She asked my father if I could borrow the car for a "night out with my friends." He agreed. With both problems apparently behind me, I now could concentrate all of my super-powers on perfecting every other angle of the date. Remember, she was the prettiest girl in the school.

All week long I prepared for that Friday night. The movie plans were set. Dinner reservations were arranged. I even had the perfect mix tape for the drive. It was all going as planned.

Friday night arrived quickly. All my anticipation had built up like an orchestra warming up for a concert. Every instrument was in tune, with every musician waiting in symphony. After reviewing my final plans for the night, I went to the garage to stash a dress jacket in the trunk of my father's Camry. As I opened the garage door, my heart came to an abrupt stop. Every muscle in my body went tight, and my stomach wound up like a clenched fist. My eyes began to glisten with tears as I noticed an unnerving absence in my father's parking spot. The Camry was gone. My father had to have taken it. My brother had already taken the minivan. With no cars left, my heart was broken.

I ran inside and quickly sought out my mother. As fearful as I looked, my mother looked worse. Unaware that my father had taken the car out, she seemed at a loss for words. My father had apparently forgotten about my little "night out with my friends." There was no telling when he would return. For once, the world seemed to stop turning without my father.

With time chasing me to the finish line, my father arrived home. Of all times, he had chosen to take the car for a stupid car wash. Upon pulling into the garage, I stood impatiently at the door. I tried my hardest to not look nervous, though the sweat on my brow was close to revealing my secret plan. In no apparent rush at all, my father appeared as calm as ever as he proceeded to clean the inside of the car as well! Steam poured out of my ears. My time was up, and I was about to explode!

I ran back into the house and asked my mother for help. "Remember Mom, don't say anything about the date," I pleaded. She calmly walked out into the garage and spoke with my father. As she walked back into the house, a smile stretched across her face. She told me there was no other option but to tell my father the truth.

"What?!" I screamed in agony. "What did you say?"

"I told him that you need the car for a date tonight," she answered calmly.

"And?" I anxiously prodded.

My mother smiled. "He said, 'I know. Why else do you think I'm cleaning it out?'"

• • •

Although my family often presumed that my father was oblivious to the random speeding ticket or sporadic bad school grade, he apparently possessed a sort of omniscience that ultimately made us all look foolish. To this day, we still do not know how my father found out about the date.

~Michael Punsalan
Chicken Soup for the Teenage Soul IV

19

TAKEN FOR GRANTED

Any man can be a father. It takes someone special to be a dad.
~Author Unknown

It's strange looking back on my relationship with my dad, because for the first thirty years of my life we didn't have much of one.

No, we weren't separated by divorce, long hours at work or even a grudge lingering from my not-so-pleasant adolescence. Over the years I'd developed a vague composite of my father—a tall, shy man who worked very hard.

I just never really paid him any mind. He was a fixture that I took for granted.

Then nine years ago, when I was pregnant in my second trimester and bleeding, my dad showed up to offer his help. I was surprised. Sure, in the past he'd given me financial aid, fatherly advice and fixed broken appliances, but money, words and tools weren't going to prevent a possible miscarriage.

Still, every day he came. He took me grocery shopping, did the heavy chores of cleaning and undeniably maintained my household.

At first I felt awkward having my retired dad around on a daily basis. I even felt guilty at times. I didn't know how to relate to this calm, quiet gentleman because at the time that's all he was to me—a nice, helpful man.

But, somewhere between folding laundry together and watching *The Oprah Winfrey Show*, we started talking. It seemed silly that it took a talk show's calamity to break the ice between us. Yet soon we were voicing our opinions on everything from politics to child-rearing. Then things got more personal, and we started swapping life stories.

My dad became a remarkable man who had a fascinating history — and a new granddaughter.

After the baby, Dad continued coming over and helping out. Our projects began extending beyond household chores, and he taught me how to hold a hammer "like a man." We built furniture, then a shed. To this day, he arrives religiously at my door every other week to help me get ready for Girl Scout meetings in my garage.

My friends find it amusing that my dad is still helping out even though my two girls have started school full-time, but they don't understand. It's not just about the work anymore. Working together broadens our understanding of one another. I doubt the issues of race, religion and morality would have come up during a brief lunch at the mall. So you're more likely to find my dad and me complaining about the inflated prices of nails in a hardware store than having a polite conversation over a hamburger. He is my best friend, after all, and that involves more than talk of the weather.

Knowing him is to understand what makes a man noble.

When he reads this, he'll probably laugh and wonder what the heck I'm talking about, but I know him now and that's an honor I almost lost.

So, to anyone searching for a true friend, I recommend starting with the person you may have taken most for granted.

~Donna Pennington
Chicken Soup for the Father & Daughter Soul

BALLERINA

My father was a tall, ruggedly handsome man with raven hair and gentle brown eyes. His name was Bernard, and he was an avid sport fisherman. He used to take my brothers and me fishing from a rowboat on a lake, or from the shore of a gently flowing stream. He ran a tackle shop in the middle of Manhattan. The store was never terribly successful, so to help make ends meet, my father sold the exquisite paintings he created without the benefit of a single day of formal training.

How vividly I still recall the endless happy hours I spent as a little girl in my father's tiny studio watching him put brush to canvas. It's like magic, I thought, of the way he could turn dollops of color into striking portraits, still lifes or seascapes.

One of my very favorites was a ballet scene a family friend commissioned my father to paint for his wife's anniversary gift. For years, the painting hung prominently in the living room of their elegant New York home. Every time we went for a visit I'd stand mesmerized by its beauty, half-convinced that any moment the graceful dancers would spring to life before my very eyes. Eventually, the couple moved away, and our families lost touch. But over the years, that painting has always kept a very special place in my heart.

My father never had much money, but he did without so he could buy me the prettiest dresses or take me out for ice cream sodas on sultry summer afternoons. He held me sobbing in his arms the day my puppy died and brought me special treats when I was sick in bed with the flu.

I felt so beautiful on my wedding day when I walked down the aisle on my father's arm. He became a doting grandpa to my three children, Tracy, Binnie and David. Once, when three-year-old Tracy drew him a picture, Dad put it in his wallet and said he'd carry it with him always. "That boy is going to become a real artist; you just wait and see," he predicted.

I was only thirty when my father died. I felt so alone and adrift. "I'm not ready to let him go," I sobbed to my mom the night of his funeral.

I missed my father terribly. There was so much I longed to share with him. How proud he would have been when I returned to school and became an English teacher after my kids were grown. He would have swelled with pride when David became a dentist, when Binnie published her first children's book, and most especially when Tracy fulfilled his grandpa's prediction and became a successful artist.

"Your father is still very much with you," my friends and family kept telling me. "He's watching over you from heaven." More than anything, I wished I could have believed them. But over the years I'd never once felt my father's presence.

"He's gone," I'd whisper sadly, poring through the family photo albums. "All I have left of Dad are a lot of happy memories."

Then tragedy struck. Pelvic pain sent me to the doctor, and the tests came back positive for ovarian cancer. The diagnosis felt like a death sentence.

Surgeons removed most of my cancer, but they couldn't get it all. "You'll need several months of chemotherapy, and even then I can't make any promises," the oncologist explained honestly.

My family embraced me with their love and support. "We'll get through this together," my husband, Barney, assured me. The chemo was so strong. A substitute teacher had to finish out my school year and begin the fall term while I lay flat on my back for weeks at a stretch. I was so frail, I couldn't stumble to the bathroom without struggling not to pass out.

Maybe I'd be better off throwing myself in front of a moving car, I thought more than once as I left the hospital after yet another infusion of toxic chemicals. How I yearned for those days long gone when I could curl up in my father's strong arms and feel safe and protected from any danger. Somehow, I survived the chemo. But I couldn't sleep at night, worrying if I'd also survived the cancer. A few weeks before Thanksgiving I went for a CAT scan. Then I returned home and anxiously awaited the results. The day before I was to learn whether I would live or die, I received a phone call from my brother Robert. "You'll never believe what happened to me today," he began, and by the time he'd completed his miraculous tale, tears of joy were spilling down my cheeks.

Every Sunday, Robert visits an open-air antique market in Greenwich Village, hoping to add to his collection of cruise-ship memorabilia. "You were so much in my thoughts today," he told me over the phone. "I was praying for you, but I kept wishing there was something more I could do." Then, from several dozen yards away, Robert spotted a painting that was instantly familiar, despite the more than fifty years that had elapsed since he'd last seen it hanging from our friend's living room wall. "I didn't even have to read the signature to know it was Dad's ballerina painting," my brother told me. "I've always remembered how much you loved it. I bought it on the spot, and I couldn't wait to get home and call you with the news." As Robert spun his tale, a radiant warmth filled my soul.

And then for the very first time since he died, I felt my father's presence. "Oh, Dad!" I thrilled. "You really have been watching over me from heaven, and now you've come back to be my guardian angel!" After I hung up the phone, I gave Barney a jubilant hug.

"It's no coincidence Robert found that painting today," I wept happy tears. "My father knew how much I needed him, and he found a very special way to let me know everything's going to be just fine. My cancer is really gone."

The next morning I telephoned for the test results, but I already knew the answer. "You don't sound at all surprised," the doctor said after informing me I was completely cancer-free.

"My guardian angel already told me," I explained happily. These days, whenever I gaze upon my father's beautiful painting, I think about how much I loved my dad and remember all the times over the years when I longed for him to be there to share in my joy or my sorrow. But my father never really left me. I know that now. He's been with me through all my days, and he watches over me still, loving me and protecting me from harm just like long ago when I was a little girl.

~Ferne Kirshenbaum as told to Bill Holton
Chicken Soup for the Grieving Soul

UNDERSTANDING DAD

A father is always making his baby into a little woman.
And when she is a woman he turns her back again.
~Enid Bagnold

It was August 1970, and at eighteen, I differed with Dad on many things. Over the last few years, my relationship with Mom had become much stronger — we now had a bond that only mothers and daughters shared — womanhood.

I wanted to celebrate my August birthday with friends and was eager to make plans with "the girls." As I rushed home from my part-time job, I found Dad in the living room, sitting on the sofa, staring pensively into space.

"Where's Mom?"

He looked up at me and immediately I could tell he was struggling to tell me something difficult. "Your mom is in the hospital. The doctors want to run some tests. I'm sure it's nothing serious, but she'll have to be there for a few days."

"Are you going to the hospital now?" I questioned. "Because if you are, I want to come. I need to talk to Mom about my birthday."

"Maybe this isn't the time to bug your mom about your birthday. Can't it wait?"

Sure, I thought, it's not your birthday. By the time Mom gets home from the hospital, my birthday will have come and gone, and she promised me a set of new golf clubs.

"Dad, Mom said that I could have a set of golf clubs, and I've been planning to golf with my friends on my birthday—but I can't do that if I don't have clubs!"

"You can rent them; a lot of people do that when they first take up the sport. I have more important things to worry about. Golf clubs are not a priority. You can rent them or you may use mine."

Yeah—right! I thought. I'm four feet, eleven inches tall, and you're five foot eight; your clubs will be too long for little me!

I pouted in my room, feeling oh-so-sorry for myself, never giving a thought to what Dad must have felt, how frightened he must have been, how he must have missed Mom.

For the next week I was unbearable. I thought only about myself, not about what my mom was going through or what the rest of my family was feeling. The only time I thought about someone else was when I stewed about my father and his stupid golf clubs.

Finally, my birthday arrived. Dad woke me early that morning and said that he and I would visit Mom because she wanted to see me on my birthday. I really didn't want to go; this was my day and I had plans, though obviously I wasn't going golfing.

Dad did not offer me the option of staying home, and I was given no choice. When we arrived at the hospital, Dad told me to go ahead, that he would join me in a few minutes. I walked into my mother's room and looked at her in that awful bed. I was overwhelmed with guilt. She looked so pale, so sickly. I could read pain in her face. Yet she looked up at me and opened her arms for me to fall into.

"Happy Birthday, Mar," she whispered. "I can't believe my little girl is nineteen."

"Mom, are you okay?" I knew she wasn't, but I wanted her to tell me differently. I wanted her to be okay—so that what I was feeling about Dad and those golf clubs would make sense. But nothing made sense now, and all I knew was that I needed my mother at home—now!

She held me in her arms and read my mind. "You know," she said, "your Dad loves you so much. He has always expected great things from you, and I think that he's having a difficult time with your independence. He still thinks of you as his little girl, and it's hard for him to let you grow up."

Just then, Dad walked into the hospital room toting a shiny set of new golf clubs, cart and all. "Happy Birthday, Peanut!" Dad shouted. And as he looked into my eyes, he began to cry like a baby. I ran to him and held him in my arms. I wanted so much to tell him that everything would be okay, but I knew in my heart that it wouldn't. Somehow, I knew that things would never be the same again.

Mom came home from the hospital the next day, and at dinner that night Dad told us that she was dying. She had only four months to live.

That night, I looked at Dad in a different light. This man was human. He made mistakes like everyone else, but he was also my best friend, my mentor, my hero. All that I expected from him as a parent was on the line. And he knew it, too.

For the next four months, my dad ran the house like a fine-tuned instrument. He made our lives as bearable as possible. His spirits were always up for us. Life went on as regularly as it possibly could. Even Christmas went off without a hitch, all because of Dad.

Mom left us on December 31. I watched my dad, waiting for him to fall apart, to scream and yell, to push us away. He never did. He instructed us on our futures. He supported us, as both Mom and Dad.

I only used those golf clubs a few times, mostly with Dad. He taught me to golf. Today, at ninety-one years old, he is still one of the kindest, most intelligent men I have ever known. My children have heard many stories about "Papa," but there is one thing they will never fully know: My dad loved me unconditionally, right or wrong, good or bad. I have tried throughout the years to be half the parent he is, making my children my first priority and sharing the unselfish love he gave me.

~Marianne L. Vincent
Chicken Soup for the Father & Daughter Soul

FATHER'S DAY

It is not flesh and blood, but heart which makes us father and daughter.
~Friedrich von Schiller

When I was five, my biological father committed suicide. It left me feeling as though I'd done something wrong; that if I had been better somehow, maybe he'd have stayed around. My mother remarried shortly thereafter, and this man was my dad until I was nineteen. I called him Dad and used his name all through school. But when he and my mother divorced, he just walked away. Once again, I wondered what was wrong with me that I couldn't keep a father.

Mother remarried again, and Bob was a wonderful, kind man. I was twenty now and no longer living at home, but I felt a great love and attachment for him. A few years later my mother was diagnosed with cancer and was not given long to live. Shortly before she died, Bob came over to my house alone one day. We talked about a lot of things, and then he told me that he wanted me to know that he'd always be there for me, even after Mother was gone. Then he asked if he could adopt me.

I could hardly believe my ears. Tears streamed down my face. He wanted me—me! This man had no obligation to me, but he was reaching out from his heart, and I accepted. During the adoption proceedings, the judge commented on all of the undesirable duties of his profession and then with a tear in his eye, thanked us for brightening his day as he pronounced us father and daughter. I was twenty-five, but I was his little girl.

Three short years later, Bob, too, was diagnosed with cancer and was gone within the year. At first I was hurt and angry at God for taking this father away too. But eventually the love and acceptance that I felt from Dad came through again, and I became, once more, grateful for the years we had.

On Father's Day I always reflect on what I've learned about fatherhood. I've learned that it is not dependent on biology or even on raising a child. Fatherhood is a matter of the heart. Bob's gift from the heart will warm my soul for eternity.

~Sherry Lynn Blake Jensen Miller
A 5th Portion of Chicken Soup for the Soul

SMEARED INK

If instead of a gem, or even a flower, we should cast the gift of a loving thought into the heart; that would be giving as the angels give.
~George MacDonald

My dad has been writing me letters every Thanksgiving and Christmas since I was able to read. When I was little, I would always find three letters taped neatly in a row, sorted by age, on the bathroom door. First Kenneth, next Kristina, then me, all sealed with our names scrolled across the white envelope neatly in blue ink. Every holiday I eagerly anticipated my letter.

"Amy, I'm so proud of you," he wrote to me when I was in fourth grade. "I know you will make a wonderful Paddington Bear in your class play... I pray for you every day. I love you, Daddy." The blue ink has smeared and faded over the years. The paper is tattered and torn because I crammed most of the letters into my childhood junk drawer.

"Amy, you will always be my baby..." Dad told me once after a very stressful teenage year. "I love you, Dad." I remember that year. I was sixteen. A sophomore. And I wanted freedom. One thing that Dad was not ready to give me.

Then one year Dad hung our letters up on the bathroom door early—before Christmas dinner, instead of after. I tore mine down, put it in my pocket and went to my bedroom to read it.

"Amy, you're growing up so quickly. I can't believe you're in your third year of college. You're turning into a beautiful woman...." I continued to read the neatly scrolled blue ink. "God has been good to you with the many gifts you have. Always use them for his glory.... I love you, Dad."

I wiped my eyes, folded the letter and crammed it in my top dresser drawer with his other letters. I opened my door, headed downstairs and met my dad on the landing of the steps.

"Thank you," I said. He smiled and continued walking. I had never thanked him or written him back. I had always expected his letters and assumed he knew I looked forward to and appreciated them.

We opened our Christmas presents after our turkey dinner. As we were cleaning up gifts and the wrapping paper that was strewn over the living room floor, Dad announced that he had one more present for the three of us.

"You can't keep them, though," he said, as he reached behind the tree and pulled out three, small, neatly wrapped boxes. "This one's for Kristina. Here's Kenneth's. And Amy's," he said, as he handed us each a shiny silver box with a blue bow on top. "Now open them together."

We eagerly ripped off the paper. Inside each box there was a Waterman pen, each a different color. We all looked at him, confused.

"Every letter that you've gotten from me has been written with your pen," he explained. "And when I die, I hope you will take these pens and write to your children."

I stared at the pen. Its tip had been cleaned; the ink removed. I knew I probably wouldn't see the pen again until after Dad had died. I snapped the box shut and handed him back his pen.

That night I ripped my drawer out of the dresser and dumped all the contents on my bed. I fumbled through junk that I had kept over the years, wishing I had put all the letters together in a safe place. I knew some were missing and that they were irreplaceable.

I reread the letters. Each ended with "Amy, I love you, Daddy" or "I love you, Dad." I wondered when he stopped being my daddy and started being just Dad. And I wondered when he had noticed the change, too.

I remember when he was Daddy. I used to grab my daddy's hand in parking lots, to cross the street, and simply just to slip my hand into his. I wondered if Dad missed those days as much as I did.

The letters not only marked the transitions of my life, but also ultimately reflected my relationship with Dad over the years. He didn't see my fourth-grade play. But he knew that when I was ten years old, Paddington Bear was very important to me. And even though he wasn't there to see it, he was praying for me. And continues to.

Years have passed since I last saw my Waterman pen. But the letters keep coming. And now I am about to become a parent. I know that someday I will hold the Waterman pen, just like Dad did, and write to his grandchild.

And one Christmas, my Waterman pen will once again be under the tree, neatly wrapped in silver paper tied with a blue bow.

~Amy Adair
Chicken Soup for the Father & Daughter Soul

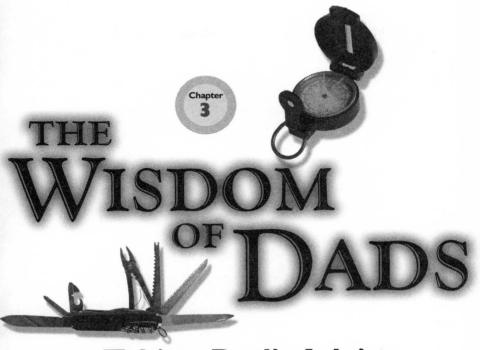

THE
WISDOM
OF DADS

Taking Dad's Advice

*I have found the best way to give advice to your children is to find out
what they want and then advise them to do it.*
~Harry S. Truman

MY DAD AND LITTLE JOE

We can do no great things; only small things with great love.
~Mother Teresa

Dad and Mom both immigrated to Canada from Iceland, their families settling in Lundar and Gimli, Manitoba. After they met and married, they moved to Winnipeg where Dad started his boat-building business in a shop attached to our house. Putting in nails was our job: As kids we were small enough to get to the underside of the boat, and it saved dad a lot of time.

Like many families, eventually we had a dog. Little Joe was a brown, short-legged, sausage-shaped dog of dubious ancestry who supposedly belonged to my sister Anna. I use the word "supposedly" because, with great tail wagging and thumping, Little Joe came to anyone who paid attention to him. We all loved him dearly, as did the rest of the neighbourhood kids.

Little Joe's lack of pedigree caused him no discomfort, nor did it cast any stigma. He trotted around the streets as though he were nobility, his foolish little head held high, bestowing an innocent doggy smile on all he met—including vehicular traffic. We tried to teach him about the dangers of the road, and finally resorted to locking him in the yard. However, on one unforgettable day, Little Joe dug a hole under the fence and bounded out to visit all the friends he knew.

Sometime later, a tearful delegation consisting of the younger members of our family, augmented by excited neighbourhood children, brought home the alarming news that a truck had seriously injured Little Joe. He now lay down the road awaiting death by a policeman's bullet, the accepted method in those days of dispatching injured animals.

We children ran to the scene of the accident, where a small crowd had gathered around our hapless Joe. Though his eyes were open, he lay pitifully stretched out, apparently unable to move. Tears filled our eyes and also the eyes of some of the bystanders as Little Joe showed that he recognized us with a feeble wag of his tail. We huddled around him, frustrated by our inability to respond to the appeal for help we read in his eyes. And we were terrified by the pistol in the holster of the approaching policeman. He motioned us away from the dog and drew his gun.

Wide-eyed, and with the defenselessness of small children looking up into a tall adult world, we began to back away with feet that seemed to be made of lead. We looked into the faces of those around us. No one could help us, and no one could help Little Joe.

Suddenly we became aware of a commotion, and the crowd parted. My father was elbowing his way through the circle of onlookers. He spoke with authority to the young policeman. "Put that thing away! You don't use a gun around children!"

Then, bending on one knee on the road, he removed his worn work jacket and carefully wrapped it around Little Joe. Perhaps many events in a child's life reach exaggerated proportions as time passes, but to this day I remember that had my father's rough, work-worn hands been those of a great surgeon, Little Joe's broken body could not have been moved with more gentleness. I cannot swear that the emotion that I saw in our dog's eyes was gratitude, but I like to think that it was.

I'll never forget that homeward journey. My father was the master of the situation. With Little Joe wrapped in his jacket, he led a procession of admiring children, tear-stained but no longer crying. We held our heads high with pride as we marched behind the man who had stopped an execution and saved our dog. He might have been a great general leading his troops but for the fact that his uniform was baggy-kneed overalls, his sword a carpenter's rule.

For many nights, we thought Little Joe's life was over. In fact, the veterinarian we summoned did not even bother to return, he was so certain our dog would not survive. But my father spoke with resolution as he knelt beside the wooden nail box that served as a makeshift hospital bed.

"He has fight in him. Wait."

So we waited. Sure enough, Little Joe survived. He went on to live a long life, and my dad—he built many more boats.

Our ostensibly stern father would probably not have stood out in a crowd; in stature he was a little above average. But I know of an army of kids and a sausage-shaped dog who, on that one special day, watched him become a giant.

~Sigrun Goodman Zatorsky
Chicken Soup for the Canadian Soul

A FATHER'S WISDOM

My father died in Vietnam when I was five years old. The last thing I expected was to receive a letter from him seventeen years later. But that is what happened one winter day when I was twenty-two years old.

It was the day my fiancé and I announced our engagement. My mom was overjoyed at the news, as was my stepfather. Such an event is a milestone for the mother of an only son. As such, it occurred to her that I had "become a man." That realization sparked in her the memory that years ago she had been given a solemn duty to discharge.

I remember being in the kitchen alone one evening. My mother walked in and handed me a letter copied onto mimeograph paper, the likes of which I had not seen since kindergarten. The seven pages were still folded, evidence of an envelope since discarded.

"What's this?" I asked.

"It's something I should have given you years ago," my mother said. "It's a letter from your father. He wrote it to you from Vietnam soon after he arrived there, just in case something happened to him. You were little at the time, of course. He said that if he didn't return from the war, I was to give it to you when you became a man. I forgot about it, to tell you the truth, although I thought I never would. When you and Claudia announced your engagement, it jogged my memory. It has been years since I had read or even thought about it. In reading it again, I realize that I should have given it to you a long time ago. I'm sorry."

It is hard to describe how jolting her words were. You would think I would have been ecstatic! Instead, I was in shock. It was too overwhelming. The letter in my hand seemed like a mysterious package with the potential to explode, depending on what it said.

While these things were racing through my mind, my body was having a reaction of its own. My face paled. I went a bit numb. My hands turned cold and began to tremble slightly. I took the letter and went to my room. I was completely unable to say anything to my mother beyond a quiet, "Thank you."

There's just something confusing about receiving a letter from your deceased father who has been gone so long that you have not one solitary memory of him. What I knew about him I had learned by asking questions of my mother, my grandmother and my aunts. I had read newspaper clippings and looked through scrapbooks. I had made peace with the fact that these tidbits were as much as I would ever know about my dad. There was no reason to expect more... certainly no reason to expect a personal letter seventeen years after a landmine ended his life.

I sat there stunned in my room. Finally, after a few minutes, I managed to unfold the pages. They were handwritten. I felt privileged to see the handwriting I had not seen before. Some words were hard to decipher, but it was worth the effort to see the personality in the handwriting that a typewriter would not have shown.

After only a couple of lines, I refolded the letter. I wasn't ready. My head had not the slightest idea how to absorb the letter. Part of me was afraid to read it, afraid that with one quarter of my life behind me, my life would not have pleased him... that I would not have his blessing. By that stage in my life, I had adjusted to not having to take into account my father's approval or disapproval. Now, all of a sudden, I might have to.

At the same time, I felt humbled that I was even getting the chance to know my father's thoughts. How many other boys, I wondered, would have this opportunity to read a letter from a father they never knew?

I set the pages on my desk and went back downstairs. My mom noticed my melancholy mood and asked, "Did you read the letter?"

"Not yet," I replied, without offering an explanation. I wouldn't have known how. I hardly understood it myself.

That brief exchange was enough to drive me back upstairs where I sat down and read the letter straight through. The words took on an almost sacred quality to me. This is part of what I read:

Dear Doug:

Your old man is writing this letter tonight because he feels the urge to share some basic thoughts with his only son. You are a very little boy at this writing, but the years will pass rapidly and someday soon you will be a young man facing the realities of life.

I fully expect to be around in the years to come and hope to assist you on your path through life; however, one never knows what the future will bring.

Someday, you will have to decide on a career. Many well-meaning people will offer their sincere advice and you will undoubtedly be quite confused. The choice of your life's work is equally as important as choosing a life's mate. Before you can do either, you must decide what you are yourself, as a person. As the years go by, you will soon discover whether you are outward or timid, adventuresome or docile, ambitious or complacent. It is no sin to be one or the other; but, it is extremely important that you discover what you are — not what at some moment in life you may think you would like to be.

After you decide what you are, think about what you would like to be within the personality and innate intelligence you possess — and then, unless you lack all ambition, pick a goal several steps higher than what you think you can achieve and work like the very devil to achieve it. Remember, son, the tallest and straightest trees grow in crowded forests where they must each individually reach for the very sun that enables them to grow into large and proud trees—in competition with the other trees. Scrub oaks only grow by themselves where they have no competition to spur them on.

Many people... exist in a dream world.... I have heard ministers and teachers condemn the war in Vietnam on many grounds they sincerely believe to be unquestionably valid. Their words of complaint have scant meaning when I watch people going to the Catholic church nearby on Sunday, and realize that until a few weeks ago, this was impossible because of Communist terrorism and military operations. I watch students, little boys like yourself, walk to school each morning under the protection of armed troops. I know that no schools or churches are allowed to operate in parts of this district I advise because they are under Communist control.

It was said centuries ago that for every man willing to lead, one thousand wait to be led. Your father is very proud of this army green he wears and would not trade his life as an Infantry Officer for any other endeavor, whatsoever. I hope someday you can say the same thing about what you have done for the first dozen years after achieving manhood.

Doug, you are a very intelligent boy and you have an extremely kind disposition. Should something happen to me, and I hope to still be serving in the world's action spots when you are my present age, do not try to emulate a way of life that may not be suitable to your own particular makeup. I do hope you will choose a way of life that holds some potential for helping to make this a better world....

Regardless of what career you choose, I do challenge you to do your part in defending the rights you have inherited. Do not rationalize and try to say you are doing your part if your conscience tells you otherwise. One must develop self-respect before he can hope to attain it from others.

Ten years from now, let's you and I sit down and discuss this far too wordy letter... and learn from each other, as I am sure that by then there will be much your old dad can learn from you.

Love,
Dad

When I finished reading the letter, it was as if the weight of the world had been lifted from my shoulders. I was not faced with trying to rebuild my life, after all. Instead, my dad had affirmed me, citing traits he had seen in me even when I was a little boy. His words were encouraging and motivating, not scolding or dogmatic. He did not lecture or warn me, but simply shared his thoughts. Instead of trying to persuade me to follow in his footsteps (which I had begun to do—even applying to West Point, only to withdraw my application), he held up virtues for which I could strive, no matter what career I chose. It felt good that, after all those years, I had some basis for thinking my dad would have been proud of me.

His letter had filled a place in my heart that I had only been partly aware of and had no idea was so large. I had received my father's blessing. It had come after many years, even from beyond the grave, but it had finally come.

Until then, even though I had a wonderful stepfather, I had not fully appreciated the power of a father over his children. This man was a virtual stranger to me, even though I shared his genes. Yet, because he was my father, his attention and affirmation in a letter mailed a week before his death profoundly impacted the course of my life as an adult. He gave me permission to proceed in a direction I would have gone anyway, but now could go with greater confidence.

I believe that God can "re-parent" us, filling in the gaps left by imperfect or absent parents. The apostle Paul even said, "You received the Spirit of sonship and by him we cry, 'Abba (Daddy), Father.'"

(Romans 8:15) But I also believe that God does not usurp the place of a human father or mother. When God established parent-child relationships, He gave them a power all their own. They have an effect uniquely their own that even God can't replace. I might not have believed that before, but I do now.

It is my wish that every father would realize the innate and powerful impact he has upon his kids' lives... the potential he can endow toward self-esteem or self-hatred, toward confidence or insecurity. It is my wish that fathers would never miss a chance to plant seeds of encouragement in young hearts. I hope that as the influence of the father's role is increasingly appreciated in our culture, it will become just as common to hear fathers say, "I love you," or "Good job" as to hear those words from mothers. A lot of fathers want to say such things, but they don't sound so familiar, or the timing doesn't seem right, or there is some other reason....

Fathers, don't let anything stop you from saying the things you want to say to your children. As my father said: "I fully expect to be around in the years to come and hope to assist you in your path through life; however, one never knows what the future will bring."

~J. Douglas Burford
Chicken Soup for the Christian Family Soul

THE GREAT CANDY BAR DEBATE

Wisdom is knowing what to do next; virtue is doing it.
~David Star Jordan, The Philosophy of Despair

Evening meals were sacrosanct at our little house in Burbank, California. Only genuine illness or events of compelling academic or spiritual importance excused us. Mother provided the food, Dad the entertainment. I was almost of age before I realized that not everyone's evening meal involved vigorous, fun, intellectual debate.

At Friday dinners, Dad took a little tablet from his left breast pocket. Every time he encountered a word he did not know, he wrote it down there. By Friday, he'd looked it up and the games began.

"What is a fillip?" he asked.

When neither my brother nor sister knew, I was relieved. As the youngest child, if I occasionally knew an answer, I felt really smart. That evening we all fell short, not knowing that a fillip was the quick, striking motion made by flipping a long finger away from the thumb. In our vernacular, it was a "thump on the head," Mother's discipline technique of last resort.

When spelling, vocabulary and current events played themselves out, Dad delighted in moving us on to his next favorite arena: ethics.

"What would you do if you were walking into a store and noticed that someone had left his car lights on?"

Of course we asked some clarifying questions like, "Was the car locked?" "Was it a nice car?" and so on.

My brother Jim came up with a plausible answer. "If the car's unlocked, you reach in and turn the lights off."

This response pleased Dad. "Yes. Would you tell anyone about it?"

"No."

"Right again. Just do the good deed and let it go at that."

The morals of these ethics discussions were consistent: do well, don't brag, be honest and throw yourself across the tracks to stop an oncoming injustice. We usually aced Dad's ethics quizzes.

The mock situation that stopped us in our tracks came to be known as the Great Candy Bar Debate. Dad brought it up periodically, and it became a chronic family controversy.

Here's the situation: You approach a candy machine, coins in hand. You can't wait for that Snickers bar to drop into the tray. But before your coin drops, you notice that there's already a candy bar in the tray. What do you do?

The only clarifying question three kids needed was, "What kind of candy bar?" Unless it was something vile like marshmallow, that candy bar was history.

"I'd take that candy bar and put my money back in my pocket," Jim said. Surely he knew this was not the right answer, although it made such sense.

"That's tempting, but that candy bar does not belong to you. You haven't paid for it," Dad instructed.

"I'd still take it," said my sister, Andrea. "The candy bar company knows they'll lose a few that way."

"That's a rationalization. Their business is not your concern. You shouldn't take something you haven't paid for."

"Well if I don't take it, the next person will," Jim said.

"Another rationalization. That next person will have to answer for stealing that candy bar on Judgment Day. You'll have done right, leaving the candy bar in the tray."

About now, Mother tried to arbitrate, asking Dad if the question about candy wasn't too tempting for three kids.

Dad became spirited. "I cannot imagine a justification for taking a candy bar you hadn't paid for! How would you explain that to God?"

I could see Dad's point, but I wondered if I couldn't find justification somewhere. I knew that in the real world, every one of us except Dad would take that candy bar and eat it.

Dad's honesty plagued him to the end of his life. As a retiree, he and Mother occasionally worked as movie extras in Hollywood. The pay was minimal, twenty bucks apiece. Sometimes it was given in cash, "under the table." Most of the folks probably had a quiet dinner out on the earnings. Dad kept books, noted every dime of income, claimed it on his IRS Form 1040, and paid the tax he owed.

When Dad's memory began to fail, things got complicated. Mother took him to the attorney to see how to get him the medical care he needed without bankrupting the family. Dad didn't comprehend much, but he wanted no legal shenanigans that might ensure his medical care but jeopardize his soul.

Fortunately, as a combat veteran of World War II, he was eligible for treatment through the VA. To qualify for the Dementia Program, Dad took a battery of memory tests, which included vocabulary.

The psychiatrist told Mother, "I can't find a word he doesn't know. When we got to 'frangible,' he gave me synonyms and antonyms."

Dad was their favorite patient after that, a kind of "dementia savant." He told the best stories and remained his charming self. He just didn't know what day it was.

The time came when the doctors could do no more. They called Mother one morning. Dad was fading fast.

By the time we got there, Dad lay still and gray against the white sheets, his pulse faint. We wept. Then we dried our tears and started telling him stories. With the family reunited there, things felt strangely festive. When we started to get hungry, I went downstairs for snacks.

The lounge was filled with patient-veterans in various states of illness and decrepitude. I bought sodas from the machine, and then decided to get a Snickers bar. Approaching the candy machine, quarters in hand, I noticed a Three Musketeers lying in the tray. I looked up toward Dad's room, toward heaven. Was this a test? Was this a joke?

Across the room, a Vietnam-aged veteran, an amputee on crutches, said, "Aw, geez! I forgot my money, and I'm starving! Can I borrow change from somebody?"

"How about a Three Musketeers instead?" I asked.

"That'd be great."

I handed him the misbegotten bar.

With drinks and candy I'd paid for, and the solution to the Great Candy Bar Debate, I returned to Dad's room. Everyone agreed that giving it to a hungry veteran was the brilliant justification that had eluded us all those years.

Later that evening Dad slipped away. I know he heard everything we said. I'm pretty sure I can explain every nuance of the Great Candy Bar Debate to the Almighty when the time comes. I just hope my explanation will satisfy Dad.

~Naida Grunden
Chicken Soup for the Father & Daughter Soul

DAD, I HAVE A BEACH BALL

*We have two ears and one mouth so that
we can listen twice as much as we speak.*
~Epictetus

I sat in the car in the driveway, listening to my daughter's pain. One of her "friends" had decided that her own self-worth needed a boost and that it would come at Betsy's expense. Every day at school, she would look for an opportunity to embarrass Betsy in front of the other kids. She would ridicule Betsy's clothes, her looks or something Betsy had said. She was making my kid's life miserable. Such are the ways of some teenagers.

"I can't go to school without worrying about what she is going to do! I don't understand why she is doing this to me. Sometimes, I wonder what she would do if I wasn't here anymore."

"What do you mean?" I asked, not wanting to know the answer.

"I mean, what if something happened to me and I wasn't around anymore? My life is miserable. If I wasn't here, nobody would care."

I held back my fears and told her, "I'd care. Your mom would care. We love you and think you're a wonderful kid. We would miss you." Our talk ended, as it was time to go in the house and get to bed.

That night, I talked to my wife, Nancy, about what Betsy had said. Besides being the "mama bear" who wanted to take vengeance for the attack on her cub, Nancy said, "We have to keep her talking to us. We have to find a way to make sure she doesn't keep all this bottled up inside." We talked late into the evening about what we could do.

The next day at dinner, I told both Betsy and our son Andy that their mom and I wanted to talk to them about something. "Remember what Mr. Tewell [our minister] said last week about the beach ball?"

In Tom Tewell's sermon, he talked about a beach ball. He talked about how light it was, and how a small wind could just blow it away. He asked us to think about diving into the deep end of a swimming pool and trying to keep that beach ball between our legs, underwater. Sure, you can do it for a while. But, after succeeding for a time, two things can happen. You get so tired you let the ball slip and it pops up to the surface. Or, in the worst case, you get so tired trying to hide it, you might even drown.

Tom asked us to think of the beach ball as a problem, a lie or an act that we had committed that we didn't want anyone to know about. We try to keep it hidden. We use all our strength, and focus all our attention, on that beach ball. It ruins our life. But, if we let that beach ball pop to the surface, to the light of day, it just becomes the piece of plastic it is and eventually blows away.

I could see that the kids wondered what the point of this story was. I told them that sometimes, we all get into situations where we have our own beach ball we are hiding. We told them that from now on, whenever they had something they felt they could never tell us, that they should come to us and say, "I have a beach ball."

We promised that the only thing we would do for twenty-four hours was to listen. No yelling, no judgment, no advice, we would just listen. After twenty-four hours, we could talk to them about how they might get out of the situation they were in. But whenever they had a beach ball, we would just be there for them and listen.

Over the years, we had plenty of beach balls presented to us, usually late at night. Some were more distressing than others. Some were even funny, and we tried not to laugh as we listened. Some never reached our ears, but they did reach the ears of friends of ours whom our children trusted. We always abided by the twenty-four-hour rule.

We never went back on our word, no matter how much we wanted to react to what they told us.

They are both young adults now. I am sure they will still have beach balls from time to time. We all do. But they know we will still be there to listen to them. After all, it's just a beach ball... a few pieces of light plastic glued together that blow away when you let it go.

~Jeff Bohne
Chicken Soup for the Father's Soul

MY FAVORITE PROFESSOR

For every minute you are angry, you lose sixty seconds of happiness.
~Author Unknown

My father was not a quiet man, and when it was his turn to drive the carpools of my childhood, we weren't going to get much time to wake up slowly.

"Top o' the morning," he bellowed, a Jewish baby boomer from New York, pretending to be Irish as he opened the doors for me and two of my friends.

"And the rest of the day to you," we groaned the response we had been instructed to on so many occasions.

He taught constitutional law at the university, and his energy instantly made him a popular professor. They loved how he once instructed a class on the first day of the baseball season dressed in a New York Mets uniform, a wad of chewing gum bulging from his right cheek. They loved how, after class, he would engage in conversations about their lives, their food preferences and their favorite sports. They loved how he cared. Three graduating classes named him Professor of the Year.

Friends and family look at me and smile.

I am the spitting image of him, they say. I have Julian Eule's mannerisms, his face, his sense of humor, his initiative, his enthusiasm, and on and on and on, to which I can only reply, "I hope so."

There was a time when I didn't quite know how special my father was, but then a time came when I realized it. I had gone to bed angry after some argument with him. I was young, probably in elementary school, and don't remember what it was about. But I do remember his response.

After the argument, I could not fall asleep. Minutes, then hours, went by. Music, then call-in talk shows, then news blared from the boxy clock radio on the night table near the head of my bed. And still I couldn't sleep.

Around midnight, my father finally came in.

I didn't say anything. He motioned for me to slide over, sat at the side of my bed and turned off my radio. And then, he began to tell a story he had read once in the newspaper.

There was an actor who always spoke of how close he had been with his own father. The two had always had a remarkable relationship. One night, though, after a slight disagreement, they left each other's company angry, refusing to even say a simple "good night" to each other. Later that night, the father died.

The son had no doubt that the love he had for his father was both known and equally returned, and yet he had to live with the memory that he and his father spent their final moments together upset, arguing over something presumably meaningless. They had not said "good night" to each other on their final evening together, and this stuck with that son for the rest of his life.

As it has with me.

I hugged my father tightly and told him I loved him. He told me the same and from then on, no matter how late I came home, no matter how frustrated I was, I never again went to bed without telling him, "Good night, I love you."

Indeed, my father was a brilliant storyteller. Yet of all the stories, cancer was the biggest. Cancer had been like war stories for my father, something he had survived when I was too young to recall, something he was proud to have defeated. Suddenly, in the summer before my senior year in high school, I learned that my father was going back to war.

It didn't seem fair, but that was not the way he chose to look at it. That was never the way he chose to look at things. When I was just a toddler, he was given an eleven percent chance of surviving a battle with cancer. With these statistics in mind, the important things in life were separated from the trivial ones. He wanted nothing more than to see his two young children grow up, a privilege denied his own father, who died of heart complications three years after my father's birth.

Eleven percent. A death sentence waiting in the wings. It amazes me that he could live with that. But he made a vow to appreciate life for all of its joy. When he beat the odds, my father kept his promise. In watching him, I learned how to appreciate life. He taught me not to get mad at the little things, saying, "Is this worth losing a day of your life to stress?"

It was a life where every day was valued, every moment treasured, every person appreciated. A life where he made sure he was where he wanted to be, with the people he wanted to be with. But after almost fourteen years of remission, my father spent a beautiful California summer evening in an ugly hospital bed, my mother by his side.

"How can I be upset when I was given the past fourteen years as a gift?" he asked. Those years, he told me, had been the happiest of his life, and if he had to die, he was more content this time.

I wasn't content. I found I needed him to remind me not to lose sight of things. He was the hand on my shoulder, calming me down without any words.

One night, during that summer, my mother called from the hospital. She was tired and wanted to go home to get some sleep. My father needed to stay. He had lost some blood, needed a transfusion and wanted someone to keep him company for the rest of the night.

I took a radio, a sleeping bag and a pillow and set off for the hospital at 10 P.M. My father smiled, glad to see me as I entered the room. I motioned for him to slide over, sat on the side of his bed, and we talked.

During the past fourteen years, there had been nothing left unsaid, so nothing specifically had to be spoken during those moments. We just sat there and enjoyed each other's company.

As the new blood entered his body, the life returned to his face.

By midnight, the radio was blasting. We sang along to every song we knew and faked those we didn't. Down the hall, a door closed. At six in the morning, the transfusion was complete, as was our pajama party.

I set off for home content, knowing that in an hour my mother would settle herself in the same spot I had occupied all night.

Exhausted, I was halfway out the door before I remembered. I turned back toward his bed, bent down and kissed him on his cheek.

"Good night, I love you," I whispered.

~Brian Eule
Chicken Soup for the Teenage Soul IV

BEYOND THE BREAKERS

On my desk there is a faded picture in an old wooden frame. It is my most cherished memento of my father. He's dressed in a pair of waders pulled down past his knees, a light wool jacket, and a faded cap cocked at a jaunty angle upon his head. He's young and robust, and in each hand he holds a striped bass weighing close to thirty pounds.

Gazing at that picture is like traveling back in time to when I was four or five, watching my father strap on a heavy canvas knapsack, grab a mammoth surf rod, and finally look down, asking, "You want to come along?"

I'd look up into his cheerful face, with his infectious grin, and my heart would leap in anticipation of spending a day with my hero—my father. He'd take me by the hand, and we'd walk the several blocks to the beach.

When I was nine, Dad gave me a rod and reel of my own. My chest swelled with pride. My initiation to fishing had begun.

"Try to get your line past the second breaker, Gary. That's where the fish will be." I always thought they were waves, but Dad explained the waves were farther out. As the wave speeds inland it swells, then breaks over itself heading toward shore. I tried to mimic my father's cast, but my sinker would land in about a foot of water several feet away. I would never be able to reach that far! Then I'd watch his cast and how the bait arched high in the air, slowly reaching its apex to curve and land with a barely discernible splash well past that second breaker. Oh, how I wanted to cast like that, but I was just a little kid. There was no way I could do it.

After many frustrating attempts, I'd quit and sit down dejected and watch as he made cast after cast. But on the days I kept trying and didn't give up, he'd make the cast for me. Then we'd place our rods in the sand spikes and open our thermoses. Coffee for him, hot chocolate for me.

He heaped praise on me when I got past the first breaker, but it took nearly two years until, finally, I succeeded. Then within several months I became nearly as proficient as he. And nearly every time I cast out he'd remind me, saying, "The second breaker, son. Cast beyond the second breaker."

After high school, I spent a few years in the Navy. When I came home on leave, Dad and I would head for the surf. We'd make our casts, then sit back in the sand and talk, catching up on each other's lives while sipping the hot coffee that was so welcome on those cold foggy days. I don't think we cared if we caught anything. We were simply a father and son reminiscing over past fishing trips and catching up on our separate lives.

It was on one of these outings that I asked, "Dad, why did you make me struggle so much by insisting that I do the casting myself? We could have caught more fish if you'd have done it for me."

He looked at me and smiled. "I guess you were a little put off, son. But it wasn't all about catching fish. You'll understand when you have a son of your own," he said, with a knowing grin.

"Wasn't about catching fish? What are you talking about?"

"It was all about doing for yourself."

I reeled in my line, checked my bait and cast it out once more. Dad nodded toward the spot where my line disappeared into the water.

"You learned that on your own, didn't you? All I taught you were the basics. In this world, Gary, nothing worthwhile comes easy."

The years passed swiftly. I married my childhood sweetheart, and before we knew it, our family grew to two girls and a boy. Unfortunately, due to my work, most of our time was spent abroad.

Dad retired to a small house in southern Oregon. It was a little over an hour's drive to the coast, and he could go fishing anytime he wanted.

One night, the phone rang. It was Dad, telling us he had been diagnosed with leukemia. We were devastated. He was okay for the time being, but eventually, as the leukemia progressed, we thought it best that I take an early retirement and return home to offer what assistance we could.

Even as the disease began to sap his strength, he still wanted to surf fish. So Dad, my ten-year-old son and I went fishing as often as possible. As my son struggled with his fishing rod, Dad smiled and said, "Don't worry, he'll catch on. You did!"

Dad seemed to grow weaker each day. On our last trip together he couldn't quite make the cast beyond the second breaker, and after several tries he reeled in his line, looked wistfully out to sea and shook his head in disgust. I took the rod from him, and with moist eyes, made his cast. He nodded in satisfaction and smiled at me with that infectious grin I remembered from my youth. Dad and I had come full circle in our lives together. I guess he sensed this, for he put a hand on my shoulder and said, "It's okay, son."

Six months later, he died.

To this day, I have tears in my eyes at the loss of him—of his wisdom, his patience and his love.

Recently, my son's family came to southern Oregon for a visit. My grandson is almost ten years old and the spitting image of my father.

One day the three of us packed up the fishing gear and headed for the ocean. Dad's old surf rod felt comfortable in my hands as I made my cast, and I have to admit I was flushed with pride and my eyes became just a little teary when I heard my boy tell his boy, "The second breaker, son, cast beyond the second breaker."

~Gary B. Luerding
Chicken Soup for the Fisherman's Soul

EAT DESSERT FIRST

The love we give away is the only love we keep...
~Elbert Hubbard

My father had his own way of imparting wisdom. He handed down stylish phrases when I least expected it. They burst forth suddenly and always came as a surprise.

One hot July Saturday morning, when I was a little girl, my dad asked me to join him for lunch. This particular day, it was just the two of us. My mother, also invited, declined the offer for nobler pursuits: a manicure and wash and set at the beauty parlor, where her standing appointment would never be sacrificed for anything as mundane as lunch.

"It looks like it's just you and me, Missy," Dad said with a twinkle in his eye, followed by one of his pat remarks. "So, let's go and raise some hell."

The restaurant was bustling with people, providing enough background noise to add an air of merriment to our meal. My dad and I parked ourselves in a booth and were handed menus so large they reached over the top of my head and offered a dizzying array of choices.

Over grilled cheese sandwiches and french fries for me and a fat hamburger, charcoal-burned and blood-red for him, my father revealed a most alluring confession: "You see that woman over there?" he pointed to a table a few feet away. I surreptitiously snuck a look.

"That's Marion, the gal who had a crush on me all through high school and into my law school years."

With that came a wink of an eye to Marion, whom I could hear giggling all the way across the room. I, the budding adolescent, sat on the edge of my seat as he regaled me with this top-secret piece of news.

"But," my father said, moving his head so close it was practically touching mine, "she couldn't hold a candle to your mother."

And so began our luncheon rituals, where we broke rules, recounted anecdotes and shared secrets. Months later, I perused the menu at a different restaurant, this time in Manhattan, twenty minutes from our home. On this particular Saturday, I couldn't decide what I wanted to eat. My father, realizing my dilemma, summoned the waitress. "Bring us the dessert menu," he said.

Obligingly, she returned with a small, leather-bound book, edged in gold leaf with a list of desserts that had my mouth watering. Profiteroles, chocolate mousse, chocolate cake and chocolate soufflé were mine for the asking. I felt as though I had entered chocolate heaven.

"But, Daddy, we haven't even had lunch."

"Even better," he winked, that same Marion wink. "When in doubt, eat dessert first!"

"What will Mommy say?"

"It will be our little secret," he said.

And there we sat on that chilly autumn afternoon in a cozy French restaurant. He, dipping a long silver spoon into a parfait, and I, gorging on layers of chocolate cake oozing raspberry and covered in a white chocolate sauce. I remember wondering if life could get any better than that.

There were to be many more lunches and dinners in our future. I accumulated a wealth of knowledge from our talks, and I was privy to personal insights and private thoughts he loved sharing with only me, mainly because my reactions were always so spontaneous and sincere. I was genuinely interested in everything he had to say, which made me, his audience of one, a perfect dinner companion.

Sometimes Mother asked half-teasingly, "Whatever do you two have to talk about?"

My dad also had a reflective side that felt protective and nurturing. He took me seriously, too, by paying credence to my individuality and giving me room for self-expression. As a lawyer, he was accustomed to problem solving. Our meals provided a venue into which I could retreat and unload my worst trepidations or, conversely, share my happiest moments. Without judging, he gently guided me through childhood, adolescence and young adulthood, and served as my one-man support system and guardian of my soul.

Even after I was married and living in Manhattan, Dad and I had a standing weekly dinner date that I came to rely on and treasure. He never once canceled out, despite his busy schedule, teaching me to honor commitment and value the importance of keeping appointments. The only Tuesday we didn't meet at a restaurant was when I delivered my daughter. That night, Mom, Dad, my husband and I dined together in my hospital room. My father brought the champagne that he had been saving for this occasion.

"Even my new granddaughter can't get in the way of our Tuesdays." And there was that wink as we clicked glasses and toasted the birth of Elizabeth.

My father was in his sixties when it abruptly ended. His death brought with it a sense of longing I have never yet been able to relinquish—longing for something that would never be the same again.

Dad died too young and had a lot more tasting left to do, but I revel in the fact that we savored much of life together. We went on for years enjoying each other's company. After his parting, despite my sadness, I was energized, knowing how lucky I was to have shared the Tuesdays of my life with him and the great life lessons he passed on to me.

I now take my two grandchildren, Andrew and Caroline, out to dinner weekly. They can choose any restaurant they want, as I was privileged to do so many years before them. Recently Andrew sighed, perusing a menu too big for a seven-year-old's eyes. "I don't know what I want to eat."

Caroline chimed in, "I can't make up my mind, either, Grandma."

My father's voice came echoing back. "Then, I guess we'll have to eat dessert first!" I told them.

And they, sitting back in wide-eyed disbelief, broke out in smiles, and "eating dessert first" was exactly what we did.

~Judith Marks-White
Chicken Soup for the Father & Daughter Soul

WHERE'S YOUR NOTEBOOK?

One father is more than one hundred schoolmasters.
~George Herbert

I was thirteen years old when Dad called my two younger brothers and me into the game room of our house. I was excited! I thought we were going to play pool or pinball or maybe even watch movies together, just us guys! "Bring a notebook and something to write with," my dad bellowed before we reached the game room. My brothers and I stopped dead in our tracks and stared at each other in horror! His request was unusual, and our excitement turned to dread as we became well aware that games or movies were not the reason we were pulled away from watching *Fat Albert*. This felt more official and tedious, like schoolwork, chores or worse, a family meeting.

As we each retrieved a notebook and pencil, we continued to ponder the reason for this summons. We ruled out a family meeting because Mom was still out shopping. We entered the game room to find three metal folding chairs facing a huge blackboard. Dad instructed us to sit in the chairs and NOT on the cushioned sofa just inches from us.

"I want your full attention. That is why I have you sitting in these chairs," he stated, businesslike.

Immediately we began to pout and whine.

"Where's Mom, aren't we gonna wait for Mom?" my youngest brother asked.

"Is this gonna take long?" my other brother sighed.

I silently squirmed in the uncomfortable metal chair.

"Your mother won't be back for hours, and if you must know, she has nothing to do with this," he said calmly. "And how long this takes depends entirely upon each of you. The more you participate, the more you'll learn, and the faster we can move on and be done. Understood?"

"Yes, sir," we responded unenthusiastically.

"Now," my father began, "we are going to have a weekly meeting with just us guys. We will have these meetings every Saturday morning, but if you have school or sports activities on Saturday morning, we'll reschedule for Sundays after church. I'm going to teach you what I have learned about life. It is my responsibility, before God, to prepare you to be strong, proud, African American men who will be assets to the community and to the world at large. It is a responsibility I take very seriously."

I just had to jump in, "You're going to teach us everything about life?"

"Everything I can."

"But that will take forever."

"Maybe." He turned to begin writing on the blackboard. "Maybe."

For the next five years, rain or shine, in sickness or in health, Dad taught us about life once a week. He instructed us on a wide variety of subjects — personal hygiene, puberty, etiquette, the importance of education, racism, dating, respect for women, respect for those in authority, respect for our elders, Christian salvation, a good work ethic, what it means to be an adult, what to look for in a wife, landscaping, minor home repairs, auto repairs, budgeting, investing, civic duties and the list goes on. We begrudgingly filled notebook after notebook after notebook.

As I approached my eighteenth birthday, the weekly lessons became monthly lessons and then every other month, until they slowly drifted away. My brothers and I were older, we had girlfriends, school activities, sports activities and job responsibilities that became extremely difficult to schedule around. I'm not sure when it happened, but the importance of our weekly lessons and notebooks began to pale in comparison to our busy teenage lives. Soon the classes and the notebooks were mere memories.

It's been years now since we had those classes with Dad in the game room. We are grown with careers and wives of our own. At every challenge in life, my brothers and I have frantically looked in attics, basements and storage sheds for our notebooks. We can't find them anywhere.

At least once a month one of us has a situation where we need to call home and ask Dad for his advice or guidance. We hesitantly pick up the phone to call him, knowing good and well he's going to laugh and say, "Where's your notebook?"

~John W. Stewart, Jr.
Chicken Soup for the African American Soul

DIRT CHEAP

May the sun shine, all day long,
everything go right, and nothing wrong.
May those you love bring love back to you,
and may all the wishes you wish come true!
~Irish Blessing

"When I die, just put me in a trash bag and set me out at the curb," my father would often say only half joking.

"I can't do that," I'd laughingly reply. "It's against code!"

"Well, don't waste a lot of money to plant me," he'd say.

A child of the Great Depression, my father lived simply, by choice. He wanted to die simply, too. Although he had a small nest egg put away, he loathed spending money on things he thought were unnecessary—and that included fancy caskets and expensive funerals.

This point was brought home to me when my mother died. The funeral director tried to convince Dad that Mom deserved only the best. Dad thought the best was wasteful.

"Why do you think I would pay for a box made of solid cherry when you're just going to plant it in the ground?" he asked the director pointedly. "Don't you have a cardboard box?"

Clearly shaken by my dad's bluntness, the director sold us the bottom-of-the-line model.

When Dad died of lung cancer fifteen years later, I knew just what I had to do. At the funeral home, I turned to the director and said, "He wanted to be buried in a trash bag and set out by the curb. What's the closest you've got to that?"

"Ah, a man like my father-in-law," the director replied. "I know just what you want." He then detailed plans for cremation and a simple church funeral. "And since your dad was a veteran, we can bury him in Denver at Logan National Cemetery."

"How much will that cost?" I asked.

"Nothing," he said.

The price was right! "Sold."

After the funeral, we were handed a plain, white cardboard box that held Dad's ashes. On the way to the cemetery, each of us wrote a parting message to Dad on the outside of the box.

"Your spot's over here," the cemetery guide said when we arrived. "They've just finished digging." He led us to a small hole less than one foot in diameter and several feet deep. "Do you have the ashes?" he asked.

I handed him the cardboard box that encased Dad's remains. As we watched, the cemetery worker took the box from the guide and began to wrap it in black plastic.

"What is he doing?" I asked, bewildered.

"I'm sorry," the guide lamented, "but we put the remains in this sack so that we can respectfully lower the box into the grave site."

"No, it's okay," I assured him. "Dad always wanted to be buried in a trash bag! I guess he got his wish, after all. It's not the curb, but it will have to do."

~Lynn Dean
Chicken Soup for the Father & Daughter Soul

STANDING BY HIS WORD

If we are ever in doubt about what to do, it is a good rule to ask ourselves what we shall wish on the morrow that we had done.
~John Lubbock

In a used-furniture business, unlike new, you cannot order stock from a catalogue. People call in, and you have to go out and make an offer. "You can't sell what you don't have," my father would say. So making his calls was crucial for him.

When I was age thirteen, my father lost his store manager, a one-armed guy who could do more with his one arm than many will do with two. With his one arm, he used to hook a chair on a long pole, then arc it upwards in the air where he would slide it onto ceiling hooks until someone wanted to purchase it. With his manager gone, my father came to me. Until he found the right person, would I come in while he went out to answer the day's calls?

The store has tens of thousands of items. "People like to bargain," he told me, "so I don't mark prices. You just have to know a range."

He took me around. "A quarter-horse motor you can sell for four dollars. For a refrigerator, depending on the condition, you can sell for thirty-five dollars to sixty dollars. However, if it has a freezer all the way across, sell it for eighty dollars, in excellent condition, maybe one hundred dollars. If a gasket's loose, it's garbage. Otherwise, I don't charge for scratches. Dishes come in with a houseful of furniture, and I don't even figure them in when I give a price. You can sell them for a nickel to a quarter. Something really nice."

Every day after school, I would pedal down to the store. Soon after, I was writing up a sales slip for an attractive plate when my father walked in. I had asked a dollar and the guy did not hesitate. I was very pleased. My father glanced down at what I was doing, turned to the customer and said, "You sure got a bargain today. My employee gave you the price and that's the price."

Afterward, I asked my father, "What was that all about?"

It turned out it was an antique plate, worth a few hundred dollars. I was devastated. Here I was trying to help my father in the business and instead I was losing money for him.

He said, "I could've stopped the sale if I'd wanted to. You were just writing up the slip and hadn't yet taken the money. Besides, by civil law, you're under age. But, a Jew stands by his word and the word of his agent."

Cost my father a small amount of money to teach me a lifelong lesson in integrity.

The event has a sequel. Years later, my wife and I needed to wire a large sum of money to our daughter in Israel. A bank teller advised my wife Loretta that a VISA check carried no service charge or interest unless late. When the bank statement showed considerable charges, I went in and tried to explain to the branch manager that we acted on their advice to avoid charges. To everything I said, all she could reply was, "We're sorry, but the teller made a mistake."

I then told her the story of my father standing behind the word of his employees. I finished by saying, "This was even when it didn't cause a loss to the customer, and when my father caught the error before the transaction. How much the more so afterward! I expect my bank to behave with at least as much integrity as my father."

The branch manager had not said a word during all of this, and her silence continued as I sat back in my chair. I had no idea of how she was going to react.

When she began to speak, her voice had softened, and she said in a dignified manner: "The Canadian Imperial Bank of Commerce will not be less than your father."

Then she promised that all the charges made to my account for that VISA check would be reversed.

As I thanked her and stood to leave, I was grateful that even in today's impersonal business world, a tale of integrity still had power to touch the heart and sway the conscience.

~Rabbi Roy D. Tanenbaum
Chicken Soup for the Jewish Soul

THE
WISDOM
OF DADS

Single Fatherhood

Most American children suffer too much mother and too little father.
~Gloria Steinem

34

SECOND CHANCE

Forgiveness does not change the past, but it does enlarge the future.
~Paul Boese

Stomach cancer claimed my mother's life three days before my second birthday. My father was devastated and never fully recovered from the heartbreak Mom's death caused him. He raised me alone, and although it was just the two of us in the house, I never really knew him. My mom's battle with cancer had been long and expensive. Insurance only covered so much, and Dad was forced to work crazy hours to keep my stomach full and the bill collectors satisfied. He wasn't home very much and was rarely in a good mood when he was home. His absence forced me to become very independent, and by the time I was twelve, I was pretty much on my own.

Left alone to do as I pleased, I was wild and developed a serious drug problem by the time I was fifteen. I did whatever it took to get high, and most times that meant stealing from my dad. I'd slip a ten or twenty out of his wallet, pawn off something small from around the house, or invent some unforeseen school-related expense. It didn't take him long to realize what was going on and confront me about it. He screamed the usual fatherly threats, and I countered with the usual obscenities of a defiant, undisciplined teenager. It climaxed when I threw and landed a punch and stormed out of the house, never to return.

I spent the next seven years bouncing around from one city to the next. Each move was supposed to be a fresh beginning, but ended the same way. I'd get into some kind of trouble with the law, or run up a tab with some drug dealer and be forced to run. I'd scrape up a few bucks, hop on a bus and move on, in search of greener pastures. Normal living was nothing but a pipe dream. I felt incapable and unworthy of living a normal life. I hated myself for what I had done to my dad.

Most recovering drug addicts will tell you that they were only able to get clean after hitting rock bottom. I met someone who helped me get clean before that happened. I was lucky. Her name was Gina. She was a bartender at Bob's Bar and Grill, a place I frequented. We struck up a casual bartender-patron friendship that slowly turned into something deeper. She knew about my addiction, but looked past it to see the real me. I fell crazy in love with her, and to my amazement, Gina fell in love with me.

Together, we confronted my addiction head on. With her love as my inspiration, I entered a rehab clinic, and on my first try, kicked my habit cold. She visited as often as they'd let her, and kept me strong with her smiles and kisses. Two weeks after I got out, we were married.

With a renewed attitude toward life, and the confidence gained from my recent accomplishment, I enrolled at the local community college. Gina kept her job and got her boss to hire me part-time. We struggled financially but somehow managed to make ends meet until I graduated with a bachelor's degree in hotel management. I found work at a five-star resort as a front-desk manager and earned enough to allow Gina to quit her job, and for both of us to concentrate on starting a family. On June 19, 1995, Dr. Barnes gave us the good news: we were pregnant.

Our daughter, Jennifer, was born on March 14, 1996. She was indescribably beautiful. God had blessed me with a new life, and with Jennifer's arrival, it was now complete. For the first time in my life, I was truly happy. I thought often about tracking down my dad, but never did. I felt too guilty, too scared to face him.

Just three months after my daughter's birth, God, in his mysterious way, tested the strength of my resolve and challenged my sobriety. On her way to the grocery store, a car ran a red light and struck Gina's car on the driver's side. She was killed on impact. I was home with Jennifer when the police officer called to inform me of the accident. I took solace in the fact that Gina hadn't suffered and probably didn't even see it coming. I hung up the phone and stared at Jennifer, who slept soundly. Tremendous grief enveloped me; I feared I couldn't handle taking care of Jennifer by myself.

The next few months were filled with anxiety, fear and depression. I found day care for Jennifer, went back to work and struggled mightily to stay sober. The emotional pain was relentless, and I was tempted every day to turn to my "old friend" for relief. Jennifer was the only reason I didn't. I would sit for hours, just staring at her, begging God for the strength to stay straight for her. I begged God to ease my pain and misery because I missed my wife so much.

One evening, after putting Jennifer down in her crib, there was a knock at the front door. I hurried to open it, and when I did, I saw my father standing there. He looked older and had less hair, but it was definitely him. He was obviously nervous and just stood there staring at me. I stared back. Several seconds had passed, when I broke the silence and began sobbing uncontrollably. My dad grabbed me, and we hugged each other tight. We stood there at the door and wept together.

"I'm sorry," I cried.

"No, son. I'm sorry."

The tears continued to flow as we held our hug. I released him and wiped my eyes. I invited him into my home; he came in and sat on the couch. I sat in my easy chair and looked at him, both of us trying to control our emotions and our tears.

"How did you find me?"

"It wasn't that hard, son. I have a friend who's made a business out of doing this sort of thing. I gave him a few bucks to track you down. I would've called but..."

"But what, Dad?"

"I didn't want... I didn't want you to say no."

I buried my face in my hands and wept again. He rose and came to me. My dad stood next to me and held me as I let out all the guilt and remorse I had carried around for years. Through my sobs, I begged his forgiveness.

"If I could take it back I would, Dad! I've hated myself for a long time because of what I did and what I put you through. You didn't deserve..."

"Stop it, son. Stop it! It was me; it was all my fault. All of it."

We talked for a while more, each of us trying to out-apologize the other. I still hadn't introduced my dad to his granddaughter, and I figured it was time.

"Dad, I have a daughter."

He looked surprised at first, then elated. It was the first genuine smile I can ever remember seeing on my father's face.

"Her name is Jennifer."

"Can I see her?"

I walked him into Jennifer's bedroom, and we both stood over her crib, watching her sleep. My dad stared at her as tears welled up in his eyes.

"She's got your mother's eyes."

"Yeah, I noticed that. Her mother passed away three months ago."

He looked at me with pity and concern, then grabbed me by the arm and led me out of the room.

"Son, I've made so many mistakes in my life. The biggest by far was letting you walk out of that house. I never got over your mother's death. I let my grief come between us. I love you; I always have. Don't make the same mistakes I made. Let nothing interfere with your relationship with your daughter. It is the only thing that matters. Her love for you will make life worth living. You are here to take care of and love that little girl. It'll be very difficult at times, but keep what happened to us fresh in your mind, and don't let it happen with her."

My dad stayed with us for two nights and then flew back home. I took his words to heart. They are always with me for inspiration and encouragement whenever things get tough.

Two months after his visit, I asked my dad if he would consider moving in with us to help take care of Jennifer—and me. He quickly accepted the invitation and moved in four days later. I miss Gina, and some days are harder than others. But I know she looks down at us and smiles because we are doing well, and Jennifer is happy.

Sometimes, a second chance is all it takes.

~Michael Shawn
Chicken Soup for the Single Parent's Soul

35

ORCHIDS AND CORNED BEEF HASH

A thankful heart is not only the greatest virtue,
but the parent of all the other virtues.
~Cicero

Rose was George's first true love. He met her at a luncheon-
ette, where she worked as a waitress. He'd always order the
corned beef hash with a sunny-side-up egg atop it and a
cup of black coffee. One day he snapped a picture of her behind the
counter serving him his plate of hash. After he had the film developed, he showed her the picture.

"Here's a picture of the girl I'm going to marry," he said, smiling.

Rose and George dated. He put the picture of her in his wallet. When he'd go out with his friends or even when he was among
strangers, he'd pull out his wallet and show them the picture.

"Here's a picture of the girl I'm going to marry," he'd say to them.
"Isn't she beautiful? Her name is Rose."

Rose fell for George just as he fell for her. They soon married.
A year later, they had a son—me. It was the three of us for several
years until my mother died suddenly, unexpectedly, from a stroke. I
remember the wake and the funeral and my father crying. I cried,
too.

Several more years passed and soon I was in high school. I was
getting ready to go to the senior prom with Jennie, my girlfriend at
the time. My father had said he'd pick up her orchid corsage at the

florist for me. Dad arrived at the florist late in the afternoon. He walked in and told the owner he was there to pick up the orchid corsage for Flynn. The man went to the case and returned with the beautiful purple and white corsage.

"That'll be fifteen dollars," the man said.

My father took out his wallet, and as he was removing the bills from their compartment, he showed the owner the picture of my mother serving him hash.

"This is my wife—isn't she beautiful?"

The old man adjusted his glasses and looked at the picture.

"Sure is," he said. "Is the orchid corsage for her?"

"No, no," my father said. "She only liked roses and daffodils. I don't think I ever gave her an orchid."

"Well, it's never too late," the man said.

My father smiled sadly and said nothing more.

Dad left the florist, and at the back parking lot, two men wearing ski masks approached him from behind. One was carrying a revolver.

"Give me your wallet," the man with the gun ordered, thrusting the revolver's muzzle into my father's ribs. My father handed it to him.

"And your watch, too," the other man said.

My father took off his gold watch and handed it to him.

"I know who you are. If you try to alert the authorities, we'll be back some night to take care of you. Understand?"

The two men fled on foot.

My father, shaken but unhurt, drove home and gave me the orchid corsage.

"Are you okay, Dad? You look pale as a ghost," I remember saying. "Is anything wrong?"

"No. Nothing's wrong. Have a good time at the prom, Son."

The next week or so my father was quiet and subdued. I knew something was wrong. After pressing him a few times, he finally told me the story.

"Did you call the police?" I asked.

"No. The robbers know who I am and where I live. If I tell the police, they'll be back for me."

Although I tried hard to persuade him to call the police, he wouldn't hear of it. What he did do was make certain all the doors and windows were locked securely each night before we went to bed. He seemed more sad, however, than afraid.

Two weeks passed. One evening, the front doorbell chimed. My father jumped — then cautiously peered out the window to see who was ringing the bell. He recognized the man as the florist who had sold him the orchid corsage. He went to the door, unlocked it, and admitted the man. The man introduced himself and then reached into his coat pocket and pulled out my father's black wallet.

"I found this in the shrubbery behind my store. I recognized the picture of your wife. It's the only thing left in it."

He opened it and showed him the picture of my mother. Gone was the name and address card, his driver's license, his union card, his social security card, the money (about forty-five dollars, my father recollected), and all other pictures and papers.

"Today is my lucky day," my father cried loudly, startling the florist. Dad tried to give him ten dollars as a reward for finding the wallet, but the florist wouldn't take it. He left and my father locked the door behind him.

"How can this be your lucky day, Dad? All your important papers and money are gone. Your watch, too."

"They can all be replaced," he said, smiling. "But there's only one picture of your mother serving me corned beef hash. Only one picture!"

~George M. Flynn
Chicken Soup to Inspire a Woman's Soul

36

WELL ENOUGH

The measure of a man is how well he provides for his children.
~Sidney Poitier

I had fallen asleep on the sofa, TV humming away in the background, when I was awakened by a kiss on the cheek—a kiss from my broad-shouldered, stubbly faced eighteen-year-old son, Dan. I groggily opened my eyes and smiled at him, glad to see he was home safely on this summer night before he was to go off to college three thousand miles from home.

"I love you, big guy," Dan said. "Very much."

"I love you, too, Dan. Very much."

We smiled at each other. He patted me on the shoulder and went to his room. I lumbered to my feet, downed a glass of water and returned to the sofa, where I sat, pondering this state of life known as single parenthood.

I'd raised Dan and his sister, Laura, now fifteen, on my own since they were ten and seven. When I use the phrase "on my own," it highlights the many faces of single parenthood. A single parent, whose ex-spouse lives a mile away and takes the kids on a regular basis, is a very different sort of single parent than the one who lives in an unfamiliar city with no close friends or relatives nearby and no child support to help. I was somewhere in between, closer to the latter. I received no child support and had a couple of people nearby who helped on rare occasion. My children's mother had had almost nothing to do with them for years, and had died a year earlier. So when I say "on my own" it really feels like I've done it alone for the most part.

Dan and I had locked horns over the years but were always close, always loved and respected each other. He was a sweet kid, but not always the most demonstrative, so a kiss and an "I love you, Dad," was always a treat for me.

I sat there and thought about raising Dan and Laura, about how this had been the best experience of my life, and how I hoped dearly it had been a good thing for them. From all outward appearances, they were happy, normal, well-adjusted kids. Having roamed the halls of their schools more than a few times, I could say with confidence they were doing much better than many of the children of "traditional" two-parent households. Much better.

I remembered the five-year, three-state custody battle that wiped us out financially and tested us emotionally and spiritually beyond what I ever dreamed possible. I remembered the happy ten-year-old boy who couldn't understand why his mother wanted his sister but didn't want him, and the tears he'd shed trying to fathom that. I remembered the little girl who was nearly catatonic for two weeks when a judge she never met ordered her to leave her mother and come live with Dan and me.

I reviewed some of the hundreds of moments we had spent together, the three of us, and whether they were fights or trips to the store or working on homework or simply sitting and talking, they were all wrapped up in my mind like tiny precious gifts.

We had come through all of it, not just intact, but stronger, closer—happier.

And now, this little boy with the bushy blond hair and the squeaky voice had become a man with a perpetual three-day growth of beard, muscles bigger than mine and a talent for jazz drumming that came from some gene pool I knew nothing of. And he was about to go off to college in California.

I got up and walked into his room, where he was getting ready to go to sleep.

"I love you, Dan. I'm really going to miss you."

He looked at me with that eighteen-year-old's "okay, we already did this tonight," kind of stare. But then, he came over, hugged me and said, "I'm going to miss you, too."

I said good night and closed his door.

I'll never know if I did this single-parenting thing right, but at that moment, I knew I had done it well enough. And I knew it was the best thing I had ever done.

~Joe Seldner
Chicken Soup for the Single Parent's Soul

37

RITE OF PASSAGE

When my son Chorus was in the sixth grade, his mother and I were divorced. No one suffered this parting of ways more than he. His whole body—the way he moved, as if carrying a hidden weight—revealed the extent of his wound. I wanted desperately to heal his pain, but felt powerless to do so.

When Chorus entered the seventh grade, he suffered from extreme sensitivity and low self-esteem. Fighting back tears, my son confided to me that no one liked him. I knew I had to do something for him—I would not fail him again—so, on his behalf, I began to investigate vision quests and other rites of passage in traditional cultures. I believed that some transitional ceremony might serve Chorus's confidence as he made the transition from boy to young man. I wanted him to experience a powerful rite of passage that would test his mettle and have real meaning for him. Since I was an experienced martial artist and instructor of Seibukan Jujutsu, it seemed that martial arts training might be a natural solution if he were willing.

Chorus's interest in martial arts was mostly relegated to the slam-bang movie fight scenes in action films, rather than to authentic training. So it required a leap of awareness and maturity on his part even to consider formal practice. I gave him the choice between learning some basic self-defense tactics, or committing to a serious training process that might one day lead to black belt ranking. Much to my delight, he chose the gauntlet of genuine training. Chorus remembers,

"Back then I was extremely shy, small and easily intimidated. I didn't want to be this way — I wanted to be outgoing and powerful, but I felt as if a weight on my chest held me down. Then, when I began my practice, I realized for the first time that with a little help from my instructors, I might throw that weight off for good."

Each time we stepped on the mat, I became Sensei (teacher) to him rather than "Dad." Some days Chorus acted sullen and punky with me, ready to collapse and quit. But he stuck with it. Weeks turned to months. A year passed, then two. Chorus persisted through the peaks and valleys of training — through the bruises, the mistakes and falls, the fatigue and pain. Progress was slow and difficult sometimes, but he learned that sweat and discomfort are part of the process. There were times he was too tired or sick to train, but he still wanted to do so. Once he insisted that we keep going despite a painful injury. During his years of diligent and faithful training, his martial arts ability improved greatly. But more importantly, I watched my son mature into a fine young man with growing confidence and physical ease.

When Chorus progressed to the brown belt level, Kancho Julio Toribio, the chief instructor, and I planned more intensive training for him, including several trips to Seibukan Jujutsu headquarters in Monterey, California. There, he trained in every aspect of the art required for the Shodan (first-degree black belt) level. Chorus recalls, "It was during this time in Monterey, while training and relating to people a lot older than me, when I first noticed changes in my personality: I started speaking to people more, and making my own decisions. I noticed that I wasn't as shy as I used to be."

One weekend in May, shortly after his fourteenth birthday, the time came for Chorus to take his black belt test. It was both significant and unusual for one so young to have advanced in the art as he had done. I believed he was ready, but the pressure encountered in this moment of truth, in a test of this nature, can make people respond in unpredictable ways. I could not know for certain if he would prevail. We traveled to Monterey to the main school, where Chorus spent all day Saturday practicing with advanced students and receiving constructive comments from the instructors, including me.

On Sunday morning, Kancho Toribio called Chorus to a special gathering. He sat in the middle of a circle of men much older and more mature than he. There, we each told Chorus about two events in our respective lives—one in which we were proud of our response to a difficult situation, and another where, in our own eyes, we failed and felt shame or regret about how we had behaved.

Each man spoke his truth openly and honestly, sometimes with great emotion. The stories ranged from heroics to cowardice in violent situations, from abuse experienced as a child to the pain of losing a loved one to death or a parting of the ways. I believe this was one of the most powerful events in my son's life—maybe in all our lives. It seemed extraordinary to see a group of men show such vulnerability for the sake of a young man's development. This sacred event had significant impact on my son. Following this gathering of men, Chorus was instructed to clean the dojo (school) in a traditional manner, and prepare for his test.

On Sunday afternoon, Chorus stepped on the mat to perform his black belt demonstration. As his father, I was pleased that, despite everyone's obvious affection for my son, they did not go easy on him during this ordeal. It was a full-out test at the black belt level, with attacks by individual and multiple assailants—empty-handed and with live, bladed weapons. It was an exhausting trial for him both physically and emotionally. I knew, because I had passed through it myself years earlier.

As his successful demonstration ended, my tears reflected the great pride and happiness I felt for my son. And when he received his black belt with great ceremony, Chorus said, "I cannot tell you all how grateful I am to my father and to those who helped me complete this process and attain the rank of black belt. This has been the most important learning experience of my life."

Something changed for us both during this whole process. The healing that I had prayed for had occurred, but even more, there was a new bond between us. We agreed we would never hold back secrets from each other and established a deep level of trust that is rare between fathers and sons in these modern times.

Recently Chorus turned seventeen, and I had the privilege of seeing him pass his test for an advanced level of black belt outranking my own. This was a proud and happy day for us both. My boy has truly become a man. I have since retired from teaching the martial arts. My son Chorus is now the primary instructor for Seibukan Jujutsu of Marin County, California.

~Robert Bishop
Chicken Soup to Inspire the Body & Soul

ARMS OF LOVE

I sat looking out the window, seeing new life growing in the early dawn of spring. The more I stared at the scenery, the more my sight blurred: I felt a warm drop—my own tear falling—as I wondered how life could be so cruel to me. What had I done to anger God so much that he would allow everything I ever loved to be taken away, one by one, piece by piece? I had made many poor choices in life, but God had always forgiven me. Where was he now? Why didn't I feel his mighty arms wrapped around me like I did when I was a kid?

Two years ago, I met a woman and saw life in a way I had not experienced before. Simplicity. Friendship. Communication. Love. I did all the things I knew to do: brought flowers, made home-cooked dinners, read books with her, watched the mist from a waterfall we'd spent all day hiking to, prayed together while holding hands.

What happened? What did I miss? What didn't I hear? I lived life to the fullest with her, and we gave God our best, inspired to live a wholesome life under his eyes. But, in our humanness, we made a choice. One that God would not overlook this time. I would be a great poster child for "it only takes once."

For the next nine months, my baby's mother vanished. It affected my work, my eating, my sleeping; anger and bitterness consumed my time and thoughts.

Then, domestic relations called to inform me that I had a son, and papers were on their way for wage attachments. Why didn't she tell me? What was his name? Did he look like me? Why, God, why?

I prayed I would find the right legal help and be able to create the income needed for funding a campaign to have my son in my life. I was able to find two attorneys and had the help of family and friends to encourage me throughout the whole mess.

Finally, eight weeks after that first call, I met my son for the first time. One look at him and love like I had never felt before overwhelmed me, accompanied by the pain of seeing his mother for the first time since the fateful evening of his creation.

The next year was spent in the courtroom. I exhausted my entire savings, sold my home, let the car go back to the bank and now rely on private funding and donations for the food on my table and the house I currently live in.

His name is Noah. He looks like his daddy. He acts like his daddy. He lives with me half the time, but we love each other all the time. I sit and stare at him for hours and watch him while he sleeps. I listen to his breath in the night while he lies next to me, asleep and snuggled against my chest. I help him count the toes he has recently discovered, as he wonders why they move by themselves.

As I sit here, I look out the window at the springtime of new life. But the more I stare out the window, the more my sight blurs. I feel a warm drop—my own tear falling—as I sit wondering how life could be so good to me. What have I done to please God so much that he would allow everything I have loved to be given to me, little by little, one day at a time? I have made many poor choices in my life, but God has always forgiven me. I feel his mighty arms of love wrapped around me like I did when I was a kid. His name is Noah. He is my son.

~Jeff Gemberling
Chicken Soup for the Single Parent's Soul

MY DAD

The most important thing in communication is to hear what isn't being said.
~Peter F. Drucker

Whenever anyone meets my dad, I imagine they first notice how handsome he is: the striking blue eyes, jet black hair and cleft in his chin. But next, I'll bet they notice his hands. He's a professional carpenter; he usually has a bruised nail or two, several fresh cuts, various healing wounds and calluses everywhere. The girth of his fingers is three times the size of an average man's finger. They are the hands of a man who started his working life at the early age of three, milking cows. His attitude toward a work crew can appear gruff; he expects them to work hard and do whatever it takes to finish the job without excuses.

Twenty-three years ago, my mom died, and this man's man was left all alone to raise a fourteen-year-old girl and an eleven-year-old boy. He suddenly had to be Dad and Mom.

It seemed easier at first. I was a rather fearless child and preferred playing with boys, doing boy things like climbing trees, building forts, playing football, baseball and with G.I. Joes. I did have a Barbie doll, but she often wore G.I. Joe fatigues and went to war with him. I even played on a boys ice hockey team. I had a lot of fun and learned many things from these activities. But none of them prepared me for stepping into my womanhood, which had to happen sooner or later.

I especially remember one day when I was about fifteen years old. We were driving down to Georgia to visit my aunt, and for some reason, every single thing my dad and my brother said or did made me crazy! I went from weepy to laughing for no reason, but my overall desire was to be left alone! It was clear they were both perplexed by this Jekyll/Hyde creature in their car.

We'd been taking our time driving and ended up spending the night at a motor lodge along the highway. Once we were in the room, Dad sent my brother out to the soda machine. When we were alone, he asked me what was wrong. There was nothing to do but admit that I'd begun menstruating for the very first time in my life. Then I burst out crying uncontrollably.

The miracle was that somehow, even though no booklet included this piece of information, Dad knew to just hold me and allow me to mourn the loss of my childhood.

He then offered to go to the store for me and buy the items I required.

We both crossed some kind of bridge that day: me into womanhood and he more deeply into the role of being mother as well as father. I think some men fear their feminine side, as if being nurturing would take away from their manliness somehow. All my dad knew to do was to love me unconditionally; not surprisingly, that worked just fine.

When my senior prom rolled around, I found myself in the happy position of dating a boy from a neighboring town; we invited each other to our proms, which were on consecutive nights.

Daddy wanted to make certain I had the perfect dress, and I did. It was a sleeveless, long white eyelet gown with a scoop neck. It made me feel like a princess. And Dad's approval was obvious; I think he was proud of me for stepping out of my tomboy image and acting the young lady—even if only for a couple of nights.

But what nights they were! Tradition at our school's prom was to stay out all night with your friends. With our parents' permission, my date and I "prommed" until 6:30 in the morning. I returned to my home to sleep for a few hours before driving to his parents' house.

I'll never forget my amazement that Saturday morning when I awoke and came downstairs to find my beautiful prom gown proudly displayed in protective plastic, like new, ready for another night's festivities.

It seems that sometime during my sleep, my dad had come into my room and found my prom gown. He had hand-washed it in a delicate laundry soap, then hand-pressed it.

My dad may not have been a man of many words when he was raising us, but he didn't really have to be. When I think of those beat-up working man's callused hands gently washing my delicate prom gown, my heart warms and relives that moment of unconditional love all over again.

It felt like the best of what we're supposed to learn from our mothers—and our dads.

~Barbara E. C. Goodrich
A Second Chicken Soup for the Woman's Soul

MYSTICAL, MAGICAL MOMENTS

A truly rich man is one whose children run into his arms.
~Author Unknown

I'll be frank. This is an eloquent piece about poop.

I have three of what I call poop-manufacturing devices. The youngest is a small puppy, the oldest is a three-year-old boy, and the last is a one-and-a-half-year-old cute-as-a-button, entirely lovable, make-you-smile-at-the-simplest-things little human girl. I added the adjectives for the third device, not that the other two aren't also cute and lovable, but because I sometimes need to be reminded that the little girl is, in fact, human. My doubts stem from the fact that she generates entirely nonhuman smells that escape from the outside garbage can and find their way back into my couch cushions.

The following is the drama I call "my family life."

Upon returning home from work, the three output devices, having not output any material for the sake of saving such output for my enjoyment, decide that it's time to get to work. Of course, the day-care provider insists that the output devices never stop working, but I find this impossible to believe since, and I could be wrong, theoretically these devices simply cannot put out more than they take in. Should their input match their output volumewise, then they would require a daily input roughly the size of a small Volkswagen.

Within fifteen minutes of returning home, it is soon apparent to me that the small, supposedly human girl has output something potent into her diaper (hereafter referred to as "the diaper"). Coincidentally, a diaper is the very same container that the small boy knows he should not output into, but does so anyway giving the following explanation: "No Daddy, no poop in the potty. Daddy poop in the potty. Robbie, diaper." So, not to be outdone by the supposedly human girl, the small boy also outputs. This sends the small puppy into an output frenzy, despite having just done the very same thing on the front lawn ten minutes earlier.

Now the stress begins (up to this point, it was only pain from the odor). Somehow, the small, supposedly human girl transforms herself into a professional wrestler about to be pinned. This transformation is triggered when she's laid down and I attempt to remove the aforementioned diaper. This is also when, for whatever reason, the little wrestler begins screaming bloody murder.

This causes the neighbors to call the police to report a case of child abuse.

The puppy shifts into red alert upon hearing the familiar Velcro sound of the diaper being taken off and waits for that brief moment when I slide the dirty diaper just out of reach of the wrestler's flailing feet while I feverishly clean the tush. Despite my knowing this will happen, despite my eyes continually scanning in all directions while also managing to be sensitive to what many call diaper rash (I call it "instant karma"), the puppy manages to bolt into the room, grab the diaper and drag it over the carpet just out of reach of my one free hand, the other not being free, since I have to hold the squirming body high enough off the carpet so as to avoid it becoming poop smeared. Throughout this ordeal, the other small human throws in expert commentary, "Oooooh, yuck!"

As the dog chews on the diaper, the wiped-as-clean-as-possible human transforms into a "greased pig," and the other, having some-how found the basketball hidden away on the top shelf of the linen closet, tosses the ball onto the greased pig's head.

It is at this point that the policeman knocks on the door.

The "greased pig" is screaming, having been bonked on the head with the basketball. The "ball player," having been reprimanded for causing potential brain damage, screams louder than the greased pig. The puppy, not to be outdone, barks uncontrollably. I smile at the police officer, who's never had children, and try to convince him that everything is perfectly fine. The dog also tries to appease the visitor by dragging the diaper to his feet as a peace offering.

We now have one small, screaming, naked child pulling on my pants pocket. An open diaper rests at the officer's legs. Yet more poop quite visibly smolders in the middle of the floor right near where we all stand. The puppy won't stop barking. And to top it off, the older boy who knows when, where and how to use the potty, has chosen not to do so and is now handing me his diaper full of poop. He, of course, is screaming because, in addition to the previous reprimand, runny poop is smeared all over his behind and running down his legs.

I can feel my head expanding as the smells accumulate, the sounds build up, and the tension increases. The policeman steps back, fearing exploding head particles, and begins to file a lengthy report.

But then something happens... something mystical, something magical.

When I pick up my little girl, she snuggles her tiny head into my neck and shoulder, then pats my back very lightly just as I do with her when she cries. The tension releases, the smells disappear, and my head returns to normal size. My boy stops crying as he realizes that if he hurries he can mow over the poop with his bubble-blowing lawnmower.

Ever receive a sincerely loving hug from a child? It's a mystical, magical thing. How can you compare poop to watching a toddler blow bubbles in the tub? Or when they shout with glee simply because you walk through the door in the evening? I look forward to each poop-filled day because every once in a while, quietly placed in between the boxes of cereal emptied onto the bed and the hands playing in the toilet, I receive yet another mystical, magical moment. These make everything that was once so overwhelming seem so very insignificant.

So, I may have several garbage cans full of freshly minted poop, and I may be on a first-name basis with both the police department and social services, but I also have happy, healthy children who are quick to jump into my arms each and every day. Of course, their diapers are full, but you know, it doesn't really matter. My children love me. And this single dad loves them.

~Rob Daugherty
Chicken Soup for the Single Parent's Soul

JUDGMENT DAY

Whant I am old and gray, judge me as a father by the number of times I said, "I love you," and how often I was able to say, "I'm sorry."

In a few days, the kids and I would mark the first anniversary of their mother's death. After dinner, we began talking about her, in a wonderfully casual manner—proof, at least in one way, that they were adjusting well.

"Have I been a good dad to you guys this past year?" I then asked daringly.

As expected, I was assaulted with, "Dad, be quiet!" and "Do you really want to know?"

I actually did. "I'll let you guys pick ten categories you want to rank me by. Any ten. You can give me any grade you want—and I promise I won't get mad," I said.

"Any grade?" Matthew asked, with a devious grin. "Are you sure we can give you any grade?"

"Any grade," I responded, with a growing reluctance. I went to get a pen and paper.

They started laughing—howling, actually—in much-too-eager anticipation.

"Should I be nervous about this?" I asked them. But it was too late.

"Laundry!" Mary shouted out, bringing all three of them to hysterics.

"Uh-oh," I grimaced. They've gone for the jugular right off the bat. This could be tougher than I thought. Comments about newly pink whites soon followed, as did complaints about mis-sorted socks and a lack of timely folding. (I absolutely hate folding.) But after careful deliberation, they gave me a B. Not bad, I thought to myself, clearly relieved.

"Personal Grooming," Anne then called.

"What does that mean?" I asked. I hoped she was referring to frequency of showers, rather than helping to braid hair. She was, and an easy B resulted.

"Cooking," they said, almost in unison, obviously getting the hang of the adventure. They gave me a very generous B-, due largely, I'm sure, to the close proximity of a McDonald's to our house.

"Clothes Shopping: B." Still quite generous.

"Food Shopping: B+." (I'd taken immense pride in this area over the past year, and was secretly hoping for an A.)

"Cleaning: C+." I exercised my first protest, pointing out to them that they were the cause of virtually all the household debris. But the judges were unmoved.

"Studying: B-." I was "too strict" when it came to homework. (I'd accept that anytime.)

"Driving Around: B+." I clearly felt I deserved an A on this one, given the amount of time I had spent in the car ferrying them to practices, activities, friends' houses and so on. But I had completely forgotten about one of Mary's basketball games the previous week. So I agreed that the lower grade was warranted.

"Gift Wrapping: B-." Do kids really care how birthday presents are wrapped? I thought that was an adult thing. Obviously not.

And finally, "Sports Fan." They gave me a well-deserved A. Far too many losing seasons had tempered my vocal competitive edge in the stands. I had reluctantly come to appreciate the value of simply participating in a sport, when a championship isn't even a remote possibility.

My overall grade as a dad?

"B," they declared. I'd done okay, according to the panel, but there was clearly room for improvement. We laughed and laughed, and they told stories about "surviving" me over the past year. It was a great moment, albeit at my expense.

After I tucked the kids in that night, I sat down and thought to myself that a B wasn't all that great. But then again, we had always been able to laugh. About their mom. About their father. In this past year, during which they could have been all too easily overwhelmed by sadness from their mother's passing, they had been able to find a wonderful measure of happiness.

Maybe as an extra-credit question I could have thrown in something like, "Don't Worry. Be Happy." It might have kicked my overall grade up to a B+. I'd settle for that this first year. For that matter, I thought, a few additional chores for three discerning judges might do wonders to help bring up that C+ in cleaning....

~Richard Zmuda
Chicken Soup for the Single Parent's Soul

THE WISDOM OF DADS

Treasured Moments

I cannot but remember such things were,
that were most precious to me.
~William Shakespeare

THE GREATEST SHOT OF MY LIFE

Golf is so popular simply because
it is the best game in the world at which to be bad.
~A.A. Milne

Like most guys I know, I was introduced to the game of golf by my father. My dad was a pretty good golfer when he was younger (5 handicap). When my sisters and I came along, he couldn't play as much as he'd like, but he still stayed in touch with the game.

In the early sixties, dad bought a bar in Portage Lakes, a nice series of recreational lakes in Ohio. My dad was in his fifties by this time and still liked to play the game. The problem was that after practically giving up the game, he would still take sucker bets from the younger guys who frequented his tavern. One guy bet Dad one hundred dollars that he could give Dad five and use only three clubs. Dad lost one hundred dollars. Another guy bet Dad fifty dollars that he could throw out his worst two holes, and once again Dad lost.

I felt bad for Pop because he was such a nice guy, and although these guys spent lots of money at Dad's tavern, at the age of twelve, I felt people thought Dad was a joke around the golf course and everyone was making fun of him.

Several days later, Jimmy Ray Textur, a young "hot shot" golfer, told my dad he would give him ten strokes and do all his putting with a driver. The bet was one hundred dollars and, of course, Dad accepted.

The following morning we met at Turtlefoot Golf Course in Portage Lakes, a beautiful course surrounded by water. On the 1st hole, Jimmy Ray hit a sweet drive, high and long, and straight down the fairway. Dad's drive sliced OB. I cringed and thought, here we go again.

After Dad's misfortune on the 1st hole, he settled down and played pretty well. Jimmy Ray didn't putt as well as he'd thought with his driver.

Dad had lost all of the shots Jimmy Ray gave him by the 15th hole. They tied on holes 16 and 17. The last hole was a par-4 straight-away with an elevated green and trees lining both sides of the fairway. At this point in time, the match was tied. Jimmy Ray hit his drive left center and had a flip wedge to the pin. Dad hit an awful slice deep into the woods where it rested on a huge clump of dirt that was the remains of a tree that was removed. By this time a few of Jimmy Ray's friends had wandered onto the course to watch the match.

I stood at the edge of the woods where I saw my dad climb onto this mound of dirt and debris and address the ball. In my heart, I figured Dad was about to lose another one hundred bucks. I felt rotten, and even worse for my dad. Just then I heard a crack echo through the woods that sounded like a cherry bomb going off under a pop can. The leaves parted, and to my amazement, the ball came out of the woods like a bullet, hit the bank in front of the green, bounced twenty feet in the air and came to rest two feet from the pin. This might have shook Jimmy Ray up a bit, for he chili-dipped his next shot. Jimmy Ray then chipped up within five feet and made the putt for par.

Dad needed his two-footer to win the match. As I walked up to the green, beaming with pride, I handed Dad his Bull's Eye putter so he could finish off Jimmy Ray. Dad walked past me and gave me a wink. He went to his bag, pulled out his driver and proceeded to knock in the two-footer!

The drive home was one I'll always remember. We drove straight to Montgomery Ward where he bought me my first set of golf clubs and a cool green, yellow and black plaid golf bag.

I'm still playing golf and running a small driving range in Mount Vernon, Ohio. Dad passed away in '93, but sometimes when I visit family in Akron, I play Turtlefoot. Whenever I come to the last hole, regardless of my score, I always feel good, for on this hole, I witnessed the greatest shot of my life.

~Del Madzay
Chicken Soup for the Golfer's Soul, The 2nd Round

THE IMPORTANT TEST

When you teach your son, you teach your son's son.
~The Talmud

I always thought Pinewood Derby cars defined your worth as a father, but my perspective may have been flawed. My father died when I was twelve, so the Pinewood Derby was one of the largest and last exams he faced. I remember with fondness how Dad passed his Pinewood Derby exam, and I knew that one day I'd have to take that same test.

When it came to woodworking, my father had a knack. I did not inherit that knack, which makes his test all the more impressive. One time, Dad gave me a pocket knife for my birthday. I'd seen him whittle, and it looked like fun. He warned me of the dangers and told me to wait until he could show me the proper and safe techniques. I couldn't wait. Almost before he had backed from our driveway, I sliced off a chunk of my thumb and had my knife confiscated.

Despite my woodworking deficiencies, Dad seemed to have confidence in our ability to make a functioning Pinewood Derby car. Perhaps the confidence came from his own abilities—knowing there wasn't any mistake I could make with a block of wood that he couldn't fix.

We sat down at the kitchen table and made our plans for our car. "Our" car. Somehow "our" plans seemed to match my limited capacity for fancy craftsmanship. The car called for two simple cuts and a whole lot of sanding. Dad knew I could sand. So he supervised my two simple cuts and turned me loose on my sanding. Each day

I sanded, and every night he'd inspect my progress and we'd talk about our project. Finally, we agreed to paint it red. He helped with the delicate wheel work, but I watched and learned. Our car won a couple of consolation speed prizes, and I thought he was just about the greatest father in the world.

The following year, we took our car-building a little more seriously.

We designed a car with wind resistance in mind and "our" design involved more complicated cuts. Our painting also addressed aero-dynamic concerns. We won major speed and design prizes, and I thought Dad was the greatest father in the world.

By the third year, Dad pretty much turned it over to me. I ran some ideas by him, but he just supported them. We talked a lot about more complex woodworking techniques. We won more major awards, but more importantly, he had helped me overcome my woodworking deficiencies. We built a display case capable of housing all three cars and several of the trophies. Dad was the greatest man in the world.

Dad died before the next Pinewood Derby, and my woodwork-ing skills seemed to always remain along the level of a twelve-year-old. Building those cars together created certain expectations—not only about woodworking and cars, but about parenting as well.

When my son brought home his Pinewood Derby kit, I remained afraid to open it—afraid I wouldn't understand the instructions, afraid I couldn't pass my fatherhood exam.

My son had no margin of error. If he made a mistake on his block of wood, I could not fix it. For that reason, I left the cursed thing inside the package for three weeks. My eight-year-old son, whom I'd lectured about procrastination, finally lost patience with me. That frightened me. If he lost patience, then I'd flunk my exam.

We sat down at the kitchen table and opened the package. We read the instructions together. They didn't make sense. So we read them again and discussed our interpretation of the instructions.

Soon we began to map out a design. He wanted a car shaped like a penguin, with wings and everything. That would have required whittling.

"No animals and no whittling."

"But a penguin is a bird."

"No birds and no whittling."

Most of my limited tool collection contained no tools suitable for an eight-year-old to operate, so we went and picked out a new coping saw together. At home, we measured and talked and came up with a modified penguin design, in which most of the penguin part of the car would be represented in an elaborate painting scheme.

"But will it look like a penguin?"

"There's lots of black-and-white critters it could look like. A killer whale, a zebra, a duck, a skunk..."

"But will it look like a penguin?"

"If that's what you want it to look like, then we'll just have to find a way to make it look like a penguin."

Find a way? That sounded like something my father would say. Worse yet, the more we worked on the car, the more and more I could see the possibilities of making a penguin sliding down the track on his belly.

"Will it be a fast penguin car?"

My son had seen my Pinewood trophies and began to talk about his expectation to build a fast penguin car so he could fill a trophy case of his own. We talked about realistic expectations. I suggested for the first year, we build a car that would make it down the track without falling apart. He wanted more. He could see the penguin, too, and if we could see a black-and-white penguin in a block of brown wood, then speed could be obtained, too. Then I remembered Dad.

"You know, the second year when we started winning our races, Dad and I worked graphite into the wheels."

"Then let's go buy some graphite," he insisted.

We did. He made the small cuts needed to outline a belly-sliding penguin. He must have inherited my father's knack. He sanded each day, and we discussed the progress each night.

The penguin-mobile did make it all the way down the track. It even won every race. In my son's smile, I saw my father's pride.

Then I realized that all along, I had been wrong. I hadn't passed my fatherhood exam. Those awards my son held were the results of my father's final exam.

My own exam would come in twenty-five years, when my son sits down with his son and the two of them plan and talk and sand.

~Brent L. Cobb
Chicken Soup for the Father's Soul

THE RUNAWAYS

You have to accept whatever comes and the only important thing is that you meet it with the best you have to give.
~Eleanor Roosevelt

One winter morning the year before I started school, my dad came in and asked if I would like to go with him to feed the cows. That sounded like fun, so I dressed in my warmest clothes, including the mittens connected by a string through the sleeves of my jacket, and went out with my dad to take my place in the world of work.

It was a pleasant morning. The sun shone brightly, but it was cold and the ground was covered with a blanket of new snow. We harnessed the team, Babe and Blue, and went over the hill with a wagon full of hay. After we found the cows and unloaded the hay for them, we started home. Then my dad came up with a good idea. "Would you like to drive?" he asked. And I responded in typical manly fashion. I like to drive anything: cars, trucks, golf carts or donkey carts. I think the attraction must be the power. There is such a sense of power to be in control of something larger than I am, and it's good for my male ego.

I took the lines from my dad and held them looped over my hands as he had shown me, and we plodded back home. I was thrilled. I was in control. I was driving. But the plodding bothered me. I decided that while I was in control, we should speed up. So I clucked the horses along, and they began to hurry. First they began to trot, and I decided that was a much better pace. We were moving along, and we would get home much faster. But Babe and Blue came up with a better idea. They decided if they would run, we would get home even sooner.

The horses went to work on their plan and began to run. As I remember it, they were running as fast as I have ever seen horses run, but that observation might have a slight exaggeration factor built in. But they did run. The wagon bounced from mound to mound. As the prairie dog holes whizzed by, I concluded that we were in a dangerous situation, and I started to try my best to slow down this runaway team. I pulled and tugged on the lines until my hands cramped. I cried and pleaded, but nothing worked. Old Babe and Blue just kept running.

I glanced over at my dad. He was just sitting there, looking out across the pasture and watching the world go by. By now, I was frantic. My hands were cut from the lines, the tears streaming down my face were almost frozen from the winter cold, stuff was running out of my nose and my dad was just sitting there watching the world go by.

Finally, in utter desperation, I turned to him and said as calmly as I could, "Here, Daddy. I don't want to drive anymore."

Now that I am older and people call me Grandpa, I re-enact that scene at least once a day. Regardless of who we are, how old we are, how wise or how powerful we are, there is always that moment when our only response is to turn to our Father and say, "Here. I don't want to drive anymore."

~Cliff Schimmels
A 6th Bowl of Chicken Soup for the Soul

DAD'S RIGHT HAND

Every action in our lives touches on some chord that will vibrate in eternity.
~Edwin Hubbel Chapin

Many of us who grew up in the '50s had dads who were more shadow than real. They left every morning to go to work (a vague concept to us) and came home every evening to eat and fall asleep in front of the TV before going to bed. We knew they cared about us, but we didn't know much about them.

My dad hauled bread for a living. Six days a week, he left the house at 3 A.M. and returned in time to eat supper and go to bed. On Sundays when he stayed home, Dad was usually working on jobs around the house while I was busy playing. Our paths seldom crossed.

So went our shared existence until the summer I was twelve. That was the summer Dad "hired" me to go along on his bread route and be his helper. Fridays and Saturdays were my designated workdays. For the princely sum of three dollars a day, I would climb into his big truck before the sun made an appearance and set out on an adventure with my dad. Off we'd go, traveling to little country stores as well as supermarkets in distant towns.

Dad stopped at most of the stores before dawn and used a flashlight to peer through a window to survey the bakery displays, then decided if they needed anything to start the day. He'd yell to me to get a box ready to pack. I'd quickly assemble a cardboard box that was stored in the corner of the truck and wait for him to tell me what to put into it. Bread and sweet rolls to start the day were bundled and left by the door of the shuttered store. Later in the day, on the return trip, we'd stop once again to replenish the bakery supply, get payment for the goods and continue to retrace our morning run.

Dad never lost his patience if I made a mistake. If he sent me to the truck for a loaf of rye bread and I returned with whole wheat, he'd grin and tell me I got the brown breads mixed up again and to go back and get a loaf in the orange wrapper. If I brought in Danish rolls instead of Bismarcks, he'd say we needed the ones with the jelly inside. Eventually, I got better at knowing the stock and made fewer mistakes. I could even suggest what was needed. I'd beam with pride when Dad told his customers that I made a pretty good bread man or that I was his right-hand man. (This was years before any of us would have thought it more appropriate to say "bread person.")

Halfway through the day, we stopped at Gracie's store in a little country village called Shennington. That little store was always a welcome sight because it meant lunch. After we finished the business end of the visit, Dad would point me toward the meat counter along the old side wall and tell me to pick out the lunch meat I wanted. I'd usually choose the ham or big bologna, and then watch in anticipation as the loaf was placed into the machine that cut it into slices. I'd wait while our banquet main course was wrapped in white paper, then I'd grab a bag of chips and a soda for each of us. By the time I got to the lone checkout counter, Dad would be chatting with Gracie and digging out his wallet. Soon, we'd be on the road again, Dad driving while I slapped meat between slices of bread to make sandwiches for both of us. Seldom have I had any sandwich that tasted as good as those unadorned meals.

Since Dad's route was mostly rural, there was a good deal of drive time between stops. The truck was noisy, so conversation was minimal, but we did manage to make short comments to each other. Our conversations consisted mostly of gestures and facial expressions. He'd point out a deer along the road and smile as I gazed with big eyes. He'd laugh when I bobbed my head in time to the rhythm of the windshield wipers. We'd share a look of disgust when some careless driver almost cut him off while passing on a narrow, two-lane road.

My workday ended when Dad pulled his truck into our driveway to drop me off, usually around two o'clock. His workday wasn't quite finished, however. He still had to return the truck to the outlet garage, clean it out and make it ready for the next day, and do his daily paperwork. I didn't see him again until supper, after which he crawled into his old rocking chair to watch a little TV before heading for bed. Though he was the same as always, I saw him differently then—he was no longer a shadow, but real.

The years have flown by, and I learned more about this mystery man as I got older. After I had children of my own, I understood the long hours he worked to support his family and the sacrifices he made. We shared many lovely times together, but nothing has ever recaptured those special days when the world consisted of Dad and me rattling around in an old boxy truck.

~Lana Brookman
Chicken Soup for the Father & Daughter Soul

A FATHER'S LOVE

Nearly fifty years ago, during one of my summer college vacations, my father drove me to my favorite fishing spot at Candlewood Lake in western Connecticut. The winding country road paralleled a beautiful little stream, about thirty feet wide, which flowed into the lake. As I soaked up the passing scenery, I decided to tell him about an idea I had been visualizing for several weeks, even if he thought it was outrageous.

We had taken this route many times before and had established a now-familiar routine. My father would bring me to the lake, carry my wheelchair to an easy location at the water's edge and then carry me to my wheelchair. He'd make one more trip from the car to bring me my fishing rod, spinning reel and tackle box, which also contained my snack. My mother was sure I'd get hungry.

Despite my cerebral palsy, I had found unique ways to cast my lure between fifty and one hundred feet. The biggest trick was how to hang onto the line after releasing the bail, and then let go of it at the right moment while casting. Believe me, there was a lot of trial and error in the backyard before I finally got the technique just right.

Truthfully, I never cared whether I caught any fish or not. I wanted to be out in nature by myself for awhile, just like other people. My father, another nature lover, understood perfectly well and, by mutual agreement, he would leave me at the lake for three or four hours before returning to pick me up. Only once did he have to return earlier than planned because of a sudden downpour; I was pretty wet by the time he arrived, but it really didn't matter. In fact, it was fun.

But on this particular day I asked him to pull over to the side of the road where we could easily see the gently moving stream.

"See that big rock out there in the middle?" I asked him.

"That flat one?" my father asked.

I had a hunch he knew what I was going to ask next. "Yes. Do you think you could carry me out there?"

He laughed at first, then said, "Let me take a look." I watched him walk to the edge of the stream, scouting for a way to step from rock to rock without getting wet. Then he began stepping carefully across the water until he was on my desired location. Though getting there did not look easy, he didn't get wet and it was obvious, as he looked all around, that he enjoyed the short journey. When he came back to the car, he said, "So you really want to fish out there?"

"Yes, I'd love to. I've always envied guys who fish standing in the water up to their knees or higher in the middle of a fast-moving stream. Several weeks ago, when we drove by here, I noticed that rock and thought it looked perfect for me, if you can just get me out there."

"Well, I'm game if you are," he said. So we began our routine, but in a different location this time. I watched him set up my wheelchair in the middle of the rock, making sure to put the brakes on, a very necessary precaution, especially in this case. Then he came back for me. Truly, I was a little scared as we went from one small rock to another because he could not use his arms for balancing as needed, but we somehow made it across the water. We were both relieved when I was sitting safely in my chair. After bringing me my usual equipment, he said he would return in a couple of hours.

And then I was alone.

The sounds of the rushing water got louder and it seemed to flow faster, as if saying, "What are you doing out here?" But I knew it was only my imagination and some of my fear of being there all by myself. "What ifs" began popping into my consciousness: What if Moby Dick grabs my lure and pulls me off this rock? What if the water rises? What if someone sees me out here and calls the fire or police department to rescue me? I quickly told myself how silly I was being and started appreciating how awesome the site truly was.

I began fishing and noticed that I could let the water's current carry my lure away instead of me casting it. I liked that. Fishermen really don't want to work too hard. Reeling it back to me was easy, despite the tug of the current, and I soon felt wonderfully calm as my lure went out and back, out and back. It was a beautiful day, and time flew by.

My father came back for me a little early that afternoon, but it didn't matter. I hadn't caught a thing, except great personal satisfaction from fulfilling a small dream. I also gained an awareness of how much my father loved me. He demonstrated it many times throughout my life, willingly taking risks for me, so that I too might experience what everyone else does.

~Donald Zimmermann
Chicken Soup for the Fisherman's Soul

BUTTERSCOTCH

What wisdom can you find that is greater than kindness?
~Jean-Jacques Rousseau

My father did not start playing golf until he was in his sixties. He used to practice putting balls into plastic cups and coffee mugs on the rug in his family room while watching the Sunday tournaments on television. He used to boast about how he had sunk fifteen of these putts in a row. I used to watch him perform these putting exercises and watched his concentrated eye focusing on the mug at the end of the room, taking two or three practice strokes, and then following through with mechanical precision, making only minor adjustments to his swing when the balls would careen off the edges of the mug. I did see him make about four or five in a row at one point, but unfortunately not fifteen.

My father did not have the best all-around golf game, but he did have an acute eye for putting. If he had started a little earlier in life, he might have even become a better and more complete player. But, his love of being outside in the sun, the long walks for exercise, and the competition we shared on the course were what really made him enjoy this game. Nonetheless, he would reward himself for any minor victory on the golf course with a piece of butterscotch candy. The candies were not only rewards for him, but for myself or anybody else who played a hole nicely. If someone sank the tough ten-footer from the rough or even just the two-footer to win the match, a butterscotch candy was his way of saying "Nice job." As long as something was done on the course that impressed him, a butterscotch candy was the victor's spoils.

When my father reached his early seventies, he developed Alzheimer's disease. His world and my family's were suddenly turned upside down. His concept of time had been wiped out, his memory was fleeting at best and his independent life was soon coming to a close.

In the beginning stages of his sickness, we would still make the occasional trek to the golf course. I did not know exactly what to expect at this point and really just characterized the memory lapses and spatial imperfections as symptomatic of old age. The frustrations of my father's illness combined with the challenge of the game made it a very tough morning.

"Dad, Dad, Dad! This way!" That's all I seemed to be yelling as my father, in the midst of disorientation, would face the opposite direction of the holes and begin to tee up. I had to physically grab him and turn him in the right direction at some holes. When I put my hands on his waist and turned him around I could feel how lost this man had become and how dependent on me he was. It felt at times like I was playing with a small child who had never stepped on the golf course before in his life.

I remember watching him walk, or better yet shuffle, around the fairway in a half-hearted attempt to find his ball, truth being he had no idea where it was. "Dad, it's over there!" I would yell and point, simultaneously waving ahead another foursome that was playing behind us.

The afternoon seemed to drag along more and more. The fifteenth hole was upon us and I had finally reached the green in about six and was prepared to putt. I had dropped a ball for my father in front of the approach just to speed up our play and let him poke it onto the green. I stood behind my ball waiting for him to chip. He had three weak digs at the ball before it finally scooted onto the green about six inches directly in front of my ball! He wore a little smile as he awkwardly shuffled around the green and waited for me to putt.

We stood and looked at each other almost comically for a few seconds—then I lost it. "Dad, mark your ball!" He still wore a face of delusion and disorientation as he meekly patted his pockets for a marker. He pulled out tees and balls—but no marker. He sensed my frustration mounting and I started to let my impatience seep into my expression.

Eventually he pulled something out of his pocket. I watched him reach down and pick up his ball and replace it with one of his butterscotch candies. He put it down and did not have the slightest clue what he had just done. The candy stood right in my putting line, the circular candy only a little bit smaller than the ball itself, its shiny gold cellophane wrapper reflecting sun and sitting so stupidly on the green.

I looked up at him and he was not even looking back at me. He was just looking around at the trees, at other golfers, wherever. I looked at him and started to laugh. I laughed hard. He looked back at me, then he looked at the candy sitting on the green. He laughed too.

The last three holes we played that day were some of the most memorable ones I have had playing this game. We both still played lousy the rest of the day, but we had fun, and my father and I would both have small awakenings amidst the green. He was freed from the delusions and disorientation of Alzheimer's for a couple of hours, and I was freed from the grasp of taking this game way too seriously.

That would be the last time I would ever play golf with my father, but it was the best time. The game became simple and fun for me again and he gave me that. Now, there are no more temptations to throw clubs or curse out loud or come home after a weekend of golfing upset because "I lost my swing." From now on, I take my time and I have fun—in all aspects of life. I carry a butterscotch candy on me whenever I play golf and when I realize I am getting terribly frustrated with this game I reach in my pocket for the butterscotch and remember that day on the course with my father—and laugh. I now enjoy golf and I am better at it. I am a pretty good putter now, too. I sank fifteen in a row in the coffee mug just a couple of days ago. Really, I did.

~A. J. Daulerio
Chicken Soup for the Golfer's Soul

ACROSS HOME PLATE

Things turn out best for those who make the best of the way things turn out.
~Daniel Considine

The wind blew through John's curly red hair as he stood at bat. Crack! The baseball connected. It sailed high over the left outfield fence. The crowd stood and cheered as he ran across home plate. Then his daydream bubble burst... and young John limped away from the empty diamond dragging his polio-damaged leg.

In 1944, a poliomyelitis epidemic ravaged the United States. This serious infectious virus hit children especially hard. It caused inflammation of the gray matter of the spinal cord and brought on fever, motor paralysis and muscular atrophy. John's concerned parents kept him away from swimming pools, from theaters, from crowds. But polio does not play fair. On a Sunday in September just after John's seventh birthday, he started walking across the living room at his home in Spokane, Washington. His legs collapsed. His stepfather carried him upstairs to bed. Three years later in 1947, Jonas Salk would develop a dead-virus vaccine that protected against poliomyelitis paralysis, but it came too late to help John.

For six lonely months, John was in the contagious-patients ward at St. Luke's Hospital in Spokane. His mother could not even visit her little boy. Many tears flowed as the hospital attendants rolled his bed to the window so he could wave to his mother standing on the sidewalk.

Treatments at that time were consistent with the Sister Kenny philosophy—moist hot packs on the affected areas, bed rest and very little, if any, physical therapy. John graduated to leg braces. Subsequent follow-up orthopedic surgeries came a few years later.

As John was growing up, his parents, six younger siblings and friends never treated him as handicapped. Therefore, John never considered himself disabled. He lived in an atmosphere of encouragement. His interest in sports remained high, and he participated as much as he could. He just did, or tried to do, what the others were doing.

John realized that having polio had turned him away from a career in sports. For an occupation, he knew he wanted to do something with his hands and help people. He enrolled in the University of Washington School of Dentistry, where he became president of his class and graduated in 1962.

As the years passed, John and his wife, Ginger, were blessed with five robust, sports-loving sons. Coaching the boys in soccer and in Little League allowed John to remain involved with sports while he watched his boys grow. On September 7, 1998, John's sixty-first birthday, he and Ginger were attending a baseball game. Their second-oldest son stepped up to the plate. He swung with powerful strength. His home run sailed over the left outfield fence and shattered the history books! Mark McGwire had hit his sixty-first home run of the season, tying Roger Maris's thirty-seven-year-old record.

"Happy birthday, Dad!" Mark yelled. He threw a kiss into the sky in Maris's memory. Then three generations of McGwires—Mark, Mark's son Matthew, and John—greeted the standing, cheering crowd. And John, leaning on his cane, crossed home plate.

~Sharon Landeen
Chicken Soup for the Sports Fan's Soul

49

NO MORE SUNDAY MATINEES

I have loved movies since I was a child. I attended Sunday matinees at the Monroe Theater, seeing films like *The Love Bug, Charlie, The Lonesome Cougar* and *The Reluctant Astronaut.* Then, in 1970, I turned ten and my hormones kicked in big-time. I got into trouble (at that time, "getting into trouble" meant lighting gasoline in the street and stealing comic books) and my tastes turned from Disney movies to more mature fare. Still, I was precluded from seeing R-rated movies.

All at once, commercials appeared on TV for *The French Connection.* They looked exciting, streetwise, powerful and testosterone-driven. This was going to be a man's movie. And I was going to miss out, because I wasn't old enough. I can remember when my dad and older brother went to see it, stepping into the freezing night calling, "We'll be back later," Peter running ahead of my father in anticipation.

The French Connection broke new ground. The car chase was daring, edgy and thrilling, like nothing ever seen before (the commercial focused on this now-famous scene and made me long to see the movie). Gene Hackman's portrayal of Popeye Doyle was far from the clean-cut cop audiences were used to seeing. Instead, he played this New York City detective as a trash-mouthed, racist and angry antihero (the film would later snag Academy Awards for best picture, director, actor, screenplay and editing). I was a movie fanatic, and I felt I was missing out on something historical, daring and new. Peter was thrilled to be seeing it. I, however, was relegated to another dreary night at home with my mom and younger brother, Steven.

When Peter and my dad got home, they expressed what I already knew. The movie was great. They talked about the car chase. "Unbelievable!" Hackman was "fantastic!" Oh, how I wished I were older and could....

"You want to go see it, Leonard?"

Was that my father who just said that? Did I hear right? Confirmation came in a second, from my mother.

"Ed, do you really think he should see it?" Oh Mom, don't kill my chances. Don't plant the seed of doubt. Be quiet for just a little longer until I can extract a promise. Then the sweet words came, and the foot gently came down with them.

"I don't see why not. I think he's old enough to handle it. We can go tomorrow night."

"But you just went with Peter tonight. You're going to go again tomorrow?"

My dad looked over at me. He must have seen my eyes, filled with excitement and anticipation.

"Sure, why not?" he said.

"Yeah!" I cried and leapt into the air.

The next night I could hardly eat my dinner. I couldn't wait to get out of the house and see something that I thought only my older brother would be allowed to see.

"Leonard, if you don't eat something you're going to be hungry at the movies," he said smiling to himself.

There it was again—confirmation of the event. Yes, we were actually going to go see this R-rated movie together. It would be my first one, my initiation. At last, dinner was over. We donned our winter coats and stepped to the front door. My dad grinned, tossed his head back and called out, "We'll be back later."

"Okay," said my mom, "have fun." I was so thrilled. Now it was Peter's turn to stay home with Mom and Steven.

We got into the car. It was freezing. My dad's Old Spice cologne gently enveloped me, and the car warmed as the heater kicked in. I could feel his love for me. This was a time for just him and me to be together. Even though he had just seen the movie the night before, he was going to take me tonight. He didn't even wait a few weeks. I was impressed and felt special.

The Monroe Theater was big (none of those shoebox multiplex theaters back then) and smelled of heat, popcorn and seat cloth. Back then, anyone under age twelve couldn't get into an R-rated movie. I looked older than I was, and my dad paid the extra money so we wouldn't have any trouble from the ticket lady. I was thrilled that my father thought I was mature enough to see an R-rated movie and that he had no problem saying, "Two adults, please," when buying our tickets.

The French Connection was better than I had anticipated. It was the most exciting movie I'd ever seen. And the most adult.

Hackman cursed like a sailor, beat suspects, crashed his car through New York City in pursuit of a sniper and shot him on the stairs of a train stop. For weeks afterward, I would stand at the bottom of my basement stairs, feign exhaustion, point my imaginary gun upward and yell, "Hold it!" just as Hackman did before he shot the bad guy.

As we walked up the steps at home after the movie, I turned to my dad and really looked at him. I wanted him to know how happy he'd made me, how wonderful it was to believe he thought of me as an adult (at least in some way), but all I could come up with was, "Thanks for taking me, Dad."

He hugged me, his big arms wrapping me tightly, and held me for just a little longer than usual. Old Spice never smelled so sweet.

"Oh, my pleasure," he said, "my pleasure!"

And it was.

After that, we went to the movies alone together all the time. The R-rating lost its importance and was no longer considered a sticking point. I had seen one and could now see all of them. My rite of passage was over. But when I was fifteen, things changed a bit and I went to the movies with my friends more than my dad.

In 1975, Peter and I, and my friends Glen Belfer and Cliff Konnerth, waited in line for two hours (this was very unusual back then!) to see *Jaws*. I went home raving about it. What a fantastic movie! I could see my father wishing he had been allowed to go with the teenagers to see this "event," because there was no way my mother was going to go with him and he certainly wouldn't see it by himself. But he was the parent now. Teenagers don't really want their parents around when going to the movies as a group.

"Hey, Dad," I said. "Ya wanna go see it?"

He seemed a little surprised. He hesitated, knowing how his place had changed, but said, "Well, yes, I'd love to."

"Okay, we'll go. Tomorrow night. Just you and me."

"Terrific," he said, turning away so I couldn't see him smiling from ear to ear.

The next night we waited in line for two hours to see *Jaws*. And this time, it was my pleasure to "take" my father to the movies. My pleasure.

~Lenny Grossman
Chicken Soup for the Father's Soul

50

FLASHING BACK

I wish we could put some of the Christmas spirit in jars and
open a jar of it every month.
~Harlan Miller

It wouldn't be Christmas without the memory of my dad taking the annual holiday photo. I carry a mental image of his hairline with the camera blocking his face and the unsnapped case dangling beneath it like the protective gear of a catcher's mask.

But nothing protected Dad from the hubbub of five kids on Christmas Day. The Christmas commotion clashed with his German temperament, driving him to create order from the chaos.

So he created the ritual. None of us could eat dinner, or even touch our forks, before he took the holiday picture. His payoff was some peace, if only for a precious few minutes.

"I need quiet," he commanded, "or else it will take me even longer to set up."

We rolled our eyes—the only things we could move without disturbing the pose. The focus of his attention was a Zeiss Ikon Contaflex I, purchased when we were stationed in Europe. A manual 35 millimeter camera, it required endless calculations and adjustments before he dared click the shutter. I'm sure it was a dad just like him who inspired some kid to invent the Kodak Instamatic!

For what seemed like hours leading up to the photo, he made us sit still in our assigned places around the table. He looked through the viewfinder every few seconds. He read—and reread—the instruction booklet. He peered through reading glasses to carefully manipulate the camera's settings.

And Mom offered us no sympathy.

"Be patient with your father," she advised. "Someday, when you're grown up, you'll thank him for doing this."

It turns out Mom was right.

Years after leaving home, I pawed through a box in her basement and discovered the Christmas pictures. I looked closely at each one and realized that, instinctively, Dad had almost replicated the poses each year. The changes were so minor that the photos resembled animation cells. I placed them in chronological order, earliest at the bottom, and began to flip through the years.

I notice how the images changed at the sides of the table where a highchair moved in and out of the frame like a ping pong ball as each toddler grew out of it. Finally, Gretchen, Carolyn, Jan and I were all seated at the table. Seven frames later the high chair moved into place again with the family caboose, Bart. Our heights increased with the years and so did our hairstyles: from pixie, to beehive, to page-boy. We were always in Sunday dress, and Mom's clothes mirrored the decades.

But little changed at the head of the table.

With no evidence of him dashing to his own spot in front of the camera, Dad sported an every-hair-in-place military crew cut. He always wore a white shirt and a necktie that exactly matched his trousers. His left hand gripped an oversized fork impaling the turkey breast. His right hand held a knife poised to carve. It is a sign of the times when I see a white cord that stretched from a wall socket to Dad's new electric knife.

It's all there, captured year after year, as we held our places and our smiles, waiting for Dad's diligently preset timer to click our pose.

My life story is told in those photographs, in all that is seen and unseen. And I smile, recalling the adage about what a picture is worth. Thank goodness Dad loved us enough to ignore our groans and snap them.

~Kathryn Beisner
Chicken Soup for the Soul Christmas Virtues

51

'TWAS THE NIGHT B4 CHRISTMAS

Old as she was, she still missed her daddy sometimes.
~Gloria Naylo

Two Decembers ago, my dad called wanting to know what I wanted for Christmas. I mentioned a particular book and then interrupted myself and said, "No, what I'd really like is for you to put *The Night Before Christmas* on audiotape."

There was this long pause and then Dad said with familiar stern emphasis in his voice, "Oh for God's sake, Mary. What in Sam Hill do you want that for? You're forty years old!"

I paused, feeling embarrassed yet determined, "Dad, I remember how good it felt when you used to cuddle us all up next to you on the couch when we were little and read *The Night Before Christmas*. I can still remember how strong your voice was, how safe I felt and how well you acted out all the different sounds. I'd really appreciate you doing this, since I live 2,500 miles away and I'm not coming home for Christmas. It would be nice to have you with me."

Dad said, with a little more softness but still incredulously, "You mean you want me to read just like I did when you were kids, with all the bells and whistles and everything?!"

"Yaaaaaah, just like that," I said.

Again, he paused a long time and then said, "I'll get you the book."

I heard the clarity of his decision in his voice and resignedly said,

"Okay. Talk to you on Christmas." We said our "I love yous" and hung up. I felt bad but tried to understand. I assumed it was too much sentimentalism for a seventy-six-year-old bear, and that in his mind it was a foolish request for an adult to ask. Maybe. Maybe not. All I knew was that each time I talked to Dad, his voice sounded more tired, and I was beginning to accept that it was no longer if, but when, the day would come that I wouldn't hear it anymore.

On Christmas Eve day, a small, brown, heavily recycled padded envelope with lots of staples and tape all over it arrived. My name and address were written out in my dad's memorable architect's lettering with thick black magic marker. Inside was a tape, with a handwritten label, "'Twas the Night b4 Christmas."

I popped the tape in my recorder and heard my father's words come roaring out. "'Twas the niiiiiiiiiiiiiiight before Christmas when allllllllllllllllllllllllllll through the howwwwwwse," just like when we were children! When he finished, he went on to say, "And now I'm going to read from *The Little Engine That Could*. I guess Dad had another message in mind when he included one of our favorite childhood bedtime stories. It was the same story we read to my mom when she was dying of cancer three years ago.

He continued with the Mormon Tabernacle Choir singing "Silent Night," our family's favorite Christmas Eve song we sang together before bedtime. And then "Oh Come All Ye Faithful" song after song until the tape ran out. I went to sleep safe and sound Christmas Eve, thanking God for giving me another Christmas miracle with my dad.

The following May, Dad passed away suddenly and unexpectedly. No more phone calls every Sunday morning, no more phone calls asking me, "What was the Gospel about today, Mary?" no more "I love yous." But his voice lives on... and continues to remind me that I can do what I put my mind to and that I can stretch myself emotionally for someone else, even when it's difficult. That's the power of love.

For Christmas this year I sent my sisters and brother and their children a copy of the tape, which they weren't expecting. My youngest sister called and left a tearful message on my machine that said, "Mary, I just got the tape. Did you know that on the tape he said it was December 19. That's today! When I put the tape on while I was in the living room, Holden [her two-and-one-half-year-old son], came running out from the kitchen full steam, yelling at the top of his lungs, 'Grampa's here, Grampa's here.' You should have seen him, Mary, looking all around for Dad. Dad was here."

His voice lives on.

~Mary Marcdante
Chicken Soup for the Soul Christmas Treasury

52

THE LAST BIG CATCH

*There is certainly something in angling that tends to
produce a serenity of the mind.*
~Washington Irving

When I think of all the fishing trips, the one that stands out is the trip that took place on November 27, 1997. Grandpa was lying in a hospital bed that was set up in Grandma's dining room. Dad had spent the night with him. Around 1 A.M., one of my aunts came in to wake up Dad. Grandpa was having delusions, thinking he was trapped in the hay barn, even though he was still in bed.

"Dad, why don't we sit on a bale of hay and take a breather," my father suggested.

Grandpa was out of breath and panicky. When Dad finally talked Grandpa out of the "barn," he suggested they go sit under the maple tree in the front yard. Grandpa agreed, and he sat up in bed. All was quiet as he looked at the imaginary land and water before him.

"Did you see that?" Grandpa asked Dad.

"See what?"

"That fish jump. There's another one," Grandpa said, as he cast out his line.

"Dad, what are you doing?" my father asked, curiously.

"Shhh," Grandpa said, "can't you see I'm fishing?"

"Mind if I join you?" Dad asked, deciding to join in on the fun. Being careful not to disturb the fish, Dad moved closer to Grandpa's bed and cast out his line.

Together, they fished from the hospital bed as if they were floating in a boat on a clear summer's day. After some time had passed, Grandpa finally got a bite. "I've got one!" he exclaimed, as he excitedly brought in his line. After much effort, Grandpa landed "the big one."

My aunt came over to the bed and asked Grandpa if he wanted her to cook his fish for supper. Grandpa was pleased with the offer and gladly handed over his "catch."

She went to the kitchen, took some haddock out of the freezer and prepared it just the way Grandpa liked it. With a flourish of grandeur, she presented the cooked fish to Grandpa. Grandpa insisted that Dad had to eat with him, so they shared the meal. Later, Grandpa told Grandma that he didn't know what that woman did with the fish, but the one he ate came from the freezer.

After dinner, my grandfather and father continued to fish until my dad had to leave for work. By then, it was early Thanksgiving morning, Grandpa's favorite holiday. All the relatives came to Grandma and Grandpa's house, but it wasn't to celebrate the traditional holiday. It was to say goodbye.

Only hours after his fishing had ended, Grandpa passed away. He had spent the last morning he had, with his son, doing what they loved to do best.

~Sonia Hernandez
Chicken Soup for the Fisherman's Soul

53

A DAD SAYS GOODBYE

Where you used to be, there is a hole in the world, which I find myself
constantly walking around in the daytime, and falling in at night.
~Edna St. Vincent Millay

I watched her and her mother decorate her college dormitory room. Everything in place, organized and arranged, just so. Attractively designed bulletin board with carefully selected, and precisely cut, colored paper. Pictures and remembrances throughout of her dearest friends. Drawers and boxes under the bed. Her room nicely accommodates not only her clothes, accessories and bric-a-brac, but her roommate's as well. I closely monitor that which I would have, in the past, ignored, knowing that this time is different. As her half of the room takes on her essence, I begin to accept that her room at home is no longer hers. It is now ours. Our room for her when she visits.

I find myself thinking of when I held her in the cradle of my arm, in the chair alongside my wife's hospital bed. One day old. So small, so beautiful, so perfect, so totally reliant on her new, untested parents. All manner of thoughts went through my mind as I examined her every feature for what seemed to be an eternity. Time marches relentlessly.

She looks up now, catching me staring at her, causing her to say to her mother, "Mom, Dad's looking at me funny."

The last few days, I touch her arm, her face—anything—knowing that when my wife and I return home, she will not be with us and there will be nothing to touch. I have so much to say, but no words with which to say it.

My life changed from the day I drove this child home from the hospital. I saw myself differently that day, and it has led to a lot of places that I would never have found on my own.

She says, "It'll be all right, Dad. I'll be home from school soon." I tell her she will have a great year, but I say little else. I am afraid somehow to speak, afraid I'll say something too small for what I'm feeling, and so I only hold on to our goodbye hug a little longer, a little tighter.

I gaze into her eyes and turn to go. My wife's eyes follow her as she leaves us. Mine do not. Maybe if I don't look, I can imagine that she really hasn't gone. I know that what she is embarking upon is exciting and wonderful. I remember what the world looked like to me when everything was new.

As I walk to the car with my wife at my side, my eyes are wet, my heart is sore, and I realize that my life is changing forever.

~Joseph Danziger
Chicken Soup for the College Soul

54

HOW I GOT INTO THE MOVIES

When I was eighteen years old, I came to America from Tel Aviv to break into the movies. It was a secret I kept from my parents, whom I had sold on the idea that I was leaving home to study journalism.

Forty-five years later, I finally lived my fantasy—a gift from my eldest son.

He is Peter David, *New York Times* bestselling author of science-fiction novels, (*Star Trek: The Next Generation, Deep Space Nine, The Hulk*), comic books, television scripts (*Babylon 5, Space Cases*) and movies.

His script, *Backlash: Oblivion II*, was being filmed in Romania. Peter wrote a cameo for me. I would have words to speak and even a close-up.

I gave up my dreams of Hollywood while in my early twenties, for a career in journalism on major city newspapers and radio. As a youngster, Peter was my faithful companion in the newsroom, pounding away on the typewriter with his little fingers, just like Dad. "Are you cloning this kid?" an editor asked one day. I thought I was.

Yet the invitation to join Peter in Romania was totally unexpected. My son and I had grown apart emotionally by geographic distance and the demands of his busy career and family life. He was a husband and father of three. My wife Dalia and I saw Peter perhaps three times a year, since we live in different states. We briefly talked on the phone now and then. I knew little about his life, nor did he know much about mine. I had feelings of loss, an awareness of my own mortality, and the sense that time was running out for my firstborn and me. But I could never express any of it to Peter. He is not one for sentimentality.

Our trip to Romania began on a clear, crisp fall day at Kennedy Airport in New York. "We're going to spend so much time together, you'll be sick of me," Peter said. I assured him this would never happen. Of course, I didn't know how he would come to feel about me.

But then, above the clouds, a few hours into the trip, Peter began to open up to me. My son, outwardly so self-confident, said he felt that nothing he was writing was ever good enough. He always thought he could have done better. He also said that he had a great need for the approval of others. And sometimes he feared that his flow of ideas would suddenly dry up.

I felt badly for him, and yet I was joyous. My son was sharing himself with me as he used to when he was at home, growing up. I never shared myself with my own father. As my son and I became distant, I knew how shut out my father must have felt. Now I was exhilarated; my son was coming back to me.

The morning after arriving in Bucharest we drove to the set. In the heart of plowed Romanian fields and small farm houses, there emerged a town from another time and place—the old American West: The General Store, Miss Kitty's saloon, the town bank, horses at the post.

Since Peter's films were a blend of westerns and science fiction, a space ship was parked at the train station. The Wild West bank was equipped with an automated teller machine.

"Incredible," I exclaimed. "This is wonderful, Peter. You have such great imagination."

He smiled. "You know how when children play, they want their parents to see them?" he said. "They want to say to their parents, 'Look at me, Mom, look at me, Dad.'"

I put my hands on his shoulders. "And you brought me here,

all the way to Romania, to say, 'Look at me Dad, look at what I've accomplished'?"

Peter nodded.

At that moment, layer upon layer of emotional distance, of defenses built against disappointment and hurt, began to peel off. I felt a wonderful sense of relief, as if a physical burden had been lifted off my chest. I realized how much he loved me, as I loved him, and how he needed my acknowledgment and approval. I told him then how impressed I was with all he had accomplished, and how proud I was of him.

In the days that followed, Peter and I talked a great deal, about his life, his hopes and dreams. And I told him about mine. There, in Romania, it was as if we were back home again and he was my kid once more.

My big day came about halfway through our eleven-day stay. Peter gave me tips on how to act in front of the camera. Clad in western garb, complete with a cowboy hat, leather gloves and boots, I was installed in the General Store to do some shopping.

"Action!" yelled the director. It was a magic word.

A seven-foot actor dressed in black, wearing a tall black hat, entered. He played a funeral director with psychic powers, and his appearance often meant death would soon follow.

Upon seeing him, I stammered to the shopkeeper, "I... I think I'll come back later." With a great deal of noise, I dropped the canned goods I had selected on the wooden floor as I dashed out, slamming the door shut behind me.

Next came the close-up. "That's a take," the director shouted. Then he, cast and crew applauded. Leading the applause was my son.

Peter thoughtfully obtained the Western hat and gloves of my costume as mementos for me. On our last evening, as cast members were writing kind words on the title page of my script, I asked Peter to do the same.

"I can't put my feelings into just a few words," he said.

But he would put some of them into the diary he kept during

the trip. He was making his final entry on his laptop computer an hour before we were to land at Kennedy.

"When I started the diary, I referred to you as my father," Peter turned to me and said. "As time went on, I began referring to you as Dad. Why do you think that is?"

Tears filled my eyes. I wanted to reach over and hug him, right there, on the plane. But I was afraid to embarrass him, and perhaps myself. So instead, I took his hand in mine and squeezed it. Tight. Real tight.

My son squeezed my hand in return.

~Gunter David
Chicken Soup for the Father's Soul

THE WISDOM OF DADS

Learning from the Kids

The guys who fear becoming fathers don't understand that fathering is not something perfect men do, but something that perfects the man. The end product of child raising is not the child but the parent.
~Frank Pittman

FAMILY PICTURE

While we try to teach our children all about life,
Our children teach us what life is all about.
~Angela Schwindt

I was sitting in my favorite chair, studying for the final stages of my doctoral degree, when Sarah announced herself in my presence with a question: "Daddy, do you want to see my family picture?"

"Sarah, Daddy's busy. Come back in a little while, Honey."

Good move, right? I was busy. A week's worth of work to squeeze into a weekend. You've been there.

Ten minutes later she swept back into the living room. "Daddy, let me show you my picture."

The heat went up around my collar. "Sarah," I said, "come back later. This is important."

Three minutes later she stormed into the living room, got three inches from my nose and barked with all the power a five-year-old could muster: "Do you want to see it or don't you?" The assertive woman in training.

"No," I told her, "I don't."

With that, she zoomed out of the room and left me alone. And somehow, being alone at that moment wasn't as satisfying as I thought it would be. I felt like a jerk. (Don't agree so loudly.) I went to the front door.

"Sarah," I called, "could you come back inside a minute, please? Daddy would like to see your picture."

She obliged with no recriminations and popped up on my lap.

It was a great picture. She'd even given it a title. Across the top, in her best printing, she had inscribed: "OUR FAMILY BEST."

"Tell me about it," I said.

"Here is Mommy [a stick figure with long, yellow, curly hair], here is me standing by Mommy [with a smiley face], here is our dog Katie, and here is Missy [her little sister was a stick figure lying in the street in front of the house, about three times bigger than anyone else]." It was a pretty good insight into how she saw our family.

"I love your picture, Honey," I told her. "I'll hang it on the dining room wall, and each night when I come home from work and from class (which was usually around 10:00 P.M.), I'm going to look at it."

She took me at my word, beamed ear to ear and went outside to play. I went back to my books. But for some reason I kept reading the same paragraph over and over.

Something was making me uneasy.

Something about Sarah's picture.

Something was missing.

I went to the front door. "Sarah," I called, "could you come back inside a minute, please? I want to look at your picture again, Honey."

Sarah crawled back into my lap. I can close my eyes right now and see the way she looked. Cheeks rosy from playing outside. Pigtails, Strawberry Shortcake tennis shoes. A Cabbage Patch doll named Nellie tucked limply under her arm.

I asked my little girl a question, but I wasn't sure I wanted to hear the answer.

"Honey... there's Mommy, and Sarah, and Missy. Katie the dog is in the picture, and the sun, and the house, and squirrels and birdies. But Sarah... where is your daddy?"

"You're at the library," she said.

With that simple statement, my little princess stopped time for me. Lifting her gently off my lap, I sent her back to play in the spring sunshine. I slumped back in my chair with a swirling head and blood pumping furiously through my heart. Even as I type these words into the computer, I can feel those sensations all over again. It was a frightening moment. The fog lifted from my preoccupied brain for a moment—and suddenly I could see. But what I saw scared me to death. It was like being in a ship and coming out of the fog in time to see a huge, sharp rock knifing through the surf just off the port bow.

Sarah's simple pronouncement—"You're at the library"—got my attention big-time.

I hung the drawing on the dining room wall, just as I promised my girl. And through those long, intense weeks preceding the oral defense of my dissertation, I stared at that revealing portrait. It happened every night in the silence of my sleeping home, as I consumed my late-night, warmed-over dinners. I didn't have the guts to bring the issue up to Barbara. And she had the incredible insight to let it rest until I had the courage to deal with it. I finally finished my degree program. I was "Dr. Rosberg" now, and I guess should have been a big deal for me. But frankly, there wasn't much joy in my life.

One night after graduation, Barbara and I were lying in bed together and I found myself working up the nerve to ask her a few questions. It was late, it was dark, and as I murmured my first question, I was praying Barbara had already fallen asleep. "Barb, are you sleeping?"

"No," she said. Rats! I thought to myself. Now I'm committed.

"Barbara, you've obviously seen Sarah's picture taped on the dining room wall. Why haven't you said anything?"

"Because I know how much it wounded you, Gary." Words from a woman wise beyond her twenty-something years. At that point, I asked the toughest question I've ever asked anyone in my life.

"Barb... I want to come home. Can I do it?"

Twenty seconds of silence followed. It seemed like I held my breath for an hour. "Gary," Barb said carefully, "the girls and I love you very much. We want you home. But you haven't been here. I've felt like a single parent for years."

The words look cold in print, but she said them with restraint and tenderness. It was just plain, unvarnished truth. My little girl had drawn the picture, and now her mom was speaking the words.

My life had been out of control, my family was on automatic pilot, and I had a long road ahead of me if I wanted to win them back.

But I had to win them back. Now that the fog had lifted, it suddenly became the most important thing in my life.

~Gary Rosberg
Chicken Soup for the Father's Soul

WHERE ARE YOU PADDLING?

'm a single dad, raising my daughter as her custodial parent (her mother lives in Canada), so these times we share together are especially memorable. My daughter, Kelcie, was in kindergarten when she taught me my biggest lesson about navigating through life. It happened when our YMCA father-daughter "Indian Princess" tribe went on a campout, and we shared our first canoeing experience. Kelcie gleefully ran to the lakeshore, climbed in front with her paddle, and I settled into the stern with mine. Five other father-daughter canoe teams pushed off at the same time.

The others paddled in different directions with varying degrees of swiftness toward the neighboring camp on the far shore, the intriguing inlet to the south or north toward a lakeshore cabin. Kelcie and I barely made any headway at all.

As a professional speaker who is always eager to educate, I presented Kelcie with a highly customized fatherly seminar on the theory of canoe physics. While stroking with my own paddle to balance her tentative strokes, all of which were on the right side of the boat, I patiently explained how one should paddle.

"Stop paddling, Dad! I want to do it myself."

"But honey, you're only paddling on the right side, and that's why we're curving to the left and hardly making any progress. Look how fast Jeff and Jessica are moving. They're paddling on both sides of their boat and they're already halfway to the cove. Now I'll paddle on the left back here to balance your strokes on the right. You see?"

"No! I want to do it my way."

"Sweetheart, if we don't paddle together and you just stroke on the right, we'll go in one big circle and we'll never get to the cove or the inlet or the boat wreck or anywhere. You do want to get somewhere, don't you? We're already way behind the others."

"I don't care. I want to do all the paddling myself."

I, the expert on all things, saw Dave and Susie's canoe already nearing the distant inlet, and Jeff and Jessica had almost reached the cove. Their wakes showed that their courses were mostly straight and true. When my daughter wasn't looking, I furtively stroked my paddle on the left side to straighten our course.

Kelcie caught me. She whipped around and shot me a defiant look: "Dad, stop it! I want to paddle on my own."

My instant seminar had not impressed her. No hint of applause. "You'll see. We'll be far behind all the other canoes. They'll be having fun at the cove, and we will have gone nowhere but in one big circle." I sat back sullenly, annoyed that my child was ignoring my excellent, wise advice. I abandoned my "let's get somewhere" strategy and let Kelcie paddle her own way. Sure enough, we slowly arced in one big lazy circle. And, as I leaned back in the stern with the paddle in my lap, I realized I was enjoying the view much more than if we had been making straight, swift progress toward a destination. Kelcie was happy, and I was, too.

That's how she taught me that the goal of father-daughter canoeing is not to reach a destination swiftly; it's to enjoy being together and to relish where you are while respecting others' wishes and learning a little something. And isn't that also the goal of life?

The lesson in the canoe helped me to determine the direction for my own life. Giving a thousand talks, making X million dollars or being featured on some TV show is not really that important in the scheme of things. My uppermost goal is to raise a loving, happy child with whom I enjoy life. Here's how I pull it off: When I first became a single parent, I closed my big impressive downtown office and added office space to my home. I get up very early, between four and five, and work in my home office until seven. From seven until nine, I'm on dad duty with Kelcie. After breakfast and schoolwork together, I walk my daughter to the bus stop and chat with the other parents and kids. When the bus pulls away, I return to my office. At 3:44 P.M., I walk to the bus stop and welcome my child home. I don't work in the evening; I parent.

My days are now more balanced, and I know I can spend more time on work later in my career. I'm content to have a comfortable life; I don't want a yacht or a mansion. Because of my priorities, my clients can count on having a happy, healthy, sane person show up in front of their audiences. And most important of all, my daughter and I both benefit from having a satisfying, loving relationship.

Knowing where I'm paddling makes the journey all the more joyful.

~George Walther
Chicken Soup for the Single Parent's Soul

IT'S HOW YOU PLAY THE GAME

I never had a policy; I have just tried to do my very best each and every day.
~Abraham Lincoln

When I was growing up, I remember hearing and reading many times, "It's not whether you win or lose, it's how you play the game." In spite of these constant positive affirmations, I didn't believe that. The real world taught me the importance of winning. Finishing first at whatever I was doing became a priority, and if that didn't happen, "how I played the game" was meaningless. In my mind, second place meant first loser.

I've since learned that this winner-take-all attitude ultimately leads an individual in any phase of life to frustration and misery. And it was the world of sports—specifically as a fan of competitive wrestling—that opened my eyes to the value of doing my best and taking pride in the results, regardless of the outcome.

My son Kevin loved wrestling when he was growing up. I remember taking him to his first practice when he was only ten years old. On that warm spring afternoon, we walked into the wrestling room at Father Ryan High School, and he immediately wanted to know what was on the back wall. As we walked closer, he could see that there were fifteen or twenty plaques, each bearing an individual's picture. I explained to him that everyone on the wall was a Father Ryan wrestler who had won a state championship.

Years later, when Kevin entered high school, it was clear he was blessed with a lot of athletic ability. Even as a freshman wrestler he showed promise, and he continued to improve each year. As a senior, he was captain of a team that compiled an incredible record, and he went into the state tournament ranked number one.

He won his first match... he won his second match... he won his third match... and he won his fourth match. Here we were, in the finals of the state tournament, ready to claim our championship. Unfortunately, the next match didn't go well. I don't know if it was the stress of the season, the level of competition or just plain bad luck, but Kevin fell behind early in the match and he never recovered. As I watched the clock wind down in the final period, it was obvious that he wasn't going to win.

His season had ended, his high school career was over, and we didn't have a state championship. Oh, I was devastated. I felt horrible, and I knew I was going to hurt for a long time. I believe at that moment you could've smacked me across the head with a two-by-four and I wouldn't have noticed. I stood there in shock, unwilling to believe what had just happened, and unable to accept it.

I painfully watched Kevin as he slowly took off his headgear, shook his opponent's hand, and stood calmly in the center of the mat as the referee raised his opponent's hand in victory. Then he quietly walked out of the gymnasium.

A few weeks later I received a newsletter in the mail from Holy Rosary Academy, where Kevin had attended grade school as a young boy. The school's principal wrote the following words:

One of our more recent graduates has been the subject of our daily newspaper's sports section. In two of the articles about Kevin Baltz, his prowess in the sport of wrestling was discussed. While Kevin enjoys an impressive reputation statewide in the sport of his dreams, it is his noble character that is the focus of the newspaper articles.

We who knew Kevin as a boy at Holy Rosary are not surprised that he should be honored. We enjoyed that same quiet heroism in him here. The impeccable courtesy now described by sports-writers was a hallmark of Kevin Baltz five years ago. His self-sacrificing manner, his respectful approach to peers, his devotion to friends and his spirit of cooperation were all very evident.

We are proud that Kevin's character has left its mark at Father Ryan High School, and in the sport of wrestling in Tennessee. We are grateful he was a part of our lives here. May his spirit continue to bless those he will touch in all his life's journeys.

When I read this, I sat down and cried. For Kevin, they were tears of joy. Wouldn't any parent be proud after hearing comments like these about his or her child? For myself, though, they were tears of gut-wrenching disappointment.

You see, I had watched every single match Kevin had wrestled in high school, yet I hadn't noticed all the outstanding qualities that the sportswriters and his principal recognized. I was focused on the wins, the victories, the championships. And when he didn't get that final win, I was especially hurt and disappointed. I'd failed to recognize that Kevin was diligently working to achieve victories, but always performing with character regardless of whether he won or lost. In that moment, my eighteen-year-old son became my mentor. He taught me that the pursuit of victory is a noble goal, but that winners in life appreciate the pursuit more than the victory itself.

I wish my son had won that state championship and claimed his plaque on the wall in the Father Ryan wrestling room. It was his goal, and I know how badly he wanted it. But really, he got so much more by not winning. That's because his championship plaque would forever be nailed to that wall, visible only to the eyes that walked into that room. Now, every second of the day, regardless of where I am or whom I'm with, I carry a much bigger announcement across my chest, which I'm sure most people see. And it says: "I'm proud of my son."

I applaud my son's effort and accomplishments, and his fortitude to accept that he had done his best. He taught me a valuable lesson about the game of life that has had a profound effect on me, and I am only grateful for his wisdom. I have now achieved an inner peace by refusing to accept losing as an outcome, rather recognizing that it is only a step in the process of growing.

In reality, all of us face adversities throughout our life, some that can destroy us physically, emotionally and financially. Our challenge is to stay in the game and enjoy the competition, whatever the outcome. Yes, we will experience obstacles, we will experience setbacks, we will experience defeat. They are inevitable. But winning in life is not based on the final score. It is only measured by "how we play the game."

~Larry Baltz
Chicken Soup for the Sports Fan's Soul

58

FISHING WITH ROBBY

My son Robby opens his tackle box and shows me his fishing lures. Each is in its own little compartment like an expensive box of chocolates. He names them, carefully holding them up between his fingers and turning them, like he is seeing them for the first time himself. Rapala, Broken Back, Jitterbug, Rattle Trap....

Fishing has brought out a new side to my son. He hoards his equipment like it's gold, preferring his old rusted fishing rod and reel than any harm coming to his new set. And this child, the same one who loses important math papers and tennis shoes, hates losing a lure to a branch on the bottom of the lake, so much so that he won't even use them.

The other day, I was stressed out and not looking forward to my evening, wondering if I would ever get to bed. Robby asked me to go out in the paddleboat with him and watch him fish. Torn, I sighed and began to apologize for how much I had to do that night.

"It's okay," he said disappointedly.

One look at his eyes and, reluctantly, I went along, all the while thinking of how much this little excursion was going to put me behind.

We paddled out to the middle of the lake, and he cast. It was long and smooth and landed with a plop about three yards from where a fish had just jumped.

"See, I don't want it right on top where that fish jumped because he'll know it's a fake worm. He won't believe a worm just dropped out of the sky right in front of him. You want him to swim to it," he explained in a low voice.

We sat quietly for a while, my son scanning the lake for his target before he drew back his arm and, in one fluid motion, floated his bait far out into the lake. I looked out over the water, beyond where he had cast. A blue heron was standing on a log by the shore, one leg pulled up under his body, his long neck smooth and elegant. He was still, like a statue. I pointed him out to Robby, and, as if the bird could sense that he was detected, it took off, its wings barely flicking the water. We watched him fly, his long neck curved in like the letter S.

"He likes that log over there," my son whispered. "He'll be back." I nodded, wondering why I'd never noticed the heron before.

"Here go the crickets," he said.

I was suddenly aware of crickets surrounding us from all sides, their grinding melody as deep as the woods themselves. I realized how much I'd been insulated by air conditioning lately, how little I'd heard of the outdoors. I closed my eyes and listened.

I heard the deep croak of bullfrogs and the far-away call of a morning dove. I heard a fish splash now and then, sometimes near us and sometimes far across the lake. And over and over, there was the slow squeak of my son reeling in the line, then a gentle whir as he cast it out again.

"I like this time of day," I said, my to-do list long forgotten.

"Just wait," he said. "In a little while the trees and the sunset will reflect off the water. It is so beautiful."

"I will wait," I said, and I thought about what I would have missed if Robby hadn't asked me to join him. I leaned back in my seat and watched my little boy, the one who, in finding his own way, is helping me find mine.

~Ferris Robinson
Chicken Soup for the Nature Lover's Soul

59

RAPID RITES OF PASSAGE

When you're pretty sure that an adventure is going to happen, brush the
honey off your nose and spruce yourself up as best as you can,
so as to look ready for anything.
~Winnie the Pooh (by A. A. Milne)

I'd come up to the Canadian wilderness with the idea of initiating my just-turned-thirteen-year-old son, Adam, into manhood, and I was ready for something wild. If I'd wanted to play it safe, I'd have stayed home. A mother's role is to teach a boy to keep out of harm's way, I reasoned; a father's job is to show him how you play the game a little closer to the edge.

So at an outfitter in Ely, Minnesota, we'd loaded up with maps, tents, fishing gear and food for five days in the wild. Then we took a float plane to Quetico Provincial Park, Ontario—seventeen hundred square miles of blue-black lakes and woods haunted by wolves, loons and moose, just over the Minnesota border from the Boundary Waters wilderness.

At the Hilly Island ranger station, where the plane landed in a wooded cove, we loaded our gear into an aluminum canoe and pushed off. As soon as we rounded the first rocky point, we were completely alone. The afternoon was overcast, and slate-colored light shimmered off the tilting panes of the waves. Around us the rocky shoreline held back a dark line of woods that stretched into wilderness.

We came to our first portage after a few hours of paddling—a short hike around Brewer Rapids, a churning chute of whitewater that dropped perhaps twenty feet over a distance of two hundred yards. We carried our gear from the bottom to the top of the rapids in two trips, then the canoe.

"Why don't we run it?" Adam asked suddenly, as we stood there at the top of the rapids with the now-empty boat. Momentarily suspending my better judgment in the interests of initiation, I responded, "Sure, why not?"

After all, it really didn't look all that bad—we'd recently been whitewater rafting on the New River, in West Virginia, and compared with the New River, it looked tame. Adam reminded me to put on my life jacket, and then I climbed into the stern, he in the bow, and we went for it. The tea-colored water sucked our boat into the surge.

"Keep to the left!" I shouted, trying to guide us out of the foaming tumult in the center of the rapids.

"Naw, let's go straight for it!" he shouted back.

So we did.

And that's when a three-foot dropoff that hadn't been visible from the shore appeared directly ahead of us. In a flash the boat caught on the lip of the precipice, swung around broadside and capsized. I saw Adam go flying over the gunwale, and then I did, too. I went under and came up choking, raking the water for a handhold. Then I went under again, dragged beneath the surface and tumbled over submerged boulders by the sheer tonnage of the torrent. My hiking boots, filled with water, instantly turned to lead weights. I glimpsed Adam's purple life jacket being swept away from me.

"Adam!" I shouted, but I couldn't hear his voice.

When I originally began planning this trip, death by drowning had not been my greatest fear. My greatest fear was that we'd have nothing to say to each other... that Adam would quickly tire of my company and begin longing for a pal or (worse) his Game Boy.

When I talked to him about taking some kind of thirteenth-birthday adventure trip, he told me that what he really wanted was to walk to the bottom of the Grand Canyon and back. He basically wanted bragging rights to a good story. But I really preferred something slower and quieter; I wanted to show him the wilderness without having to prove anything to anybody. But most of all I wanted to reacquaint myself with my son, whom—in the bustle of boyhood, Smashing Pumpkins, Nintendo, backward ball caps and all the rest of it—I seemed to have lost. He was passing from the sweet vulnerability of childhood to the hulking sullenness of adolescence so fast, I sometimes imagined I'd wake up to discover he'd grown a full beard overnight.

Like many fathers of my generation and my culture, I also longed for some sort of celebration, some rite of passage that would clearly delineate my son's child-self from his impending man-self—preferably an event more spiritual than getting a driver's license and less painful than circumcision.

We settled on a canoe trip. To my relief, my worries about having nothing to say to each other proved absurd. In fact, he seemed almost as famished for my company as I was for his. I rediscovered the delightfully daft and ingenious mind I remembered from his childhood. A steady machine-gunfire of questions came back at me from the front of the boat: "What's a hide-a-bed?" "What's an epiphany?" Then suddenly, his voice filled with dismay:

"Dad, I forgot the words to 'Frosty the Snowman'!"

Paddling through those lovely, glimmering lakes, the two of us riding a slender vessel across the dark water, I was startled to discover how much the kid weighed—since in order to keep the boat from tipping over I was forever trying to strike a balance between the ballast of our two bodies. With a surge of sympathy I realized that his skinny, little-kid's body was shuddering under the onslaught of testosterone, and he'd been packing on muscle mass by the hour. I also became acutely aware that his movements were like a series of kinetic explosions—he'd abruptly rock from side to side, bang on the side of the boat, not paddle at all and then suddenly start paddling like fury. My job, I reckoned, was not to squelch that riotous energy, but to teach him how to steady it.

In the back of my mind, I think I'd also intended to use this trip to have serious fatherly talks about Growing Up, Taking Personal Responsibility and all that. My prepared text was boring and pretentious. When my own father took me aside and furrowed his brow like that, I didn't listen, either.

All these thoughts swept over me in a rush of panic and longing as the two of us tumbled helplessly down through the rapids. I glimpsed again the purple flash of Adam's life jacket and spotted him frantically dog-paddling toward me. Then, abruptly, we were both swept out of the main channel into a deep, still eddy. To my amazement, I could hear him laughing and shouting: "Awesome, dude!" I was scared to death, but he was having a ball.

Finally my feet made contact with the bottom and I was able to stand. When Adam gained a footing, I looked over at him, still wearing a sopping Redskins cap, and then we both started laughing and shouting deliriously. The canoe, upright but so full of water that only the tips of the bow and stern were showing, had drifted out into the cove and was now perhaps two hundred yards away. We'd have to swim across the channel, floating a log ahead of us for safety, then hike through the woods to fetch the badly banged-up boat.

Only later did it occur to me that during the whole misadventure, we'd been swapping roles of boy and man. My son made the suggestion that we take a wild chance and ride the rapids in the first place, and he reminded me to put on my life jacket. I agreed to his ill-considered plan and then tried to play it safe like a grown-up. My boy laughed all the way downstream while I—like my own father—wound up desperate with worry.

I was teaching Adam to be a man, but at the same time, he was reminding me not to forget my own boyishness. He was also demonstrating something else: that he could occasionally be more sensible and grown-up than I am; that he could sometimes be right when I am wrong; that some small part of him already is an adult. I found this revelation both comforting and unsettling. After all, inherent in the notion of initiating my son into manhood is the idea of my own demise. I was training my own replacement. In the end, my original highfalutin' notion that I was going to take my son into the woods to be initiated proved to be a bit too prideful, and a bit too simple. In truth, I seemed to have almost as much to learn as to teach.

We waded up out of the water onto the rocky shore, and for a few moments we just felt exhilarated and supremely alive — soaked, baptized, awakened. We'd had an adventure together. We'd actually done something, been somewhere. Something had happened to us, and we'd survived.

The journey had just begun.

~Stefan Bechtel
Chicken Soup for the Father's Soul

THE WISDOM OF A CHILD

*Sadness flies on the wings of the morning
and out of the heart of darkness comes the light.*
~Jean Giraudoux

Never had life been so difficult. As a veteran police officer, exposed to the constant stress and pressures inherent in the profession, the death of my life partner struck a hammer blow that pitched me into the depths of depression. At twenty-eight years of age, my beloved Liz had suffered a perforated colon as a complication of Crohn's disease and died tragically after several operations and six agonizing weeks in the intensive care unit. Our firstborn son, Seth, celebrated his fourth birthday the day following his mother's death, and Morgan, our youngest boy, would reach his third exactly three weeks later.

Liz, who had been a stay-at-home mother, excelled at cooking, housecleaning and all the other domestic chores that embellished our lives. In true macho-cop, chauvinistic fashion, I had taken her generosity for granted, never having time to take on any of these responsibilities myself. As a result I found myself suddenly, in the midst of my grief, thrust ranting and screaming into the role of maid, shopper, driver, launderer, childcare professional, cook and dishwasher.

We had moved into a heavily mortgaged new home only weeks before Liz's death, and our financial situation was already precarious. I soon realized that police work, with its rotating shifts, would necessitate a live-in nanny, further taxing my already overburdened salary.

To my great dismay, the constant demands for attention from two preschoolers left me exhausted and irritated, until I began to resent their very existence.

In the following days, loneliness and pain gave way to guilt, anger and, eventually, self-pity. I spiraled deeper and deeper into despair, and it wasn't long before my body began to display its inner turmoil. Despite my efforts to veil my grief from the children, my eyes became dark and baggy, my weight plummeted, and on one occasion, the boys watched me spill milk all over the table as a quivering hand thwarted my efforts to fill a glass.

Although I dreaded the moment, I knew at some point I would have to delve into the task of sorting through Liz's personal effects, cleaning out the closets and boxing up her clothes and other belongings. One evening, the boys tucked away for the night, I began. Each dress, that scarf, this pair of shoes, one by one, evoked its treasured, if not painful, memory and feelings of overwhelming guilt. It was in a small fold, deep within her purse, that I found almost by accident a neatly folded, tiny slip of yellowed paper, its creases, tight and crisp with age, protecting a carefully printed message.

"Dear Kevin," it began, "these are all the reasons that I love you..." and as I read on, her words obscured by tears, my heart ached and my body shook with convulsive, painful sobs of loneliness. I had hit bottom.

Slowly, in that hopeless fog of despair, I became aware of two small arms wrapped around my legs as I sat at the edge of the bed. A small voice asked in all the innocence of his three years, "What's the matter, Daddy?"

"I feel sad, Morgan, that Mommy's gone to heaven, and we won't see her for a very long time," I said, struggling vainly for composure.

"Don't worry, Daddy, we'll help you. When Seth and I get up in the morning, we'll put the cereal on the table and all you'll have to do is make the toast."

With those few, simple, loving words, my three-year-old child taught me a greater lesson than any other. His thoughts were sunlight filtering into the dreary, winter landscape of my soul, and I knew at that instant that life would be okay.

~Kevin D. Catton
Chicken Soup for the Grieving Soul

61

MY DREAM HOUSE AND MY BOY

The world is round and the place which may seem like the end
may also be only the beginning.
~Ivy Baker Priest

I t seemed the perfect place to raise a family: a beautiful lot in Spokane, Washington, surrounded by ponderosa pines, near forests and streams. When my wife, Joy, and I found it, we knew it was the ideal site for our dream house.

The lot was expensive, far beyond what I could afford on my modest salary as a philosophy professor at Whitworth College. But I started teaching extra classes and moonlighting in real estate.

We finally bought the lot. Sometimes I'd put my infant son, Soren, in a backpack and take him for walks in our future neighborhood. "You'll love roaming these fields and streams," I'd tell him.

Then came the wonderful summer when I helped the contractor build our home. My brother-in-law, a California architect, had designed elaborate plans as a gift. I'd work sunup to sundown, rush home for dinner and often go teach a night class. Confronted with choices for materials, I'd always answer, "Give us the best. We're going to be here for a lifetime."

I'd take one of our girls, Sydney, five, or Whitney, seven, with me whenever I had errands to run. But at the dinner table, I'd just nod as the girls tried to tell me about their day. Rarely was my mind fully with our family. Instead, I'd be worrying about the escalating costs of the house.

But we made it—a four-year goal fulfilled! I felt pride and satisfaction the day we moved in. I loved helping my children explore the neighborhood to meet new friends.

Only a week later, we had to move out.

Unable to sell our other home, we'd arranged to rent it to meet the house payments. At the last minute, the renters backed out. "We can make it somehow," I assured Joy. But she faced the truth of our overextended finances, "Forrest, we wouldn't own the house; it would own us."

Deep down, I knew she was right. The exquisite setting and distinctive architecture meant our new home would sell faster than the old. I reluctantly agreed, but disappointment led to lingering depression.

One afternoon, I drove to the new house just to think. To my surprise, I was engulfed with a sense of failure and started to cry.

That fall and winter, I kept wondering why this loss bothered me so much. My studies in religion and philosophy should have taught me what really matters—it's what I try to help my students understand. Still, my mood remained bleak.

In April, we all went on vacation to California with Joy's parents. One day we took a bus trip to the Mission of San Juan Capistrano, where swallows return each March from Argentina.

"Can I feed the pigeons?" begged Whitney, heading toward the low, stone fountain inside a flower-filled courtyard. The four adults took turns taking kids to feed the birds, visit the souvenir shop and enjoy the manicured grounds. When it was time to get back to the bus, I looked for Joy and found her with the girls and their grandparents.

"Where's Soren?" I asked.

"I thought he was with you."

A horrible fear hit as we realized it had been nearly twenty minutes since anyone had seen him. Soren was a very active twenty-two-month-old who loved to explore. Fearless and friendly, he could be anywhere by now.

We all started running through the five acres of the mission grounds. "Have you seen a little red-haired boy this high?" I asked everyone I saw. I ran into back gardens, behind buildings, into shops. No Soren. I started to panic.

Suddenly I heard Joy scream "No!" Then I saw Soren, lying on the edge of the fountain, arms outstretched. He was blue, bloated and looked lifeless. The sight burned like a branding iron in my mind. It was one of those moments when you know deep inside that life will never be the same.

A woman cradled Soren's head as she gave him mouth-to-mouth resuscitation, and a man pressed on his chest. "Is he going to be all right?" I yelled, fearing the truth.

"We're doing the right things," the woman said. Joy collapsed on the ground, saying over and over, "This can't be happening."

Lord, don't let him die, I prayed. But I knew he couldn't be alive, not after nearly twenty minutes underwater.

In less than a minute, paramedics arrived, connected Soren to life-support systems and rushed him to the hospital. A trauma team pounced on him, led by a specialist in "near drownings."

"How's he doing?" I kept asking.

"He's alive," said one of the nurses, "but barely. The next twenty-four hours are critical. We want to helicopter him to the Western Medical Center in Santa Ana." She looked at me with kindness and added, "Even if he lives, you must realize there's a strong chance of significant brain damage."

Nothing could have prepared me for the sight of my young son in the intensive care unit at Western. His limp, naked body was dwarfed by the machines connected to him by countless wires. A neurosurgeon had bolted an intracranial pressure probe into his head between the skull and the brain. The bolt, screwed into the top of his head, had a wing nut on top. A glowing red light was attached to his finger. He looked like E.T.

Soren made it through the first twenty-four hours. For the next forty-eight hours, we stayed by his side while his fever skyrocketed past 105 degrees. We sang his favorite bedtime songs, hoping we could soothe his hurt even in his comatose state.

"You both need to take a break," insisted our doctor. So Joy and I went for a drive and started to talk.

"There's something besides Soren that's really bothering me," I told her. "I've heard that when couples go through a tragedy like this, it may separate them. I couldn't bear to lose you, too."

"No matter what happens," she said, "this isn't going to break us up. Our love for Soren grew out of our love for each other."

I needed to hear that, and then we started to cry, laugh and reminisce, telling each other what we loved about our mischievous son. He delighted in balls, and before he was even a year old, I'd hung a miniature basketball hoop in his bedroom. "Remember how he scooted in his walker and tried to land one, squealing 'yeaaa' if he came near?" I asked.

We also discussed our fears about brain damage. "The doctor seems more hopeful now," I reminded Joy. He had told us Soren was alive only because all the right things were done immediately after he was found. Thinking earlier that we'd lost him, we felt grateful he even had a fighting chance. We'd take him any way we could get him. But we wondered what the impact would be on the family if brain damage was extensive.

"Can you believe that, for these past months, what mattered to me was losing that house?" I asked. "What good would a new house be if we came home to an empty bedroom?"

Even though Soren was still unconscious, that conversation gave us some peace. We'd also been receiving wonderful support from friends, family and strangers and felt the power of their prayers.

In the following days, four visitors dropped by to see Soren. First came Dave Cameron, who had discovered Soren underwater. A Vietnam veteran, he led tours at the mission. "I arrived early that morning. Standing near the fountain, I suddenly had this strong sense of foreboding," he said. "That's when I saw the backs of his tiny tennis shoes. Instinct and training took over from there."

Soon after came Mikiel Hertzler, the woman who applied mouth-to-mouth resuscitation until the ambulance arrived. "I've been trained in CPR," she told us. "When I first saw him, I couldn't find a pulse.

But faint bubbles in the back of his throat made me think he was trying to breathe."

I shuddered. What if someone with less medical knowledge had discovered him and given up sooner?

Then two strapping paramedics, Brian Stephens and Thor Swanson, told us that they were usually stationed ten minutes away, but that day they were on an errand a block from the mission when they got the call.

As we remembered the doctor's words about Soren being alive only because all the right things happened immediately, their stories touched us deeply.

On the third night, the phone woke me in the hospital room my wife and I were using. "Come quick," shouted Joy. "Soren's waking up!" When I got there, he was slowly stirring, rubbing his eyes. In a few hours, he regained consciousness. But would he ever be the same boy who had brought such exuberance to our home?

A couple of days later, Joy was holding Soren in her lap. I had a ball in my hand. He tried to get it—and he said, "Ball." I couldn't believe it! Then he pointed to a soda. I brought it to him with a straw, and he started to blow bubbles. He laughed—a weak, feeble laugh, but it was our Soren! We laughed and cried; the doctors and nurses did, too.

Just a few weeks later, Soren was racing around our home, bouncing balls and chattering as usual. Full of rambunctious energy, he gave us all a sense of wonder at the gift of life.

Almost losing Soren helped me look closely at my role as a father. What really matters is not that I provide my children the ideal house, the perfect playroom, even woods and rivers. They need me.

Recently, I drove back to my dream home. Prisms of sunlight shone through its fifty-two windows and, yes, it has a beautiful site. But I wasn't troubled anymore, and I know why. As I returned home to take the kids on a promised picnic, all three ran out. Soren squealed, "Daddy, Daddy, Daddy!" And I had time to play.

~Forrest Baird as told to Linda Lawrence
A 6th Bowl of Chicken Soup for the Soul

62

SLEDDING

One day in early December, we woke up to discover a perfect, freshly fallen snow. "Please Mom, can we go sledding after breakfast?" my eleven-year-old daughter Erica begged. Who could resist? So we bundled up and headed over to the dike on the Lincoln Park golf course, the only hill in our otherwise flat prairie town.

When we arrived, the hill was teeming with people. We found an open spot next to a tall, lanky man and his three-year-old son. The boy was already lying belly-down in the sled, waiting to be launched. "Come on, Daddy! Come on!" he called.

The man looked over at me. "Okay if we go first?" he asked.

"By all means," I said. "Looks like your son is ready to go."

With that, he gave the boy a huge push, and off he flew! But it wasn't only the child who soared—the father ran after him at full speed.

"He must be afraid that his son is going to run into somebody," I said to Erica. "We'd better be careful, too."

With that, we launched our own sled and whizzed down the hill at breakneck speed, the powdery snow flying in our faces. We had to bail out to avoid hitting a huge elm tree near the river, and ended up on our backs, laughing.

"Great ride!" I said.

"But what a long walk back up!" Erica noted.

Indeed it was. As we trudged our way back to the top, I noticed that the lanky man was pulling his son, who was still in the sled, back up to the summit.

"What service!" Erica said. "Would you do the same for me?"

I was already out of breath. "No way, Kiddo! Keep walking!"

By the time we reached the top, the little boy was ready to play again.

"Go, go, go, Daddy!" he called. Again, the father put all his energy into giving the boy a huge send-off, chased him down the hill, and then pulled both boy and sled back up.

This pattern went on for more than an hour. Even with Erica doing her own walking, I was exhausted. By then, the crowd on the hill had thinned as people went home for lunch. Finally, it got down to the man and his son, Erica and me and a handful of others.

He can't still be thinking the boy is going to crash into someone, I thought. And surely, even though the child is small, he could pull his own sled up the hill once in a while. But the man never tired, and his attitude was bright and cheery.

Finally, I could stand it no longer. I looked over at him and called, "You have tremendous energy!"

The man looked at me and smiled. "He has cerebral palsy," he said matter-of-factly. "He can't walk."

I was dumbstruck. Then I realized that I had never seen the boy get out of the sled in all the time we'd been on the hill. It had all seemed so happy, so normal, that it never occurred to me that the child might be handicapped.

Although I didn't know the man's name, I told the story in my newspaper column the following week. Either he or someone he knew must have recognized him, because shortly afterward, I received this letter:

Dear Mrs. Silverman,

The energy I expended on the hill that day is nothing compared to what my son does every day. To me, he is a true hero, and someday I hope to be half the man he has already become.

~Robin L. Silverman
Chicken Soup for the Unsinkable Soul

THE
WISDOM
OF DADS

Father Knows Best

*I watched a small man with thick calluses on both hands work fifteen
and sixteen hours a day. I saw him once literally bleed from the bottoms
of his feet, a man who came here uneducated, alone, unable to speak
the language, who taught me all I needed to know about faith and hard
work by the simple eloquence of his example.*
~Mario Cuomo

THE GARDEN GUARD

Few things help an individual more than to place responsibility upon him,
and to let him know that you trust him.
~Booker T. Washington

Both my parents, Hungarian immigrants, were born with green thumbs. Our family of ten depended on the food we grew in our huge vegetable garden. My mother canned much of the produce for winter, and my father sold potatoes and cabbage to the local stores and high schools. Our garden was the pride of the neighborhood.

But then, one summer when I was quite young, we had a problem. Someone was stealing some of our vegetables. My parents were dumbfounded. "I don't get it," my father said. "If someone wants vegetables from us, all they have to do is ask. If they can't afford to pay for them, they could just have them."

Then one of the neighbors tipped us off that an old bachelor who lived a short distance from us was seen selling some vegetables in a nearby town. It didn't take long for my parents to put two and two together. Benny did not have a garden. So he was obviously getting his vegetables from someone else's garden.

Now, Benny was not a bad old fellow. My dad often hired him for haying and other odd jobs just to help him out. Benny had no steady job and lived in a small cabin that looked rather bleak to me. My parents figured he was taking our vegetables to earn a few extra dollars. But stealing is stealing, and it just isn't right. My father decided to handle this situation his own way.

"I'm going to hire Benny," he announced one day.

"What?" my mother exclaimed. "Joseph, we don't have enough money to hire anyone. Besides, why would we hire the man who's taking our vegetables?"

My father only smiled and said, "Trust me, Mary, I've got a plan."

"What are you going to do?" my mother asked.

"I'm going to hire him to guard our garden."

My mother shook her head. "What? That's like hiring the fox to watch the henhouse. I don't understand."

"Well," my father said, "here's what I think. Benny's got himself backed into a corner. And I'm going to give him a way out. The way I figure it, he can't turn me down. And he sure can't take the vegetables that he's guarding."

When my father approached him about the job, Benny was obviously a bit shocked. But Dad handled it pretty well.

"Benny," he said, "someone — probably some kids — has been taking vegetables out of our garden. I wonder if I could hire you to guard it for me?"

Benny hemmed and hawed for a bit, but after Dad explained that he would also be eating supper with us (and Mom's cooking was legendary), he finally agreed.

Needless to say, there were no vegetables missing the next day. Whether or not Benny slept most of the night was not important. The fact was that Dad's plan was working. We were not missing any vegetables and Benny had a job... of sorts. I don't think my folks could have been paying him much. But he was being paid. And just having a job gave Benny more than a little pride.

That solved our problem. But that wasn't the end of the story. Things worked out even better than my father had planned. You see, each morning, after Benny got done sleeping — er, guarding the garden — he'd stick around long enough for breakfast and then follow us around in the garden.

Now, Benny got to kind of liking this garden business. He'd ask questions like, "Why do you plant these carrots here? How come some of these peas are growing faster than those over there?"

My parents were patient with him, answering all his questions. Then my father suggested something. "You know, Benny, the growing season is just about over, but I could take my team of horses over to your place and plow you up a nice patch of ground where you could plant a garden next spring."

"You would do that?" Benny asked.

"Certainly," my father replied. "That's what neighbors are for."

By the following spring, Benny had his garden spot, all plowed, disked and ready for planting. In fact, my parents gave him various seeds that he could use: corn, peas, pumpkins, potatoes and such. Benny caught on to gardening as if he'd been a born farmer.

As we drove by his place in our old rattletrap car one day, Dad slowed down and pointed at Benny's garden. "Look at that, would you? He's growing nicer sweet corn than we are. And he's so busy gardening that he doesn't have time to guard our garden. Of course... for some reason, we don't need a garden guard anymore."

We all chuckled a little at that. But our smiles lingered for a long time after—smiles of pride in the new gardener we had helped create, and pride in our remarkable father.

~Tom R. Kovach
Chicken Soup for the Gardener's Soul

64

THE LESSON

The greatest gift I ever had
Came from God; I call him Dad!
~Author Unknown

Screech! Crash! The old black pickup truck in front of me stopped. I didn't. I slammed into its rear, crushing the fender and bending the driver's door of my car. Except it wasn't my car. It was my father's. I shouldn't have been driving it, and now I had destroyed it.

The farmer climbed out of his truck, slowly and deliberately, and looked at the damage. I sat sobbing, my lip bleeding where I'd bitten it. He was quite concerned, but we managed to exchange names and phone numbers before he pulled out onto the highway again. I cautiously followed, knowing I dared not go home. I'd be in big trouble.

It was my high school graduation day. I drove to school and crawled out through the passenger door. Surveying the mangled fender, contorted door, scrapes and dents, tears flowed down my face, which was rapidly becoming more swollen by the minute—I didn't cry "pretty." I climbed up a ladder in the gym and began draping crepe paper for the dance that was to follow the ceremony. Word traveled fast, and soon a teacher stood at my feet.

"You'll have to go home to get dressed for graduation sooner or later," she reasoned. "Sooner would be much better; you have to tell your parents."

I finally agreed and slowly drove home. The "Death March" sounded in my ears.

My mother took one look at my face when I walked in the door and screamed, "What on Earth happened?"

I hung my head and tears spilled from my eyes again. "I crashed Daddy's car."

She threw up her hands in dismay and rushed to the backyard where Dad was grilling burgers.

"Stop cooking, Ted. We're not going to eat. Jean has wrecked your car."

He looked at her and quietly said, "Is she hurt?"

"No, except for biting her lip."

"Well, then, what does that have to do with eating dinner?" He flipped a burger, piled it on a plate with the others, then walked across the yard and put his arm around me. "Let's go in and hear all about this — if you're sure you're all right."

I sniffled and nodded.

The phone was ringing when we got to the back door. The farmer wanted to make sure I was safe and had no other injuries. He refused to let Daddy pay for the scrapes on his truck.

I pressed ice to my lip while Mother brought cold washcloths for my swollen eyes. My father smiled at me and whispered, "Cars can be repaired...."

I graduated that evening with my family in attendance, joyful I had earned my diploma, yet knowing my greatest lesson had come from my father. High school taught me what is important in books. Daddy taught me to value what is really important in life.

~Jean Stewart
Chicken Soup for the Father & Daughter Soul

65

LEGACY

I was fortunate to grow up in a household where books were treasured. My parents were voracious readers and, early on, they taught my sister, Ann, and me the pleasure of the printed page. My father C. W. "Chip" Grafton, was a municipal bond attorney in Louisville, Kentucky, and spent forty years of his professional life dedicated to his passion for the law. In his spare time, he nurtured a passion of a different sort—writing. Many evenings he returned to the office after hours to devote his energies to the crafting of fiction. In his lifetime, he published two novels of a projected eight-book mystery series, a mainstream novel, and a "stand-alone" crime novel, entitled *Beyond a Reasonable Doubt*. His first mystery, *The Rat Began to Gnaw the Rope*, won the Mary Roberts Rinehart Award in 1943.

During my childhood, he often talked about writing. He was a teacher at heart, having taught both college English and law school classes in the course of his career. Listening to him, I had no notion in the world of being a writer myself, "when I grew up." In those days, women were generally encouraged in one of three vocations: you could be a nurse, a teacher, or a ballerina. Since I was ill coordinated and was not only squeamish at the sight of blood, but also phobic of needles, I had naturally fixed my sights on teaching. As to subject matter or grade level, I had no clear concept.

My father's lessons about writing, while peripherally entertaining, seemed to have no relevance to my goals. Still, I absorbed his advice, which he might well have offered as a way of reaffirming his own self-generated code of writing conduct. He used to say, "You have to keep your writing simple. It's not up to you to revise the English language. You should always spell correctly and use proper punctuation." He thought it was a miracle that a writer could conjure up an image in his own head, translate that image into marks on a page, and then, through the catalytic action of reading, have the same image appear in another person's head. How could an idea leap like that from one mind to another? I'm not sure my father ever figured out how such alchemy transpired, but he believed that a writer's first responsibility was to foster and promote that magic. In his mind, good grammar was essential to keeping the communication pathway clear.

He believed in plain old hard work. He believed that in a novel the transitions were important. He'd tell me, "Every writer has the big scenes in mind, but if you don't take particular care with the scenes in between the moments leading up to the crowning moment in your book, the reader may not be with you. The reader may, in fact, become bored or impatient and toss the book aside before reaching the critical passage that inspired you to begin work." He also felt minor characters were important and took special delight in making them come alive in his own books, even if their appearance was confined to a paragraph.

Probably the most important advice he ever gave me was how to handle rejection. He'd say, "Bend with the wind. When disappointments come along, as surely they will, don't stiffen with bitterness. Be graceful. Submit. Think of yourself as a sapling, yielding to circumstance without cracking or breaking. Bending with the wind allows you to right yourself again when adversity has passed." At the ages of eight and ten and thirteen, none of this seemed pertinent, but I recognized the sincerity with which he spoke and unconsciously took note.

Not surprisingly, in time, I too began a lengthy love affair with the written word. In college, I wrote poetry and short stories, graduating with a BA in English, still convinced that I'd teach. By the time I moved from Kentucky to California in the early sixties, I was married, raising a family and working full-time as a medical receptionist.

Like my father, I, too, returned to my desk at the end of the day and devoted myself to writing.

At the age of twenty-two, after an adult education creative writing class, I started work on my first full-length novel, *Maggie*. This book was never published. I suffered my rejections (not always gracefully, I confess) and set to work on my second full-length novel, *The Monkey Room*, which went nowhere. The third completed novel, *Sparrow Field*, was summarily dismissed, garnering as many form rejection letters as the first two. Sometimes, a kind soul would pen a single sentence of encouragement at the bottom of the page. I didn't even know enough to take heart from this anonymous support. All three early novels ended up in my "bottom drawer" where they remain to this day.

Looking back, I can see that the writing in these manuscripts, while earnest, was nonetheless amateurish. The characters were either flat or manufactured. The story lines were poorly realized, clumsily executed, or sometimes absent altogether. Without knowing it, I was now teaching myself three vital lessons about writing: persist, persist, and persist. The fourth full-length novel I wrote was completed under the unwieldy title, *The Seventh Day of Keziah Dane*. I entered this manuscript in what was then called the Anglo-American Book Award Contest, probably long-since defunct. If memory serves, no award was given that year.... At least, I didn't win one... but I did receive an offer from a British publisher, a sum that in those days translated into perhaps as much as three hundred and fifty dollars. I was thrilled, ecstatic. I thought I'd died and gone to heaven. With the counsel of an experienced writer of my acquaintance, I used that publishing offer to net myself an American agent, who then secured me an American publisher. *Keziah Dane* was published in 1967 and a fifth novel, *The Lolly-Madonna*, came out in England two years later.

Soon afterwards, a British producer bought the film rights to this novel and together we wrote the screenplay, a form he taught me in ten days flat. Eventually, we made a deal with MGM and the movie, *Lolly Madonna XXX*, was released in 1973, starring Rod Steiger, Robert Ryan, Season Hubley, Jeff Bridges, and Randy Quaid, among luminous others. While the film itself was not financially (or aesthetically) successful, I earned sufficient money to begin to write full-time. I suppose at that juncture, having sacrificed my R.N. and my appearance in *Swan Lake*, I must have realized I wasn't going to be teaching elementary school, either.

I spent the next fifteen years working in Hollywood, where I supported myself and my children writing numerous movies for television. At the same time, I completed yet another full-length novel, my sixth... never published... and followed that one with a seventh, which has never seen the light of day. By then, I was restless writing teleplays, and even more restless with the necessity for writing by committee. Film is, by its very nature, a collaborative medium, and I was not suited to the impact of all those egos. By 1977, I was keenly aware of how destructive group writing was to someone of my stubborn and recalcitrant disposition. It occurred to me I'd best get back to solo writing if I hoped to reclaim whatever talent I had left. I began work on my eighth full-length novel, a mystery, which I knew from the outset would be entitled *"A" Is for Alibi*.

I relate this progression in some detail because at every step of the way, I was utilizing the precepts I'd literally learned at my father's knee. Meanwhile, he — pragmatic, hard-headed, practical soul that he was — had one day added up the total of all the monies he'd earned from his books and realized he couldn't support his family on the proceeds. At that point, he set aside his publishing ambitions, moved his literary projects to the back burner, and renewed his commitment to municipal bonds. He still wrote when he could, but he'd relinquished all hope of trading in his career as an attorney for one as a novelist. He intended, on retirement, to write full-time. To that end, he'd completed a portion of *The Butcher Began to Kill the Ox*, the third in his mystery series. He'd also written a hefty six-hundred pages of a novel about his experiences growing up in China, the son of Presbyterian missionaries in Shanghai.

At the age of seventy-one, still actively engaged in the practice of law, he began teaching bond law to young attorneys coming up behind him in the firm. He had, by contract, only three years to serve until his long-awaited freedom. One Sunday morning in church, he was stricken with a heart attack and died within hours. This was January 1982, four months before the publication of *"A" Is for Alibi*. The dedication to my first published mystery reads:

For my Father, Chip Grafton, who set me on this path.

In dying, my father taught me yet another lesson, one I wish I'd had the power to teach him. Follow your heart. Summon the courage to live out your dreams. None of us really know how much time we have left. Writing is our task. It's what we were put on this earth to do. If you're passionate about writing, don't postpone the process. Write every day, filling your life with fearless imagination. Your writing may prove to be a struggle, but the discipline will give form and shape and substance to your life. Work hard. Persist. And remember—please—to spell correctly. Use proper grammar and punctuation. Keep your writing simple and mind your transitions. Tend to your minor characters and above all else, dear hearts, learn to bend with the wind.

~Sue Grafton
Chicken Soup for the Writer's Soul

66

KNOWING WHERE TO TAP

*It is a thousand times better to have common sense without education than to
have education without common sense.*
~Robert G. Ingersoll

Before setting off to college, my father sat me down and
shared this memorable story with me. It is one I shall never
forget. My father is not college educated, yet he possesses
more wisdom and insight than most college professors I have met.
After you read this story, you'll know what I mean.

> There is an old story of a boilermaker who was hired to fix a
> huge steamship boiler system that was not working well. After
> listening to the engineer's description of the problems and ask-
> ing a few questions, he went to the boiler room. He looked at
> the maze of twisting pipes, listened to the thump of the boiler
> and the hiss of escaping steam for a few minutes, and felt some
> pipes with his hands. Then he hummed softly to himself, reached
> into his overalls and took out a small hammer, and tapped a
> bright red valve one time. Immediately, the entire system began
> working perfectly, and the boilermaker went home. When the
> steamship owner received a bill for one thousand dollars, he
> complained that the boilermaker had only been in the engine
> room for fifteen minutes and requested an itemized bill. So the
> boilermaker sent him a bill that reads as follows:

For tapping the valve:	*$.50*
For knowing where to tap:	*$ 999.50*
TOTAL:	*$1,000.00*

"Tony," he said, "I want you to go to college so that you can get your degree, but more important, I want you to return with an education."

~Tony D'Angelo
Chicken Soup for the College Soul

67

MY FATHER'S VOICE

Dad, your guiding hand on my shoulder will remain with me forever.
~Author Unknown

My father raised me mostly by example. He was a doctor who also had a farm in the Midwest on which he raised cattle, horses and hunting dogs. I learned by watching how to work; how to handle animals and the kinds of unforeseen events that are so frequent in the life of a doctor's family.

My father took things as they came, dealt with them and, as he used to say when some obstacle had been overcome, "Let's move right along." He had a few precepts I was expected to live by, and he always referred to them by their combined initial letters: DL! DC! SDT! And DPB! They stood for Don't Lie; Don't Cheat; Slow Down and Think; and Don't Panic, Bud! I was amazed as a boy how often he found occasion to say one or another of those things.

He thought animals were splendid teachers, and he taught me to watch them carefully. One winter, a squirrel invaded our house around Thanksgiving. We never saw or heard it, but I found stashes of nuts hidden under the cushions of the couch and almost every chair. The fascinating thing is that the nuts were always one of a kind. Acorns in my father's chair. Hickory nuts at one end of the sofa and almonds in their shells—stolen from the holiday bowl that my mother kept on the coffee table.

I thought the squirrel was very smart to sort out his larder that way. My dad said the squirrel was even smarter than I had imagined and gathered only one kind of nut at a time. And that would be much more efficient than gathering a mix and then having to sort them out.

That kind of teaching did not alter much even when I was a grown man, even to the day he died. I was thirty when he became ill on Christmas Eve. We buried him on the third of January, his coffin draped in an American flag. The United States soldier who received the folded flag from the bearers handed it to me without a word. I clutched it to my heart as my wife and I left that most sorrowful of places for the long, forlorn drive to the airport.

The world seemed darkened by his absence. There was an emptiness so great that at times I thought I could not bear it. At his funeral, the minister told me that all he had been to me still lived. He said if I listened I could hear what my father's response would be to any concern I needed to bring him. But after I left the small country town where he lived and returned to the large city where I was making my way, I never once heard his voice. Never once. That troubled me deeply. When I was worried about leaving one job for another—something I would have talked over with my dad—I tried to imagine that we were sitting in his barn having one of our "life-talks," as my mother used to call them. But there was only silence and the image of me alone, waiting and profoundly sad.

Although I worked in the city, my wife and I bought an old farmhouse on a few acres of land some forty miles away. It had a pond where I could teach my son to fish and a meadow where we could work our dog.

One day during the same dreadful winter that I lost my father, I set out with my young son to do a few errands. We drove out into the country to look at some antique dining room chairs I was thinking of buying as a surprise for my wife. I said we'd be home by suppertime. We had gone a few miles when my son saw deer grazing just beyond the edge of a parking lot that belonged to our country church. I pulled in the lot, turned off the engine and let the car glide as close to the deer as I could without spooking them.

A buck and three does rummaged in the snow for grass and leaves. They occasionally raised their heads and took a long slow read of the air. They knew, of course, we were there. They just wanted to be certain they were safe.

We were as still as we could be and watched them for some time. When I took my son's hand and turned around to leave, I saw a pall of smoke coming from under the hood of my car. We stopped in our tracks. Oh God, I thought, the engine is on fire. And I am alone with a child in the middle of winter in the middle of nowhere. I did not have a cell phone.

I told my son to stay where he was, and I went to the car to investigate. I opened the driver's door, pulled the hood latch and went to the front of the car. Gingerly, I opened the hood. As soon as I did, I saw that the right front of the engine was aglow with fire, and smoke was coming out of it at a pretty good clip. I closed the hood without latching it down and went to where my son stood in the snow, excited and amazed.

"Daddy, is the car gonna blow up?"

"No. But I sure have to do something, and I don't know what...."

"Snow will put it out," he said.

"Snow might crack a cylinder, too." What could be the matter? I thought. Engines just don't catch fire like that. My mind began to move irrationally. I would have to find a house along the road, call for help. I would have to call my wife, frighten her probably. There would be the expense of the tow and probably a new engine. Then as clearly as I ever heard it in my life, I heard my dad say, "DPB!"

I am still astonished that I was immediately calmed. The frantic racing of my mind ceased. I decided to see exactly what, in fact, was burning. I retrieved a stick from a little oak and went to the car, opened the hood and poked at the glowing red place on the engine. Coals fell from it, through to the ground. I could see then, sitting on the engine block in a perfect little circle—a small collection of acorns, cradled by the shape of the metal.

I laughed out loud. "Come here," I said to my son. "Look, a squirrel stowed its treasure in our car. And when the engine got hot, his acorns got roasted."

I knocked the acorns and the rest of the glowing coals off the engine, closed the hood, put my son in his car seat and got in beside him.

When we drove away to finish our errand, I knew—for the first time since my dad died—that I could get on with my life. For on that snowy day in the parking lot of our country church, I discovered that his voice was still in my heart, and his lessons would be with me forever.

~Walker Meade
Chicken Soup for the Grieving Soul

WHAT I LEARNED AT THE OUTHOUSE RACES

My seventy-five-year-old father, Ed Kobbeman, is one of the all-time-great, get-it-done, do-it-now kind of guys. He built his own home in 1946, and it's a veritable showplace of repair and improvement. He's often out in the barn fixing things before they break, restoring antiques, building things from scratch or designing and creating amazing gadgets and gizmos.

It wasn't too surprising, then, when Dad proudly showed me his latest creation... the outhouse he'd built from the rough wood ripped from an old wooden crate. The traditional sun and moon were cut out of the front door, and the sloped roof had shake shingles. Dad had fashioned a fancy seat inside, within arms reach, of course, of the supply of corncobs dangling on strings. The dual-purpose Sears Roebuck catalog hung from a hook on one of the inside walls. There was even an American flag waving off the back end. It was, indeed, a fine outhouse.

Why a man who built an all-electric home in the 1940s with a beautiful modern bathroom, would build an outhouse in the 1990s was something of a puzzle to me at first, until Dad explained that he intended to enter his creation in the First Annual Rock Falls Days Outhouse Races.

To be in this grand event, one's outhouse had to have wheels. These he found in his neat-as-a-pin storage area outside the barn, taken off some old contraption he'd worked on years before.

The day of the race, Dad's nephews arrived to load his pride and joy into their pickup truck. The four made up the outhouse racing team, along with one great-niece weighing in at under a hundred pounds, chosen to ride on the seat inside, per race rules. They all wore red look-alike, tank-style, T-shirts, looking so spiffy they could have been vying for a medal at the outhouse event at the summer Olympics.

The contraption arrived safely in the heart of downtown Rock Falls, Illinois. In the blazing sun of that scorching June day, the five outhouse teams lined up. The four muscular nephews in charge of the Kobbeman outhouse grabbed the pole handles and rocked ole Bessy back and forth, chanting, "Feel da rhythm, hear da rhyme, come on team, it's outhouse time!"

The starting shot rang out. The red-shirted Kobbeman clan, out in front by a foot, screeched around the markers thirty yards down the parking lot and turned 180 degrees to make their way back to the start/finish line.

Just then, disaster. The hard rubber on the wheels started peeling off. One at a time, hardened black tires split off the wheels as old rubber gave way to new asphalt. The nephews hung on for the last few yards, barely winning the first race by sheer strength of will and brute muscle power as they lifted that outhouse off the ground, niece and all, and drag-carried her across the finish line. But now there was no hope for the second heat.

I stood there, ready to cry. My father had put so much time and talent into making what was obviously the most superior outhouse in the race, and now it was all over. Without wheels, an outhouse cannot run.

Out of the corner of my eye, I saw Dad walking like a mad man away from the race. I wondered if he, too, was as disgusted with those old tires as I. What a shame, I thought, to lose the contest because of some stupid old wheels. Considering the strength and enthusiasm of the red-chested manpower, it was a low blow, indeed.

Five minutes later I realized Dad hadn't come back. Where is he? I wondered. Thinking he'd gone off to the restroom at the corner tap, I suddenly realized that if he didn't get back soon he'd miss the rest of the races.

Minutes ticked by. By now my cousins were using the old standby, gray duct tape, to wrap the wheels in hopes that they could patch them together enough to at least try for the second race.

Five minutes later Dad was still nowhere to be seen. Doggone, him, I thought. Where could he be? Gone off, upset at himself for using old tires on a new outhouse? How could he just leave like that? This was my dad, the man who spent a great deal of my childhood teaching me to be a good sport, to enjoy life, but to always play the game fairly. And now, just because the wheels fell off his outhouse, he's acting like a poor sport?

The announcer was on the microphone telling the participants to get their outhouses lined up. Just then Dad ran up to outhouse row clutching four brand new wheels. He tossed me a few tools.

"Here, hold these. Hand me those needle-nose pliers."

Within seconds the nephews and Dad had that wooden, shake-shingled wonder on its back, ripping the duct tape off with the pliers, undoing rusty nuts and bolts, and attaching the brand new wheels. It was a scene straight out of a pit stop at the Indy 500. Fifty seconds flat and those new wheels were in place.

The Kobbeman clan won the next four races amid plenty of good-natured hooting and hollering from the folks on the sidelines. In the ceremony that followed, Dad, his nephews and his great-niece were presented with an outhouse trophy so spectacular it could only be given to the finest of privy makers. That shiny, blue-and-gold, two-foot-tall trophy even had a tiny little outhouse on top with the door wide open, as if to say, "Come on in, friend!"

After the presentation, photo session, lots of backslapping and congratulatory kudos from the townspeople, including the mayor, we headed home. In the car I asked my dad, "Where'd you go when you ran off like that? And where'd you get those new wheels?"

My father took a deep breath. "Well," he said, starting slowly, then speeding up his words as he told the story. "I ran two-and-a-half blocks to the car. Unlocked it, drove home like a bat out of Bangkok, ran in the house, got the key to the barn, ran out there, unlocked the barn, pulled my new lawnmower out on the grass, grabbed some tools, pulled off the first two wheels and threw 'em in the car. Then I decided I could take the other two off downtown while the boys were puttin' the first two on the outhouse. So I lifted that lawnmower into the back end of the station wagon. Then I decided that was dumb. I could take the wheels off there at home just as fast, so I lifted the lawnmower back out of the car and unbolted the second pair of wheels, threw 'em in the car, put the lawnmower back in the barn, locked the door, jumped in the car, drove back to town and just happened to find a parking place right in front of the start of the race. Must have been a guardian angel. Best luck I ever had findin' a parking place."

I couldn't believe my ears. "Dad, you did all that in the fifteen minutes you were gone, between the first and second races?"

"Yup."

I just shook my head. "Why? Why did you do all that in this heat? You had a heart attack ten years ago, remember? And how did you know you wouldn't miss all the rest of the races when you took off for home like that?"

He smiled, "Well, I just couldn't let the boys down. They worked so hard to win that first race, I just couldn't let those old rotten wheels ruin their chances for the rest of the races. Besides, there was a problem, and it just needed to be fixed, that's all."

Well, one thing's for sure. On that hot afternoon in June in the heart of middle America, my father gave a whole new meaning to the phrase, "Race to the outhouse." He not only saved the day for his nephews and great-niece, he also taught me a valuable lesson: No matter how grave or impossible a situation seems, just bulldoze ahead. Don't hesitate. Just fix it.

Follow this advice and, who knows? You just might end up with a two-foot-tall trophy with a shiny little outhouse on top with the door open, welcoming you inside.

Don't you just love America?

~Patricia Lorenz
Chicken Soup for the Father & Daughter Soul

MARKING THE TRAIL

Sometimes I wish I were a little kid again,
skinned knees are easier to fix than broken hearts.
~Author Unknown

I sat in the front pew holding hands with my mom and sister as the choir sang, "I go before you always, come follow me...." I took a few deep breaths to quiet my pounding heart and allowed my mind to wander to one of my favorite memories.

I loved that early morning hike with Dad. The smell of Rocky Mountain pine and the chilly air filled me with energy as I hustled behind him on the trail. I had hiked with Dad a dozen times in my eleven years, but I still worried when the trail disappeared.

"Is there a trail, Dad? I can't find it." I ducked under the aspen branch he held back with his large, sturdy frame. "The scouts and their dads following us are never gonna find us," I said, with mixed delight and concern. "If you weren't here, how would I ever find the way?"

He gave my shoulder a reassuring squeeze. "We'll mark our trail."

On his instruction, I gathered rocks and stacked them in a pile. Next, we arranged stones to form an arrow pointing uphill. "This shows anybody behind us which way to go," he coached.

Around the next bend I collected stones and formed them in another small heap. "Now they can follow us easily," I beamed.

We repeated these rock formations several times as I panted and stumbled over the steep terrain, following his big footprints in the soft dirt.

Feeling more exhilarated than tired, we reached the summit. There we sat in silence on the rocky peak listening to nature's concert. Wildflowers blanketed the meadow stretching between the rolling foothills. Dad gestured toward an eagle soaring in the cobalt sky.

I knew my dad created these moments especially for me. I was always the youngest scout and frequently missed out on adventures my older brother and sister experienced. Dad loved his role as an adult leader because it allowed him to combine the three loves of his life — family, faith and the great outdoors.

Storm clouds gathered over a faraway ridge. Thunder rumbled as the distant clouds collided in a clash of lightning.

"Did I ever tell you about how I really found God during the war?" Dad asked, breaking the silence. I knew he enjoyed telling that story almost as much I as enjoyed hearing it over and over again.

I knew it by heart. He had taken a break from maintaining the generators that provided electricity for his platoon. Sitting atop a hill, he watched the Earth burning in patches below. When a magnificent lightning storm illuminated the blackened sky, he realized no man-made electricity could compare to that of the Divine Creator. "That's when I knew, and I have never doubted Him since," Dad nodded with a smile.

I reached for his hand and held it tight as we watched power sparks in the distance.

When he said it was time to leave, I groaned in protest. I didn't want this treasured moment to end. He reminded me that, while we loved the trail, there are often better things at the end. "Like Mom and her pancakes waiting back at camp!"

Before beginning our trek back, Dad arranged rocks in a circle, then placed a single rock in the center. "This marks the end of the trail," he said. "This will tell those who follow that we went home."

Several years later, Dad was diagnosed with Lou Gehrig's disease. His most difficult path of life lay ahead. We learned all we could about the incurable, debilitating illness, while Dad's ability to eat and speak gradually diminished. Accepting his impending death with courage and faith, he still showed me the way.

He led me through earning my Eagle Scout award.

I followed in his footsteps when I was confirmed in my faith.

He guided me through the rocky path of high school graduation and choosing a college.

He gathered me with my mom, grandma, aunt and uncle to pray together after church every Sunday.

In written notes, he told us that, while he loved life's journey, he looked forward to eternity with the Master Electrician.

My sister tugged gently on my hand. The choir ended the refrain, and the piano played softly as Father Bob offered the final funeral prayer. Dozens of scouts and former scouts came forward, placing a circle of rocks on the altar. Together my sister, brother and I placed the single rock in the center.

It was the end of the trail.

Dad had gone home.

~Tim Chaney as told to LeAnn Thieman
Chicken Soup for the Christian Teenage Soul

TAKING CARE OF THINGS

"You're going to be alone on the place this weekend," my father said as though that was no big deal. "I expect you to handle it." We were walking back toward the barn from the fenced pasture where we kept our best brood cows. The ladies—as my dad called them—turned their white faces toward us, then went back to grazing the sweet short grass of their pasture.

"For how long?" I said, trying to control my uncertain voice that now and then still turned squeaky.

"Two days. I have to go to a medical conference in Chicago. There're a couple of presentations I need to hear. You'll be okay."

I had never been left alone on our farm, and the only thing I was ever in charge of was the dogs. My father always found time for the cattle, even if he'd had one of those days when everyone in town seemed to get sick. It didn't matter if he was tired to the bone when he came home, he still made the rounds of the place, looking after his herd of Herefords. My mother had gone to Canton, Ohio, to visit her sister for a few days, and now my father had to go away, too. I thought they could have planned things better, but it gave me a chance to show my stuff. I knew I could take care of just about anything that might come up, and I was ready to prove that to my dad.

I finished my chores at the barn and went to wash up for supper. The kid I saw in the mudroom mirror looked confident, even sort of smug. I gave him a thumbs up and went into the kitchen.

I had, in my fifteenth year, got the idea that I knew more than most people. Certainly more than my parents. And I did not hesitate to demonstrate how smart I was. If my father, for instance, started holding forth at dinner on baseball — a sport he cherished — and got a fact wrong or quoted a player's stats incorrectly, I would point out his error, whenever I could. My father wasn't always happy that I knew so much.

One summer night a while back, as he pushed some green beans around on his plate with his fork, he got to talking about responsibility and quoted a remark of Connie Mack's. Then my dad rested his chin on his hands thoughtfully and began by saying what a great baseball manager he thought Connie Mack was. "He knew what really matters. Once he told a·reporter, 'I guess more players beat themselves than are ever beat by an opposing team. The first thing any man has to know is how to handle himself.'"

"He said 'licked,'" I said, correcting my father. "It's 'licked themselves' and 'licked by an opposing team.'"

He folded his napkin, laid it carefully on the table, leaned forward on his elbows, stared me in the face and said, "So what?"

"So you got it wrong," I said, emboldened by the plain fact that I was correct.

"I got the spirit right," he said. "You missed the point. The point is you got to know yourself. Know what you can do and what you can't. So why don't you just let up on the rest of us a little instead of missing the gist of what I'm saying to you?"

"Try not to be so annoying," my mother said. I thought for an instant she was talking to my father, but she was not.

My dad was often put out with me, and so I was a little surprised — a few weeks later — that he would go to Chicago and trust me with the cattle.

Our farm wasn't as large as most, but there was a lot to be responsible for, and I was determined to handle whatever came up, to show my dad I wasn't just all talk.

As soon as he left on his trip, I headed out to the barn lot to see that everything was okay when I noticed the water in the cattle trough was low. I didn't understand how that could be since a float and lever maintained the level.

When I investigated, I saw the float hanging in mid-air and not a drop of water came from the filler pipe.

I checked the pump. The casing was hot. I checked the fuses in the barn, and one was blown. So I disconnected the pump, took it into the workroom and in a half-hour had replaced the carbon brushes and repaired the short—the source of the problem.

When I turned the system back on, the sweet purr of the pump engine as it kicked made me feel like an old hand. But the problem with the pump turned out to be a breeze compared to the disaster that confronted me the very next day.

I mucked out one of the stalls in the barn where my father kept cows that were close to calving. Only Low Loretta was close to her time. She got her name because her unusually short legs kept her pretty low to the ground. She was not much to look at, but she threw some fine calves and was my dad's favorite.

She liked the orchard pasture especially because of her fondness for apples. She was allowed in that pasture during the day, as long as someone was working around the barn to keep an eye on her. And my dad always put her up at night when she was close to her time so she could be checked on easily. She often had trouble at calving. On Saturday afternoon, I went down to the pond in the afternoon to fish a little and take a swim. I left Loretta in the orchard lot. She was basking in a spot of sun under a tree and looked too content to move. I wasn't planning to be gone for very long.

As I lay on the raft I'd built a summer ago, I thought of how the first words out of my dad's mouth would be, "Everything okay?" I'd be able tell him that everything went fine. Nothing I couldn't handle.

My daydream ended abruptly, however. On my way back to the barn, I heard a sound I'd never heard before. There were two distinct and terrible noises. The first was like water gurgling through mud that was followed by a gut-wrenching cough.

I ran toward the orchard and found, about twenty feet from the barn, Loretta down on her front knees, throat stretched skyward, eyes rolled back in her head, looking as though she were about to die.

I knelt beside her and began to stroke and soothe her. She made a gasping sound and her sides heaved as though she was having a hard time breathing. I felt under her jaw and down along her throat. About a third of the way from her breastbone there was a hard place in her neck. I knew right away that she'd got a green apple stuck in there. Even though she was about to choke to death, I was determined to handle the problem myself.

I massaged her throat to try to force the apple loose, but I couldn't budge it in either direction. The apple was lodged too far down to pull out. I told her I was going to get someone who could fix her up and ran to the tack room to call our vet, Dr. Carrico.

When I told him what was the matter he said, "Stay with the stupid critter, keep her head up and I'll get there as quick as I can."

Doctor Carrico was an outspoken man of strong opinions and plain language. When he arrived and saw Loretta near death, he gave her a cussing like I'd never heard. "When's her calf due?"

"Week, maybe."

"I sure hope we don't lose it."

He felt around her neck studying the situation. Dr. Carrico moved deliberately. I never saw him hurry even in an emergency. Finally, he told me to go to the barn and get him a couple of short boards. When I found what he wanted, he pushed Loretta over on her side, placed one board under her neck where the apple was and another one on top. My dad's favorite cow was very near her last breath and suffering badly. I could not imagine what he was thinking of doing. Then, as I watched in horror, Doctor Carrico put his foot on the uppermost board and stomped hard on it. Twice.

There was a squishy sound, Loretta gave a great wheezing cough and swallowed the now-crushed apple. I sat back on my heels staring at the vet in amazement. I would never have thought of doing what he did. Never. If Loretta had to depend on me to save her, she'd be dead. I felt inadequate and ashamed. I even thought about not telling my dad, but dropped that stupid idea in a hurry. He was not a man you kept things from. Loretta, now free to breathe, struggled to her feet, regarded us both with a baleful eye as though we were the cause of her problem, and then walked off toward her stall in the barn. I guess she felt safe there.

"It'll be awhile before she eats another green apple," Doc said.

"I bet you're right about that."

"Where's your dad?"

"In Chicago."

"And he left you to see about things?"

"Yes, sir, he did."

"Well, he's lucky you know when to holler for help. Good thing you didn't wait one more second."

Late Sunday afternoon, I began watching for my dad's car to turn in our road from the highway just below the south pasture. I rehearsed telling him what had happened, hoping I could find a way to hide how much of a failure I felt. But when he finally got home, there was nothing to do but tell it straight.

My dad didn't say anything much when I told him what had happened to Loretta. I said that I went off to fish and left her in the orchard. I even admitted I tried to treat her myself instead of calling the vet right away.

He didn't seem to react much, just kept saying, "Hmm, I see," a lot. I guessed he was very disappointed in me.

Almost two weeks to the day after her terrible ordeal, Loretta had her calf. We were in the barn with her when she delivered. My dad wiped the newborn off with a burlap feed bag, and Loretta waited patiently while it stood for its first nursing. The calf was a pretty little heifer, wonderfully proportioned and strong boned. After a while my father said, "What are you gonna name it?"

That surprised me because he always named the cattle. Then he said, "She's yours. You earned her." I looked at him in wonder. He smiled at me and slapped me on the shoulder as he left the stall. "Take good care of her," he said as though he trusted I could do that. That evening, I went down to the pond to be by myself for awhile. The sun had set, but the sky still glowed. I looked up the gentle hill toward the house. Lights were now on in the living room, and I could see the shadow of my father as he got up from his chair and crossed the room to get something or other. On that evening, in the fading light, I decided a few things: to stop tormenting my dad all the time, to give up being such a wise guy and to name my little Hereford calf after a legendary baseball manager. I called her Connie Mack.

~W. W. Meade
Chicken Soup for the Father's Soul

71

A HOMECOMING
OF A DIFFERENT SORT

There's one sad truth in life I've found
While journeying east and west —
The only folks we really wound
Are those we love the best.
We flatter those we scarcely know,
We please the fleeting guest,
And deal full many a thoughtless blow
To those who love us best.
~Ella Wheeler Wilcox

Jeff and I had many conversations during the year, but I will always remember the time he told me about his family. His mother, a loving, caring woman, was the one who held the family together. She died shortly before Jeff graduated from high school. His father, a successful physician, cold and stern in Jeff's words, had firm beliefs that a person would never make a valuable contribution to the world unless they attended and graduated from college by the age of twenty-three. His father had even paved the way for Jeff to attend the same college from which he graduated, and had offered to pay Jeff's entire tuition and living expenses. As an active Alumni Association member, he was excited that his son would someday follow in his footsteps.

Jeff was twenty-seven and a successful business planner at a Fortune 500 company—without a degree. His passion was skiing.

When he graduated from high school, he decided to decline his father's offer and instead move to Colorado to work with a ski patrol. With pain in his eyes, Jeff told me that he still remembered the day he told his father he was going to forego college and take a job at a ski resort. He remembered every word of the short conversation. He told his father of his passion for skiing and for the mountains, and then of his plans. His father looked off into the distance, his face became red, and his eyes squinted and bore into Jeff. Then came the words that still echoed in Jeff's mind: "You lazy kid. No son of mine is going to work on a ski patrol and not attend college. I should have known you'd never amount to anything. Don't come back in this house until you have enough self-respect to use the brains God gave you and go to school!" The two had not spoken since that conversation.

Jeff was not even sure that his father knew he was back in the area near where he grew up, and he certainly did not want his father to know he was attending college. He was doing this for himself, he said over and over, not for his father.

Janice, Jeff's sister, had always remained supportive of Jeff's decisions. She stayed in contact with their father, but Jeff had made her promise that she would not share any information about his life with him.

Jeff's graduation ceremony that year was on a hot, sunny day in June. As I walked around talking to people before the ceremony, I noticed a man with a confused expression on his face.

"Excuse me," he said as he politely approached me. "What is happening here today?"

"It's graduation day," I replied, smiling.

"Well that's odd," he said. "My daughter asked me to meet her at this address." His eyes sparkled and he smiled. "Maybe she completed her associate's degree and wanted to surprise me!"

I helped him find a seat and as he left me he said, "Thank you for helping me. By the way, my name's Dr. Holstrom."

I froze for a second. Jeff Holstrom. Dr. Holstrom. Could this be the same person I had heard about over the last year? The cold, stern man who demanded his son attend college or never enter his home again?

Soon the familiar strains of "Pomp and Circumstance" could be heard. I turned around in my chair to get a glimpse of Dr. Holstrom. He seemed to be looking for his daughter amongst the graduates on stage. Speeches were given, the graduates were congratulated, and the dean began to read the names of the graduates.

Jeff was the last person to cross the stage. I heard his name being announced: "Jeff Holstrom, magna cum laude." He crossed the stage, received his diploma from the college president, and, just as he started down the stairs from the stage, he turned toward the audience looking for his sister.

A lone figure stood up in the back of the audience—Dr. Holstrom. I'm not sure how Jeff even saw him in the crowd, but I could tell that their eyes met. Dr. Holstrom opened his arms, as if to embrace the air around him. He bowed his head, almost as if to apologize. For a moment it seemed as if time stood still, and as if they were the only two in the auditorium. Jeff came down the stairs with tears in his eyes.

"My father is here," he whispered to me. I smiled.

"What are you going to do?" I asked him.

"Well," he said. "I think I'm going home."

~Vicki Niebrugge
Chicken Soup for the College Soul

THE WISDOM OF DADS

The Lighter Side

Nothing shows a man's character more than what he laughs at.
~Goethe

72

ONCE WAS ENOUGH

When you stretch the truth, watch out for the snapback.
~Bill Copeland

The first time my father and I ever went fishing became a family legend.

We spent hours waiting for a nibble. The sun was blistering, and this was back in the days before sunscreen. We were hot, sticky, and mad that the fish refused to suck up our night crawlers.

Being only seven years old, I observed that perhaps the worms were the problem. Maybe the night crawlers only wriggled at night, and now they were just lying there limp on the hook. Dad ignored my assessment of the situation.

We began to pack up to leave. As we headed back to our truck, we heard tires spinning in the distance. Getting into our truck was a grim affair. Having sat in the boiling sun for six hours, the seats were blistering. Naturally, I was wearing shorts.

I shifted from side to side in the seat so as not to cook my backside. While driving out we saw a truck with a boat trailer and boat that was stuck in the mud. That explained the sound of spinning tires we'd heard.

Being a nice guy, my dad helped pull the man from the mud. In return, this fellow gave Dad some fish for being a Good Samaritan. As Dad climbed back into our truck with a brown bag full of fish, we waved goodbye to our newfound friend.

On the drive home, we agreed to take in the fish as if we had caught them. We were sure there was no way for Mom to know the difference. It was just a little white lie.

We arrived home hot, sweaty, and smelly, and went to clean up while Mom prepared the fish. We made a big deal out of the fact that we had already cleaned them and put them in the bag so as not to make a mess.

After showering, Dad and I met in the hall and exchanged conspiratorial grins. Sitting down to freshly fried catfish, hush puppies and coleslaw, we dug in heartily. In the spirit of embellishment, we both went on about how good something tasted that we had actually caught ourselves. Mother looked suitably impressed.

As we got up to do the dishes, Mom cleared her throat. "I just have one question of you two great fishermen," she said. We looked at her expectantly, thinking we had another opportunity to regale her with our great fishing ability. With a tiny smile, Mom asked, "How was it again that you two managed to not only clean your fish, but also freeze them before you got home?"

~Karri J. Watson
Chicken Soup for the Fisherman's Soul

73

NERD DAY

Know, first, who you are; and then adorn yourself accordingly.
~Epictetus

You know it's going to be a bad day when your teenager knocks on your bedroom door first thing in the morning and says, "Today is Nerd Day at school, Pop. Can I borrow some of your clothes?"

~Ron Chapman
Chicken Soup for the Father's Soul

74

FATHER KNOWS BEST

You must lose a fly to catch a trout.
~George Herbert

Tepid days and cool nights are the greeting cards of summer in the lower Sierra Nevada mountains. What better place to escape the stifling summer heat of the Sacramento Valley? My eight-year-old son Logan, his Uncle Neal and I did just that, traveling to the cooler high country of the Feather River region for some camping and fishing fun.

After setting up, Neal headed upriver to fly-fish the pools and riffles, while Logan and I fished a little closer to camp. It wasn't long before Logan hooked a nice-sized rainbow trout and landed the brilliantly colored prize by himself. His excitement about catching the fish puzzled me.

"Logan, why are you so excited?" I asked.

He looked at me and said with a prideful grin, "Because this is the first fish I ever caught."

"No it isn't. You've caught fish before, even bigger than that one," I reminded him.

"No, Dad," he patiently, but excitedly, explained. "This is the first fish that I've ever caught. You always hooked it and then handed me the pole."

Logan was right—this was the first fish he'd ever caught by himself. But this was just the beginning of the ensuing dilemma.

"So, Logan," I asked, "are you going to throw your fish back so it can live, or are you going to eat that sucker for dinner tonight?"

Logan was perplexed by my question, not knowing how to respond. Very much an animal lover, this was a big decision for him. To help ease his mind, I finally put the fish in an old bucket filled with river water while he pondered his answer.

Over the next half hour, Logan continually talked to the fish, so much so that he and the fish were becoming fast friends. Much to my chagrin of missing a wonderful fish-fry dinner, I figured the fish was going back into the river. But that was okay—it was Logan's fish and Logan's decision.

"Dad, do you think I should throw him back or keep him?" he asked, glancing at the bucket and his new fish friend. It was obvious that Logan didn't want to make the final decision and was hoping I'd do it for him. After a few fatherly moments trying to figure out the best way to help my son with this impasse, I came up with an idea.

"Tell you what, Logan," I said. "If Uncle Neal comes back with a creel full of fish, then we'll keep him. If he doesn't, then we'll throw him back because even though he's a big fish, there's not enough of him to feed all three of us. How does that sound?"

"Oh, that sounds great, Dad!" Logan thanked me and turned to the bucket to share the decision with his friend.

Soon after, a small figure could be seen in the distance—it was Neal slowly working his way downstream. Logan spotted him and took off running. Did Neal have a creel-full or did he get skunked? I looked at Logan's landlocked friend waiting patiently to learn its fate. In a way, I felt sorry for the fish. I was also worried about Logan if his uncle was successful in his outing; would he honor the decision?

When the two were within earshot, Logan was talking excitedly to Neal, telling him all about his catch. Suddenly, Logan darted past me and flashed a grin. Okay, I thought, his friend's going to be saved, returned to its mountain stream for another day and another fisherman.

As Logan raced by, I looked at a beaming Neal. He opened his creel, showing off a basket full of sparkling rainbow trout, which totally threw me off. I quickly turned to Logan, ready to offer fatherly advice to my devastated son.

Logan was on his haunches and staring in the bucket. Knowing his intense love for animals, I waited for Logan to apologize to the fish.

With all the courage he could muster, Logan had only six words for his friend.

"I'm going to eat you, sucker!"

~Jeff Wise as told to Dahlynn McKowen
Chicken Soup for the Fisherman's Soul

75

IN THE PINK

When in doubt, wear red.
~Bill Blass

I had several choices on Saturday. Clean the garage, wash the car or go to the golf store and waste hours looking at a bunch of stuff I couldn't afford.

It was crowded at the golf store. I like it when it's that way. The salespeople are too busy to pester you, and you can play with the putters all day long. I have won many imaginary tournaments on that little carpeted green.

I was heading to the front of the store to forage in the "experienced" golf ball jar when I saw three familiar kids—mine—coming in the front door. At first I assumed my wife sent them on a search party and that I'd have to clean the garage after all. Then I saw the sign over the checkout stand, "Ask About Our Father's Day Specials." They were here to buy me a gift! Not another Three Stooges tie. Not another Handy Mitt, the greatest car-washing aid since water, but a golf gift. Cool.

I ducked down behind the shoe mirror as they headed toward the golf ball section. Would they buy the Tour Edition Titleists? Probably not without help. I dashed down the club display aisle and slipped behind the mountain of shimmering red and gold boxes.

"What about these yellow balls?" I heard my youngest child ask.

"Or these orange ones?" my daughter added.

I poked until a box of Titleists fell on the floor a few feet from them.

"Whoa, dude. This whole thing could fall," said my older son.

"Yeah. Let's look somewhere else."

Darn. I followed in a crouched position as they walked slowly by the golf bags and over to the glove display. Perfect. One of those double-thick, imported gloves with the removable ball marker. They walked right by. Okay. Maybe they'll pick out one of those electronic distance calculators or a six-pack holder. They ambled on.

Finally, they entered the clothing section and headed for a rack full of Ralph Lauren Polo shirts. Yes! I could already picture myself standing in the fairway, contemplating my approach shot, while the others in my group commented on my impeccable taste.

"Hey. Look over here." The enthusiasm in my daughter's voice meant they had found the perfect gift. I felt bad that they were going to spend all that money, but who was I to question their immeasurable affection?

"Cool. And they're cheap, too."

Cheap? I peeked through some women's sweaters. My daughter was holding up a pair of pink polyester pants that had been on the clearance rack since day one.

"And we could get this to go with it." My older son held up a lime-green mesh shirt.

I gasped audibly. They looked in my direction, so I slipped further back into women's wear, bumping into the store manager.

"Just browsing," I whispered.

He looked at me strangely and I realized I was holding a pair of extra large women's shorts and an athletic bra. Behind me I heard, "Look. The final touch."

I got down on all fours and stuck my head out. My youngest son was holding up a hat that said "Tee-riffic Golfer" in type large enough to see four blocks away.

"But it's red," my younger son said. "Does that matter?"

"Naw," said my daughter. "Golfers always dress weird."

I watched them walk toward the front, then I turned and looked at the manager. "I don't suppose...?"

"Nope. All sales final. Besides, you'd break their hearts."

I slept in on Sunday. At about nine they marched into the room, placed a package on my chest and said, "Happy Father's Day."

I tore the wrapping slowly, hoping I could muster up enough excitement when I held up that hat. But the package contained only a note.

"Look beside you," it said.

I turned slowly and there on the pillow was one of my favorite putters from the golf store.

"I don't understand," I said.

"Dude," said my older son. "We, like, knew you were there. Your car was parked out front."

"Are you disappointed?" my daughter asked.

"No! This is perfect." I stroked my new putter lovingly. "So," I laughed. "Guess they let you take those dreadful pink pants back, huh?"

Just then my wife entered the bedroom carrying a carefully wrapped package.

"Ahhh. Not exactly..."

~Ernie Witham
Chicken Soup for the Golfer's Soul

76

FISH PUNKS

Tell a man there are 300 billion stars in the universe and he'll believe you.
Tell him a bench has wet paint on it and he'll have to touch it to be sure.
~Murphy's Law

Every year, my dad, affectionately called the "Fish Master," goes on a weeklong executive fishing trip to the Kenai Peninsula in Alaska. This is no ordinary fishing trip. It's an all-inclusive, cigar-smoking, hanging-with-the-guys salmon fishing trip. It usually consists of my dad, a few of his close friends and some family members.

Last year, my cousin Pete and I were invited. We were instantly coined the "Fish Punks," partially because Pete hadn't fished since summer camp, and I hadn't reached "Fish Master" status yet at the ripe old age of twenty-six.

In my mind, these were going to be the best seven days of salmon fishing in the world. We started out each morning with a gourmet breakfast at 4:30 A.M., and then tour guides picked us up and drove us to the river, where we were separated into small boats to fish. Thousands of salmon were spawning; you could almost reach in and grab one. We usually caught our limits by 7:30 A.M., then it was on to bowling and the movies, ending with a dinner and a few rounds of drinks at the local night spot.

After a few days of reveling in this, we chartered a small seaplane to take us across Cook Inlet to a remote river site in search of a true wilderness experience and more of the greatest fishing on earth.

Roll call included the "Fish Master," my uncle, a judge, an

attorney and us, the Fish Punks, who brought up the rear carrying all the gear. The guide and his black Lab, Buddy, met us at the airport. They lived in a tent next to the river and guided city tourists like us into unforgettable, amazing backwoods fishing holes.

One night, at about 11:30 P.M. (Alaskan dusk time), our guide asked if anyone wanted to fish at a secret hole upriver. Room was limited, so two members of our group would not be able to go. Relegated to the bottom of the fishing totem pole, Pete and I were left behind.

After a bit, Pete and I became bored and decided to fish off the banks about one hundred yards downriver from our tents. We felt confident in our fishing abilities and secure with my field training in the army.

So, on a quiet summer evening, two Fish Punks were on their own in the woods. Two trumpeter swans trumpeted overhead, two beavers beavered across the river; it was a scene from Noah's ark. I had my line in the water trying to catch that champion king salmon and become a "Fish Master," when all of a sudden we heard some loud ruffling in the bushes across the river. Just as I yelled "Fish on!" Pete yelled, "Bear!"

I wasn't giving up a potential trophy salmon because of some bear across the river, even if it stood ten feet tall. I saw the bear look across the river at me with a fish on my line, then at Pete who was freaking out. The bear didn't seem to have any interest in the beavers, which didn't bode well for us.

Pete dropped his fishing pole and ran off, quickly returning with a chain saw he tried to start. Rummmm ummmmm... spatter spatter... Rummmm ummmm cough, puff, ummmm rumm hmmmmmmmmm. Finally, he got it going.

The bear remained on his side of the river, just a stone's throw away; I was still yards downriver fighting my champion salmon. The swans flew overhead, the beavers hid under a fallen tree in the river. The bear calmly went about his bear business, then disappeared back in the bushes.

Pete killed the chainsaw and ran to where I was still trying to land my fish. My heart raced as I reeled it in: a midsized, nothing-spectacular fish! I started to unhook it, feeling pangs of disappointment, until I noticed a rainbow hue reflecting in the water. It was a champion-sized Dolly Vardon trout. A glimmer of hope returned. I ended up catching that fish—it was the biggest one caught in the river that season. And to think I might have forgone the opportunity to avoid an old bear.

The fellas came home with a boatload of fish. We told the guide our story about the bear, and he laughed, saying it was probably a beaver, not a bear. Even so, he suggested putting the fish in garbage bags and leaving them in the boat on the riverside to protect them from the bear or other hungry animals.

John, the attorney, decided he would stand guard all night to protect the fish from whatever might steal them—just him and his old buddy Jack Daniels. He set up a lounge chair next to the fire as the rest of us settled into our small tents for the night.

In the morning, we were awakened by Buddy's barking and our guide yelling, "Get out of here!" The ruckus was accompanied by several gunshots. I jumped up and ran out of the tent to witness a huge brown bear running away with a bag of fish over its shoulder looking like Santa scurrying off to deliver Christmas presents. In his other paw he had a six-pack of beer to wash it all down, or at least it seemed so in my state of drowsiness.

We all regrouped around the remainder of the campfire. The fish guard was happily laid out, fast asleep, on his very comfortable beach chair. We saw the bear's footprints walking through camp: step, step, step, step over John, step, step, step, bag of fish, turn around, step, step, dropped parts of fish, step over John, step, step, bear scrambles, step, run, running full speed from the crazy shooting man and the barking black Lab.

John swore he hadn't fallen asleep while protecting our catch. Since we know all attorneys are true to their word, it must have been the bear that finished the bottle of J.D.

~Rod Scott
Chicken Soup for the Fisherman's Soul

PUNCH LINES

Above all else: go out with a sense of humor. It is needed armor.
Joy in one's heart and some laughter on one's lips is a sign that
the person down deep has a pretty good grasp of life.
~Hugh Sidey

My dad is an hour late when he shows up at my house for dinner.

"I can't believe the traffic," he says, as he takes off his coat. "There I was, stuck behind a huge mattahue. What a nerve-wracking experience."

He follows me into the kitchen and accepts a ginger ale.

"I'm sorry the drive over was so hard," I say. "By the way, what's a mattahue?"

"I don't know. What's a matta you?" he says.

If restaurants were divided into joking or nonjoking sections, I know where my father would sit every time.

As a child, I did not appreciate my father's persistent sense of humor. He lay in wait for me every morning. Wearing a respectable gray suit, reading the newspaper and drinking coffee, he looked like an ordinary adult. I knew better.

"Want a bagel?" he asked, as I dragged in.

I analyzed the question, wary that a joke lurked in its shadows. "Okay," I answered. I had learned monosyllabic replies made me less vulnerable to the pitfalls of punnery.

My father calmly sliced, toasted and buttered a bagel for me. I took a bite and relaxed. "Interesting article about the space program," he said. I nodded and kept chewing. He continued, "Johns Hopkins is doing a study on the nutritional impact of space. Do you know what those fellows eat?"

"Some sort of capsule or algae," I said.

"According to this article, all they eat is launch meat." One bite later, the pun sunk in. He'd gotten me again! I clutched my stomach and groaned. Dad smiled and returned to his newspaper.

Every neighborhood gathering, every family social, every Sunday school picnic, my father rolled out his stories and jokes. I envied my friend Susan whose dad quietly flipped hamburgers and freshened drinks. I wished for a father like Camilla's, who puffed on his pipe and occasionally interjected a philosophical comment. I yearned for a parent like Uncle Frank, who inconspicuously lounged on the sofa, absorbing wrestling matches. My father was at the center of every event, milking the crowd with the expertise of a Wisconsin dairy farmer.

When I reached high school age, I avoided outings with my father. Why did such a smart man stoop to such fourth-grade humor? And why did the adults all eagerly wait for that lull when my father said, "Oh, by the way, did you hear the one about...?"

I dreaded a new boyfriend walking into my father's web. My father would be sitting there, looking middle-aged and innocuous in his La-Z-Boy. My friendly father would then gently draw out the boy until he found what he was looking for: the excuse for a joke.

"So where are you taking Debbie tonight? Dinner and a movie? You know, I recently ate at a Howard Johnson's. I ordered soup. The waiter brought my soup, and there was a stick right in the middle. 'Waiter,' I said, 'what is this twig doing in my soup?'

"'Oh, that's nothing, sir,' the waiter said. 'We have branches all over the country.'"

I'd enter the room just in time to see my potential Romeo roll his eyes and clear his throat. Then he'd crank out the smile. "Good one, sir. Do you think Debbie will be ready soon?"

Recently, my friend Philip dropped by to meet my family. My mother offered him a glass of orange juice, and my father graciously weaved Philip into the conversation. Philip told my father how he loved the desert, and my father listened attentively. After a pause, Dad said, "Speaking of the desert...." Mom and I glanced at each other. The joke unfolded as casually as white bread. At the end, we all laughed and my father settled back, like a chess master contemplating his next move.

"Your father is great," Philip said afterward. "I never felt so at home meeting a new person."

"Well, he goes overboard sometimes with the humor," I said.

"I loved it," Philip said.

Suddenly, I realized my father does not just work for laughs: With his jokes and stories, he makes people feel welcome, comfortable and part of the group. My father has been quietly accomplishing the things I've been reading and studying about for years.

I often attend seminars on how to network. I read books on how to bring people together in groups. I attend conferences on speaking and storytelling. Yet I'd been in the presence of a master all these years without even realizing it.

One night, my daughters and I were gathered around the supper table. I passed the baked potatoes and said, "I got a speeding ticket today."

"Mom, I can't believe it. You just had one last month."

"The policeman who stopped me was nice—and a real body builder. I asked him why he was so strong." I lowered my head and sliced my tomato into quarters.

"So, what did he say?" Sarah asked, taking a sip of iced tea.

"He said he's strong because he's constantly holding up traffic," I answered.

My daughters stopped eating and gave me "the look." They raised their eyebrows and shook their heads.

"You're as bad as Grandpa," Jessica said.

I smiled and basked in the praise. Then I wondered if they'd heard the one about...

~Deborah Shouse
Chicken Soup for the Father & Daughter Soul

78

HOOKING GREENBACKS

I n 1988, I took my twelve-year-old son Jason on one of our annual father-son summer vacations to Yellowstone National Park. It was an exceptionally hot summer, the same year the great fires swept through.

Jason and I had already been fishing inside the national park, where there were lots of rules protecting the fisheries. With few exceptions, only lures and flies could be used. Dead or live bait was taboo. We'd fished the Madison, Gibbon and Yellowstone Rivers, and Jason tried to blame his lack of success on his fishing pole. I had to admit his old spinning rod had seen better days.

One morning we left the park and drove about twenty miles out to Hebgen Lake. The idea was to rent a boat and try some trolling. As it turned out, a strong wind kicked up by the time we arrived, and the lake was much too choppy for fishing. Jason and I tried fishing from the dock in the marina's sheltered waters. A short while later, I headed up to the marina's combination bar, restaurant and tackle store to meet an old friend and enjoy a cold brew.

My friend asked about Jason.

"Yeah, he's down on the dock, catching some strange-looking fish," I said, "and he's still complaining about that old fishing pole of his."

Someone else piped up, suggesting I buy the kid a new one.

"Oh, I will, but I was holding off until his birthday next month," I answered.

About fifteen minutes had passed when we heard someone

running up the wooden ramp to the side screen door that led to where we were sitting.

"Dad! Dad!" Jason yelled as he burst through the door. He was carrying his old fishing pole with something dangling from his hook. "Look what I caught!" he exclaimed. He was grinning from ear to ear.

Several of the bar regulars and I did double-takes at his prize catch. There — green, dripping wet, but the real thing — was a twenty-dollar bill attached to his hook.

I must say, the sight of that greenback immediately grabbed our attention. I surmised that Jason must have spotted the bill in the clear water while standing on the dock and used his lure to drag the bill across the lake bottom to shore. He then stuck it on his hook for a more dramatic presentation, and it worked! Jason turned and quickly headed back outside, obviously still excited. He said something about catching enough money so he could buy that new fishing pole. I remember quite a few chuckles at the bar.

Ten minutes hadn't passed when Jason returned with another dripping wet twenty-dollar bill attached to his hook. We made him show us the first one to be sure he wasn't pulling some kind of practical joke. The chuckles turned to laughter, with more than one of the regulars looking out the window toward the dock.

Jason quickly unhooked the second soggy twenty-dollar bill, stuffed it into his pocket with the first and ran back out the door and down the ramp with his fishing pole in hand. When he returned ten minutes later with a wet ten-dollar bill attached to the same hook, a couple of the bar regulars quickly downed their beers and cleared out, we assumed to get their own fishing poles. But by that time Jason had snagged all the greenbacks out of the old marina fishing hole, and there was nothing left but those strange fish.

Someone took a Polaroid picture of Jason proudly posing with his fishing pole and greenbacks and added it to the bulletin board that displayed other lucky Hebgen Lake anglers proudly showing off their catches.

I took Jason back to West Yellowstone where he bought that new fishing pole, and we returned to Yellowstone National Park so he could break it in on the real thing. The good news was that Jason's luck changed. Although he didn't spot any more greenbacks, he did out-fish me during the remainder of our father-son vacation. I still grin every time I remember that picture on the marina bulletin board of Jason holding his greenbacks alongside photos of other fishermen holding their trophy fish. You have to wonder who had been the most excited.

I returned to Hebgen Lake and the same marina about twelve years later and the photo was still there. Today, I have it as a souvenir from that most memorable trip.

~Ken McKowen
Chicken Soup for the Fisherman's Soul

79

OUR FIRST MEETING

When you realize you want to spend the rest of your life with somebody,
you want the rest of your life to start as soon as possible.
~Harry to Sally in When Harry Met Sally

As a college student in the '70s, I belonged to a youth program called "Contact Canada," whose purpose was to attract potential college immigrants to Canada. I was one of only four Americans in an international group of two hundred young adults who toured in teams to several provinces.

Along the way, I met a lovely Brit, and we became friends. But our three weeks quickly came to an end, and we returned home to our respective countries. Sue and I exchanged letters over the next year.

The following summer, she flew to California to stay with my folks and me for a month-long holiday. I was immediately entranced by this exciting woman and asked her to marry me after two short weeks. We consulted an immigration attorney, who recommended that we marry on U.S. soil to shorten the laborious green-card process. After six months, we could then have a formal church wedding.

With that, my best friend Joel, Sue and I drove to Reno for a one-day trip to tie the knot after a two-week engagement. We intentionally downplayed the ceremony, telling ourselves that this was only "for the government." We had no rings, no formal attire, and of course, no honeymoon. Aside from being love struck, our official marriage in the U.S. would shorten her request for residency to months rather than years.

The following day, I reluctantly watched Sue board a Pan Am 747 through tear-filled eyes. I hid in a corner of the airport lounge to compose myself. We would be separated for one hundred and twelve days—a time in which I would receive a letter a day from my long-distance bride.

I didn't have the courage to ask her how her parents handled the news that their only daughter was returning from a holiday married to an American. Somewhere in the hour drive between Heathrow and their home near Gatwick, she made the announcement. As much as I missed her, I'll admit I was relieved to have missed that awkward moment. Especially telling her father.

Each day seemed like an eternity waiting for the end of my college semester. My flight to England was scheduled two hours after my last final at San Jose State, but even that wasn't enough time. I would have to finish my three-hour test in only one hour. Nobody has ever whipped though an archeology final with such enthusiasm.

On the plane, I sat in my window seat in a complete daze. I was desperate to see Sue again and excited to stand before God and family to exchange vows in a real wedding.

But amidst the excitement, I was absolutely terrified—a nervous wreck, wondering what fate had in store for me when I finally met my father-in-law. After all, his daughter and I only dated a month before getting engaged for only two weeks. My worse crime, I was sure, was not properly asking him for her hand with European formality.

I pictured him basking in the same aura of anti-Americanism that was prevalent all over Europe in the mid-'70s. My stomach twisted and burned, and my excitement was waning as the fear grew.

After my plane landed, I found my luggage and stood in the long line at Immigration, in dread of the meeting. I prayed the drive to her family home would be quick and the impending explosion of anger even quicker.

As I cleared customs and entered the concourse, a sea of faces surrounded me. From the crowd, a gentleman broke free and raced towards me. Although I had not met her father yet, I knew who this man approaching me was. It was time. The long wait was over, and I was prepared for my fate.

He ran up to me, grabbed my hand and pumped it up and down in a warm handshake. His left hand slapped my shoulder as he said, "Thank God, lad. I thought she would never leave the house!"

And so began my relationship with a man that I've loved and respected for twenty-seven years. He's given me the gift of his daughter, my best friend and soul mate. Unexpectedly, he also gave me his gift of acceptance.

~David R. Wilkins
Chicken Soup for the Bride's Soul

FATHERS ARE GOOD AT TELLING TALL TALES

I thought I would share with you a father's greatest fear: answering a five-year-old child's question of "Where do babies come from?"

Even though I've reached an age at which I could be a grandpa (a young and virile one, I might add), it doesn't seem that it's been more than twenty years since I gave the "birds and bees" speech.

Because I did such a magnificent job of bungling my first attempt, my wife didn't entrust me with that chore a second time.

Although time has a way of mercifully erasing embarrassing moments from memory, I can recall, with depressing clarity, the circumstances of my father-son talk.

One night while Nancy and I were watching *All in the Family*, she said calmly, "Jim, I think you should find time to tell Shawn about the facts of life. Soon."

"Aw, Honey," I whined, "the little guy is too young for that sort of thing."

"I don't know about that." She smiled and raised an eyebrow. "Yesterday, Shawn wanted to know if he could trade his G.I. Joe for a Raquel Welch."

"They don't make Raquel Welch dolls, do they?" I asked.

"No," she said, "but he didn't want a doll, he wanted Raquel Welch. THE Raquel Welch!"

I cleared my throat several times, fidgeted quite a bit and finally said, "Wellll... well, Honey, I guess you're right, but he's so young."

"Kids mature faster nowadays," she said comfortingly. "The curse of television and movie previews, I suppose."

"I better do it now and get it over with," I said.

If I remember correctly, our little talk ended with "...and so you see, an Indian shoots an arrow into the sky. If it lands in an oyster bed, the mommy will have a boy. If it lands in a strawberry patch, she'll have a girl."

"Then does the mommy have to eat the oyster?" asked Shawn.

"Ummm... ahhh... yeah, sure. And that's probably why there are more girls than boys," I said.

Suddenly, the bedroom door swung open. "Jim, JIM HORNBECK! How could you tell a story like THAT?" shouted Nancy. "Why, that's the most ridiculous thing I've ever heard."

"Mommy," said Shawn, "don't be mad. I knew it was just one of Daddy's stories."

"You did?" I said, overcome with relief.

"Sure," said Shawn, "Mikey already told me where babies come from."

"He did?" we chorused.

"What really happens," he continued, "is a man and a woman go to Hollywood and get married. After they do a bunch of kissing and hugging, they have a party and get lots of presents."

"Oh, good grief," sighed Nancy.

"And two of the presents are catalogs."

"What?" we chorused again.

"Then they choose a boy baby from Sears," said Shawn, "or a girl baby from JC Penney. That's what Mikey said."

"Who told him that?" I asked.

"His dad," said Shawn.

Nancy frowned. "Oyster beds and catalogs. Now, where would you men ever learn stories like that!"

I smiled sheepishly and said, "From our fathers, of course."

~Jim Hornbeck
Chicken Soup for the Father's Soul

Chapter 9

THE WISDOM OF DADS

Fun and Games

It isn't the big pleasures that count the most;
it's making a great deal out of the little ones.
~Jean Webster

STEAL WHAT?

There is more logic in humor than in anything else.
Because, you see, humor is truth.
~Victor Borge

This story took place several years ago, when our boys were about eight years old. It was the first game of the season, and the first game in which the boys began pitching. I went out to discuss ground rules with the umpire and realized that this was also the first year that the boys could steal bases. Unfortunately, we had not gone over this in practice. So I hurried back to the dugout, gathered my players and proceeded to go over the rules. As I got to the subject of stealing bases, I announced enthusiastically, "And this year we get to steal!" The news caused the boys to erupt into yelling and cheering. Their response left me thinking positively that this might all work out okay after all. Then the cheers died down, and as our team was about to take the field, one player loudly exclaimed, "Steal what?!" I let out a groan as I realized that the question had come from my son!

~Cary McMahon
Chicken Soup for the Sports Fan's Soul

FINAL SEASON

The other night, after the parents had all come to pick up their sons and I was picking up catcher's equipment, bats and, of course, one forgotten mitt, it dawned on me that this was it: the last season I would coach one of my sons' baseball teams.

Two sons. Twelve seasons. Hundreds of games. Maybe three decent umps. And thousands of memories, hidden in my mind like all those foul balls lost in the creek behind the Ascot Park backstop.

Sitting in the rickety bleachers that spring evening after everyone had gone, I found myself lost in thought, mentally walking along the creek, finding those long-forgotten foul balls and listening to the stories they had to tell.

The time our left fielder got locked in a Dairy Queen bathroom during a postgame celebration. The time I handed a protective cup to our new catcher and he thought it was an oxygen mask. The time a tee-baller cleanly fielded a grounder, picked it up and tossed it to his mom, who was sitting behind third base reading *Gone with the Wind*.

For something that became more than a decade-long family affair, it had begun casually enough. While watching one of my five-year-old son's tee-ball games in 1985, a manager asked if I would coach second base.

"Uh, second base?"

"Yeah. At this level you need coaches at second base or the kids will forget to take a left and wind up at Safeway."

So I coached second base. And before long, our family's summers revolved around a diamond: me coaching, my wife Sally keeping score and the boys playing. Like the Israelites trudging out of Egypt, we hauled our equipment—lawn chairs, video cameras and sixty-four-ounce drinks—from ball field to ball field, week after week, summer after summer.

The time our right fielder turned up missing during a championship game, only to be found at the snack bar eating licorice and flirting with girls. The time we showed up at an empty field, only to discover that I'd read the schedule wrong and our game was actually ten miles away.

The time I explained to my fifth-grade team that, because we'd given up eighty-nine runs in the last four games, we needed to set a defensive goal.

"It's a six-inning game," I explained. "Let's just try to hold them to twelve runs per game. Two per inning. Can you do that?"

Silence. Then my philosophical right fielder spoke up.

"Coach," he said, "do we have to give up the runs even like that, or could we like give up all twelve in the last inning?"

Our teams were more than a collection of kids. They were extended family, some of whom would end up sleeping overnight and going to church with us. And some of the boys desperately needed that. One year, of fifteen players, only five had a mother and father living together under the same roof. Once, a boy missed practice because his aunt had been murdered. And I can't count the number of times I took kids home, because nobody came to pick them up.

But I've always remembered the advice I heard at a coaching clinic: "Who knows? The six hours a week you spend with a kid might be the only six hours that he actually feels loved."

The out-of-control coach who pushed me off the field. The kid who didn't get picked for my team firing a splat gun at our left fielder. The father who dropped off his son, Willie, and told him to get his own ride home; he and his girlfriend were going to a tavern to throw darts. We went into extra innings that afternoon, and the man's son played the game of his life, going all nine innings at catcher and making the game-winning hit.

We tried to make it more than just baseball. With help from our sons, we established a team newspaper. A few times, I'd put candy in the sack at second base and let players dig in every time they threw out a runner. (Best defensive practice we ever had.)

Sally was our DH—designated healer—with her ever-present cooler of pop and packages of frozen corn for sprained ankles and bruised arms. Once, we had pizza delivered to the ball field just after we'd lost to a team with one of those scream-and-yell coaches. I think we had more fun that night than the team that won.

The time we won with only eight players. The time Michael, a friend of my younger son, spent the night at our house and played hours of backyard baseball, the rules stipulating that you must run the bases backward. The next morning, in a regulation game, Michael hit a hot grounder and promptly took off—for third base.

Over the years we won games, we lost games and we lost baseballs—zillions of them. But for every ball we lost, we gained a memory. As a family, we laughed together, cried together, got dusty together—as if each of those hundreds of games was a microcosm of real life, which it was.

A weak-hitting kid named Cody stroking a three-run double and later telling his mom, "I'm trying to stop smiling, but I just can't."

My oldest son becoming my assistant coach and reaching a few kids in a way that I could not.

Kids I coached as third-graders, now taller than I am. And, of course, the night we were going to win the city championship. But for the first time in two months, it rained. Instead of playing on a field of dreams with perfectly straight white lines and a public address system, some official handed us a bunch of medals and called us co-champs.

Later that night, after the post-season pizza banquet, the restaurant manager approached me, broom in hand. "Excuse me, but are you the coach of the Washington Braves?"

"I sure am," I said, figuring he was going to pull me out of my doldrums by congratulating me on the co-championship.

"Coach," he said, handing me the broom, "your team trashed the indoor playroom. Wanna help sweep?"

Two sons. Twelve seasons. Hundreds of games. As a family, we had shared them all. But what, I wondered, had we missed in the process? What had we given up in order to pursue what some might see as trivial?

Nothing. Because whether your family is together at baseball games or camping trips or rodeos or dog shows or soccer tournaments or swim meets, the common denominator is this: families together—a rarity in our busy times—making memories. Learning lessons. Sowing seeds that can be nourished only by time.

Regrets? Only one. I wish Willie's father had considered his son more important than a game of darts. He missed seeing his teammates mob him after making the game-winning hit.

The time a tall third baseman was making fun of my four-foot-nine son at the plate—until my son nearly took off his head with a line-drive double.

My oldest son proudly posing for pictures with his grandparents after the team won a city championship.

The time he played his final game, and walking to the car afterward it hit me like a line drive in the side of the head. This was it. I'd never coach him in baseball again.

Dusk was descending. It was time to head for home where my family—the boys were now seventeen and fifteen—would be. As I slung the equipment bag over my shoulder and walked down from the stands, I noticed a young father and his son playing catch between short and third.

I smiled slightly and headed for the car, leaving behind plenty of lost balls for others to find.

~Bob Welch
Chicken Soup for the Father's Soul

LIFE ON THE BACK NINE

The first time I played golf—real golf where you keep score and putt everything out and take it seriously—was in a father-son tournament. I was ten. I remember thinking it would be cool to drive the golf cart. I was right. It was very cool driving the golf cart. Did I already say I was ten at the time? I think we shot about a 65 for nine holes, which is all we played because the attention spans of young golfers really don't allow for a full round.

The golf course I grew up playing, Meadowbrook Country Club, has a 609-yard par-5 that wore us out. I think we made a 12. But I was very proud of the fact that I didn't whiff any shots. And I was hooked. My dad had introduced me to a game that would forever be a part of my life.

It would also test the boundaries of our bond.

By the following summer, I was playing golf every day, which included sneaking onto the course on Mondays, when it was officially closed, and squeezing in three holes on the front nine on Tuesdays before the Ladies Day crowd would make it around to the seventh tee.

I even found what would be the family dog on the golf course that summer. A stray collie mix met me on the third tee one morning and followed me for the rest of the front nine. After I fed her half my hot dog from the snack bar, she was mine.

By the time the next father-son tournament rolled around, I would have cried if I'd shot a 65 on my own ball. I had developed a strong short game and expected my dad's length off the tee to make up for my shortcomings. If he could get us within 135 yards on the par-4s, I could get us on the green. And one of the best things about Meadowbrook back then was there was hardly any water and—except for one par-3—you never had to carry a water hazard to reach a green.

We shot 48, and I was miffed. I rolled my eyes every time my dad mis-hit a shot. I grimaced when my putts didn't fall. I kicked at the grass and mumbled to myself. I had a miserable time. We finished third. I thought we should have won.

That afternoon and evening, I moped around the house like it was the end of the world. This pattern carried on for years because, although my dad and I were both accomplished players, we never learned how to play together. By the time I hit my mid-teens, I was regularly shooting in the 70s. I won the club junior championship when I was fifteen, and the members had to put up with a five-foot-nothing squirt playing in their club championship that summer because the junior champ got an automatic invite.

Life was good, except for when Dad and I would tee it up as a team. We could go out on Saturday and both shoot in the 70s—I remember both of us had 6 handicaps when I was sixteen—then turn around the following day in that hate-inducing alternate-shot format and fire an 85 in an event in which you were allowed to choose the better of two tee shots.

I was so disgusted one time that I putted the last three holes left-handed. Not a word was spoken on the ride home. The crazy thing was that we'd take this act on the road to play in the Tommy Galloway Father-Son at Hermitage Country Club, which was a big regional to-do. Winning the low gross in our age group was impossible because we were bound to make a couple of 7s. We'd always get to the sixteenth tee and one of us would say, "Well, there's always the net. If we shoot 82, they take away our two worst holes."

One time, we reached the par-4 seventeenth hole 7-over for the day and looked like we'd break 80... until we both dunked it into the lake running down the right side of the fairway. It was negative on negative. The problem was, we couldn't learn to accept each other's faults. He sprayed drives and had a tendency to severely misclub himself. I was into go-for-broke golf. By the time I was sixteen and had hit a growth spurt, I figured there wasn't a par-5 I shouldn't reach in two. And I had turned into a terrible putter. My dad fretted over my jab stroke, which was either on fire or ice cold; I, meanwhile, fretted about his desire to play it safe.

By the time I was seventeen, we'd accepted the fact that we weren't much of a team. We were at the peaks of our games—my high school team won the 1981 state championship and I signed a golf scholarship with Virginia Commonwealth University. Dad was as consistent about shooting in the 70s as he'd ever be. But together we were mush.

I went off to school and lost myself in books and knowledge and a hunger to be a newspaper writer. And I lost my interest in playing competitive golf. After two seasons, I was through as a college golfer. There were some memorable rounds, but they were too few and far between.

Meanwhile, we had aged out of the father-son tournament. But a few years ago, Dad called and asked if I wanted to play in the father-son again. Turns out they'd changed the name to the politically correct parent-child and had created an over-eighteen age group.

Did we really want to put ourselves through that turmoil again?

I was playing rarely, and Dad had developed shoulder problems and was playing even less.

"Sure," I said. "Why not?"

A funny thing happens when you reach adulthood. All of a sudden, you can accept your dad's faults because you start to realize you have your own. And why in the world should four hours of golf with Dad be so stressful?

We hit a bucket of balls to warm up, and I don't think either of us hit more than three practice shots on the sweet spot. I would have hated to pick up the range that night; Team Radford had sprayed shots everywhere. But we must have left all the bad shots on the range. We birdied the first hole when I hit a wedge to about ten feet and Dad ran in the putt. Then we birdied the fourth hole, a par-5, when Dad hit a 200-yard 5-wood onto the front of the green, and we two-putted from forty-five feet. By the end of the round, we'd made four birdies. We had some ugly holes, too, but they weren't too ugly. And the amazing thing was that after an ugly hole, we always followed it with a chance for birdie. I remember laughing when I signed the scorecard.

Here were two hacks who had never played well together and they'd just shot 4-over 75 in an alternate-shot format. A lot of the guys I had grown up with, and who had always trounced us as a father-son tandem, had decided to play that Sunday. I scanned my age group's scores—81-77-85-76-82-90.

We'd won? Unbelievable. When we came home with the hardware, Mom also couldn't believe it. For years, she'd had to hear us trash each other for hours after every father-son event we played. Now she had to hear us gloat.

Suddenly, Dad's 220-yard drives into light rough were a thing of beauty. And just as suddenly, as long as my putts went into the hole, Dad didn't care what my awful stroke looked like. We laughed about the fifteen-inch putt he missed on the fifteenth hole, something I was constantly guilty of.

Two holes later, I air-mailed a par-3, something he was more prone to do in the past. The following year we shot 72. By the back nine, we weren't worried about beating the field, we were wondering if we could beat par.

All of that negative energy that had followed us for years had become positive power. For years, we had been in situations where we would ponder whether to play the ball out of the woods or the one that was buried under the lip in the bunker. Now, we were having to choose between a ten-foot downhill putt or a fifteen-footer uphill for birdie.

We haven't played in a parent-child tournament for a few years now. Dad's shoulder became so aggravating that he quit playing and gave up his membership at the club. But I was in the attic of my parents' house the other day looking for some old Batman comic books for my own son when I came across a box of old golf trophies. The first one I picked up was the first-place trophy for the 1989

Meadowbrook Country Club Parent-Child, unlimited age group. The second one was a third-place cup for the 1973 father-son, eleven-and-under. It took sixteen years to get it right. But finally we did.

~Rich Radford
Chicken Soup for the Golfer's Soul

LIKE FATHER, LIKE SON

Giving your son a skill is better than giving him one thousand pieces of gold.
~Chinese Proverb

Like many fathers and sons, Bob and Dave like to play an occasional round of golf together when they can find the time. Nothing serious: Ten bucks a hole; bonuses for birdies and "polies" (approach shots that come to rest within a flagstick-length of the hole); optional presses whenever you're steamed—pretty much the same kind of convivial game fathers and sons enjoy in every part of America. The competition is fun, sure. But it's the being together that really matters. Because of career commitments and travel and all the other complications of being two working stiffs, they don't have a chance to see each other as much as they like. Even though they're in the same line of work, both master practitioners of the same profession, Bob and Dave's paths cross with depressing rarity. Like so many fathers and sons in our increasingly turbocharged world, they communicate mostly electronically, over the phone or—and this is one of the benefits of doing what they do—the television.

So when these two fellows do come together on the links, every moment counts.

When they arrive at the golf course, filled with the same kind of heightened anticipation most dads and sons feel before they're about to display their game to the most important male in their life, the conversation usually goes something like this:

Dad: "How many strokes am I getting today?"

Son, scoffing: "None."

Dad: "All right, fine. What tees do you want me to play?"

Son, indicating the back markers: "The same as me, of course."

Dad, pleading: "You may not be aware of this, Son. But the old guys? We don't play these tees. We start a little closer to the hole."

Son, resting his hand on Dad's shoulder: "You got your freakin' name on your bag, don't you? Quit your crying, and play some golf."

These days, Bob, who is one of the longest hitters you've ever seen for a guy in his fifties, is about fifteen yards shorter than his son off the tee. But as old Pops likes to remind his precocious kid, the game of golf is not merely a driving distance contest. And every now and then he proves it to young Dave. "There are days I make him dig into the wallet," Bob says proudly. "And, man, he's as tight as can be. It kills him!"

Bob laughs heartily. "It doesn't happen all the time. I'm not ashamed to admit it: He's definitely got the best of me these days. But you know what?" he says, smiling contentedly. "It's pretty cool to be able to compete with the number-two player in the world. And to know he's your son."

Bob and David Duval are both touring professional golfers. They both crisscross the United States in search of birdies and the monster paychecks that accompany them. They are both winners on their respective Tours.

And they are father and son.

Fathers try to teach their sons well, and watch with pride and contentment as their boys blossom into the men Dad hoped they would be.

Fathers serve as role models for their blooming offspring, idealized examples of the fully realized adult man young sons hope to become. Fathers show the way, and sons try earnestly to follow.

Sons try to make their fathers proud. Sons try to learn their fathers' lessons well. Sons hope to live up to their fathers' guiding example.

Which is all to say that Bob Duval, professional golfer, Senior Tour champion, and, yes, father, is in the peculiar and enviable position of having a son who has become the man his old dad hoped he would. And then much more.

David Duval, PGA Tour superstar, is one of the most famous golfers on the planet, a stylish, enigmatic athlete who has at times been capable of dominating his sport more completely than anyone but Tiger Woods.

Bob Duval has finished in the magic Top-31 his last three campaigns on the Senior Tour.

David Duval earns multimillions in both prize money and product endorsements. He travels the country in a private jet. He cannot go anywhere near a golf course without being mobbed by autograph-seeking fans.

Bob Duval earns a healthy six-figure income. He flies commercially. Only friends and family members recognize him.

David Duval is Bob's son. But that's not how the world sees it.

"No, David used to be Bob's kid," Bob Duval tells me, chuckling at the thought. "Now I'm definitely David's dad." He thinks for a moment.

"Everything has sort of flipped around," Bob Duval says. "The father has become the son."

We're sitting on the back deck of Bob's Jacksonville Beach home. With Buddy, Bob's faithful dog patrolling for lizards and the ocean crashing into the shore just a wedge away, it's a perfect afternoon to reflect on what it means to be a dad. And not just any old dad—though dads of any sort are cherished by their sons—but a member of the Senior Tour dad, and the father of a PGA Tour superstar dad. "I remember when it happened," Bob recalls. "It was David's first time being in contention down the stretch as a pro on the PGA Tour—and my first cigarette in several years! I was so nervous. He was battling with Peter Jacobsen at Pebble Beach. I remember having an overwhelming sense of pride—and it just got bigger when the phone didn't stop ringing for two hours, even after he finished second. At that point, in the eyes of a lot of people, he stopped being my kid and I became 'David's Dad.'"

Bob Duval doesn't say this with even the faintest trace of bitterness or remorse. He says it like a proud papa.

"I mean, my son chose the same path, the same business, as old dad. I couldn't be prouder. I don't think any dad could be prouder," Bob Duval says, smiling.

As if on cue, the phone rings. It's David, who lives a little ways down the road, in Ponte Vedra. Wants to know what time they're meeting this afternoon, for a round of golf. And if they've got a tee time arranged.

For some reason this thought amuses me immensely: David and Bob Duval showing up at a nearby golf course, wondering if, perhaps if it wasn't too much trouble of course, if they might, you know, hop on to the 1st tee? And then I realize: Today they're just a father and son looking to have an impromptu round of golf together.

And that's pretty sweet.

~Michael Konik
Chicken Soup for the Golfer's Soul, The 2nd Round

HUNTERS' BOND

Fortunately for me, the war in Vietnam ended before I received my draft notice. This was good for world peace, and especially for my own inner peace. Guns, senseless bloodshed, fear—I couldn't understand any of it. I was lucky not to have to face the killing in Vietnam, and I managed to successfully avoid any involvement with firearms for many years thereafter—that is, until about middle age when my only son reached adolescence.

My son's childhood preoccupation with weapons gave me little concern at first, since it did not seem an unusual fascination among young boys. However, just when I thought that his interest in guns would begin to fade, it escalated instead. He began to openly express his desire to take up deer hunting. In fact, on several occasions, he proposed this to me as a good idea for a father-and-son activity. Now, this was not what came to my mind when I thought about ways in which my son and I could find common ground. I hoped that I could placate him with "maybes" or "we'll sees," and that his idea would eventually fade away like earth shoes did in the seventies. After all, I had watched him go through phases when his life focused on Tonka toys and Legos, and they passed. But his preoccupation with firearms was tough. His interest only intensified and so, too, his incessant hounding of me to go hunting with him. So I began to give the matter my serious attention, trying to figure out ways to dissuade him from living out his fantasies.

This was a difficult one, and I decided to call in reinforcements. I consulted several of my friends, one of whom was an FBI agent, a man I always found to be levelheaded and a source of good advice. I thought that he could especially appreciate my concern about firearms. But much to my surprise, he was all for it.

"Let him learn the right way," he said. "Better under your supervision than with anyone else. Besides, hunting is probably the most appropriate use for a gun anyway." My friend's words hit home. If my son was eventually going to do it with or without my consent, it was better if we learned together.

Reluctantly, I entered into the wide world of sports, a world that was essentially foreign to me. Eventually, I went shopping for a rifle. I started by trying to persuade my son that a light .22 was the way to go. However, I was repeatedly informed by the experts that you couldn't hunt deer with a .22, and I was forced to purchase higher-powered equipment.

After buying our rifles, we joined a rod-and-gun club, which had a rifle range and provided us with paper targets for practice. Even at this stage, I held out the hope that it would go no further than the rifle range and that somehow my son would be satisfied with shooting cardboard figures. I was wrong again, and his interests continued to grow, particularly after talking to several hunters we met there.

One older fellow, who actually belonged to a hunting club and owned land in the mountains, invited us to come up for the first day of deer season. I thought of every possible excuse to get out of it, but found myself once again purchasing hunters' gear — boots, camouflage clothing and all the accessories that went along with joining the brotherhood of hunters.

This was a paradoxical experience for me, since I had such an aversion to the entire concept of hunting animals for sport. At the same time, I was intrigued and most inspired by my son's obvious sense of excitement in preparing for our expedition. But I found myself wondering how he would actually react upon coming face-to-face with the game that he was supposed to shoot. It all looked so easy in the hunting films that we viewed during the hunters' safety course and, on some level, I was thrilled by the chance to bond with my son who, up until this point, had not been motivated by very much in life. After months of practicing at the rifle range and conversations about the ideal hunting situation, deer season finally arrived. It was time to become bona fide hunters.

On the day of the big hunt, I was as nervous as a kid on a first date. The prior night's sleep was interrupted by nightmares and harrowing screams in the night—most of which were mine. We rose at three in the morning in order to arrive at the mountains before dawn, so that we could set up our stakeout post. We laid out all of our clothing and paraphernalia the night before, including thermal underwear, backpacks, boots, gloves with the fingers cut out, 150 square inches of orange cover material (so that we wouldn't be mistaken for deer), a knife, toilet paper, a Thermos with coffee and, of course, our weapons of destruction.

As we climbed toward our mountain destination, snow flurries became a steady snowfall, which I was told is ideal for hunting. While my son slept in the seat next to me, I drove like a white-knuckle flyer through a squall of snow in the early morning darkness, asking myself repeatedly why in God's name I was doing this. Of course, glancing to my right—where the great white hunter was sleeping like a baby—somehow helped me to reconcile my avoidance and his enthusiasm.

On the mountainside, the newly fallen snow sparkled a fresh and clean scene in the first rays of sunlight. What a beautiful and serene setting—the stillness and silence of this enchanted forest. How could such a murderous act, tracking down innocent prey in their own domicile, take place here? I felt like a ruthless assassin.

We pulled off the main road and onto an abandoned dirt path. The ground was littered with Styrofoam cups and fast-food wrappers—all of the evidence of salivating predators out for the kill. We unloaded our equipment and made our way through the thick brush, hauling our gear into the dense, dark woods. I trudged along like a schoolboy on his way to the principal's office, all the while attempting to hide my anxiety behind a bravado and a false display of enthusiasm for my son's sake. So this was the hour of reckoning, I mused. Facing our foe. All those months of target shooting have led to this day, when a father has to challenge his long-held beliefs and a son has to follow his own distinct dream. I wondered who was the more anxious, me or the deer, which no doubt had already sensed our presence.

Now, the hunters' task is different, depending on what is being hunted. With fowl such as pheasants, it's the hunter's chore to walk through wilted cornstalks, usually with a trained hunting dog, and roust the pheasants from their hiding place. But with deer, as with many other large game, the hunt consists of waiting quietly in one spot—sometimes for hours—until your prey crosses through the line of fire. As fate would have it, my son and I share one trait that would have a powerful effect on our success as hunters; we have no patience. We sat back-to-back, my son and I, camouflaged against a mound of brush, shivering in the cold morning air. My son anxiously prayed that he would soon see a deer in his sights. I anxiously prayed that the deer would have the good sense to go in the other direction. It didn't take long before these brave hunters broke the golden rule of silence. We began to chat.

"Dad, what if we get a deer, what will we do with it?" he asked me innocently. Yipes! Now there's something that we hadn't thought about. What would we do with it? Part of the art of hunting is also knowing how to gut the animal and field dress it and prepare it for the trip to the butcher.

I had forgotten about those horrible parts of the training film that showed the gruesome technique of eviscerating your catch and hanging it upside down to drain.

"Well," I said, "you remember what we saw in the films about cleaning the deer and preparing the carcass for butchering."

"Yeah," he muttered with the same enthusiasm he responds with when asked to clean his room. "That's the part that I don't want to do. I'll let you do it, Dad."

"Oh no," I snapped, "the hunter who bags the trophy does it. That's part of the experience."

"I don't know if I can," he sighed. "I feel like I am kind of hurting the deer."

"Well, what do you think you're doing when you shoot it?" I asked. The look on his ashen face told me that it had really never sunk in until now.

This was my opportunity to make my move. I leaned into him gently and whispered, "Are you trying to tell me that you have second thoughts about killing these animals?" He tried to speak, but couldn't. As a knowing smile slowly crossed his face, I realized that he was just like me, except that he had become caught up in the whirlwind and excitement of being a hunter with all of the gadgets and glory. I inched over to him and put my arm around him.

"Listen," I said, "there is nothing wrong with having those feelings. Lots of people have them." I winked at him and smiled. "How many guys do you think froze out there when it was time to pull the trigger?" My mind shot back in time to the popular movie of the 1970s, The Deer Hunter, in which Robert DeNiro—sighting a buck in the scope of his rifle—suddenly let it get away, shouting, "Alright, we're even." We are even, I thought to myself.

From that day on, that time spent "hunting" with my son became an intimate and precious activity. We would talk about all kinds of things, from cars to girls—just plain guy talk. We would always quit by 9 A.M. and stop for breakfast at a bleak little diner that we had found on that first ride up, one with lousy pancakes.

In all of our years of hunting, we have never even seen a deer, except the one that happened to leap through the parking lot of the diner while we were eating breakfast one morning. Very cunning of that animal to jump through enemy lines while our guard was down.

Perhaps the best was when my son and I were so anxious to get up to the mountains that we actually forgot to pack our guns. Clearly, hunting had never been the point anyway. We never did bag a deer, but we did manage to bag a trophy far more valuable to both of us—a hunters' bond!

~Frank M. Dattilio
Chicken Soup for the Father's Soul

FISH TACOS

The gods do not deduct from man's allotted span the hours spent in fishing.
~Babylonian Proverb

Oh, how my dad loved to fish! He fished when it was hot enough to fry eggs on the road beside his favorite hole along the Yellowstone River. He fished when the ice flows were challenging the accuracy of his fly casting.

For my dad's birthday one year, instead of a gift, I gave him myself for two hours as designated rower of his boat on any river of his choosing.

He opened up his present and laughed. "I have just the place for that trip. We can float and talk and watch the fall colors together on the Yellowstone River, and it's only a two-hour trip, no more." This suited me fine, since I didn't care for the sport.

Our chosen day was beautiful, the air cool but not cold. The sky was the blue that only a clear, cloudless day in Montana can offer. As we launched the boat, I looked at my watch and sighed to myself. It was ten o'clock in the morning. If everything worked out, I'd be pulling this boat out of the Yellowstone River around noon. My old man was happier than a dog with a new bone. Wearing his new vest from my mom and his new hat from my sister, he looked great standing there wedged into his casting station.

"Here's my offer," I said. "You get me off this river by noon and I'll buy the tacos. Later than noon and you're buying. Deal?"

"Deal," Dad said.

With a devilish grin, he asked if I wanted to fish while he

rowed. Just for that I gave one of the oars a good pull and almost tipped him into the river. We both laughed. I watched as my dad cast his line out. His casts were that of a master. Quickly he started pulling in fish. He loved the excitement of the fish hitting his flies and didn't care if the fish stayed on the line or not. Fishing had been a lifelong project for him; he first learned how to fly-fish as a young boy in Minnesota, and sixty years later he was still fly-fishing.

Dad knew the river well, and he knew each hole with intimate detail.

"This hole has a great fish in it. A great big one that broke my line before," he'd say. Or, "See that ripple up ahead. There's a big ol' rock behind it, and we need to steer clear of it."

The morning was great, and as we drifted downriver I watched my dad and the birds in the sky, and otherwise kept myself entertained as best I could. People who knew my father and me laughed because of the differences in speed. My father was the turtle and I was the hare.

I had made the taco bet because I wanted tacos for lunch, and I didn't mind paying if it meant spending only two hours on the river. I was positive I could get us down that river in record time. With me working the oars, my dad did the casting. I kept moving the boat along, but I didn't seem to be making the kind of progress I thought I should be making. The river was flowing really well, but the boat seemed to be moving too slowly. I was also having some trouble controlling the boat.

"Everything okay back there?" I asked my dad.

"Yup, everything's okay. You're doing great. No problems."

He cast out his line. It was obvious he was having a really good time. I wasn't having a really good time. I was struggling. I felt like I was trapped like a rat in a maze. But it was a maze of my own creation since I had volunteered for the job.

It was funny thinking about the two of us. My father was in heaven, fishing away. I was in hell rowing like a madman trying to get us off that river within two hours, watching debris float down the river faster than we were. I decided to make the best of my punishment. I turned it into time with my father on the Yellowstone River.

I bounced off a few rocks that I should have missed. "You sure we're doing okay?" I asked again.

My dad looked around us again. "Yup. We're doing great."

Cool. Old age has to be mellowing him a bit after all, I said to myself. On previous trips, when I hit rocks that hard I'd get the "Dad look." Everybody alive knows it—the look that makes anyone of any age feel like they're three years old again. I looked at my watch, "Dang." We were only two-thirds of the way to the end. I looked up at my dad. "It's noon; you're buying."

"Really!" he said in disbelief. "Look again. You've got to be wrong."

"Nope," I said. "It's twelve, and I'm getting hungry."

I knew where we were, and I knew the end was near. I felt like a marathon runner. I checked my reserves of strength and recommitted my tired arms to the task of getting this stupid, broken-down, miserable boat to the end of the line. Another really frustrating and torturous half-hour, and I was able to get our boat to the bank where I could back the truck up to it.

As I cranked the winch to pull the boat onto the trailer, I noticed my dad at the back of the boat doing something.

"Dad, what are you doing back there?" I yelled to him.

"Nothing! Just keep winching her up."

I continued cranking, but the boat felt awkward. I stopped and went back to see what my father was doing.

My father, who loved fishing more than anything, was trying to hide his secret weapon—a large tin can filled with cement was hanging over the back of the boat!

"What's that?" I asked.

"Nothing!" he said.

"I can't believe it! You just made me row that dumb boat for two-and-a-half hours dragging that anchor in the water the whole time, didn't you?"

He was caught and he knew it.

"I did," he said sheepishly. "But I lost the bet, so I'm buying the tacos!"

~Joseph T. Lair
Chicken Soup for the Fisherman's Soul

87

THE U.S. OPEN

Golf combines two favorite American pastimes:
taking long walks and hitting things with a stick.
~P.J. O'Rourke

When I was seven, my dad introduced me to golf by taking me to Houston's Memorial Park Golf Course to watch the gentle giant who strolled the fairways of professional golf. It was there that I first laid eyes on Arnold Palmer and his swashbuckling style of playing golf. I was mesmerized by his charisma. I told my father that I wanted to be just like him! My dad saw that I had every chance to succeed, and twenty years later I was blessed with the fulfillment of that dream.

But as good as I was, I wasn't nearly good enough to be an unqualified success. I struggled and persevered, but fell short time and time again. More than anything, I wanted to play in a major championship and experience what that was like. It took me eleven attempts, and ten straight years of disappointment, before I finally qualified for my first U.S. Open Championship in 1979.

Qualifying was a rigorous test of thirty-six holes in one day, usually played in one-hundred-degree heat, with only a couple of players from a very strong field advancing to the championship. For every golfer who ever dreamed of playing golf against the greats of the game, competing in a U.S. Open was always the pinnacle.

After so many failures, simply qualifying to play one Open was almost more than I could anticipate. Expectations ran high and hope eternal. I couldn't wait to get on the plane, fly to Toledo and drive to the course. When we finally drove through the gates of Inverness Country Club, the relief and the emotions of the moment brought my family and me to tears.

I played well in practice, but once the Championship began, my game deserted me when I felt pressure the most. I started poorly and finished even worse, to miss the 36-hole cut by only two shots. My wife and parents both walked every step of the way, in some ways living my dream vicariously. It was a huge disappointment to come up short, because we knew that I might never have another chance to play in a U.S. Open.

On Sunday, while waiting in Chicago's O'Hare Airport for our connecting flight home, we saw the opening moments of ABC-TV's national broadcast. Jim McKay's opening oratory was so stirring that I saw my father moved to tears. He turned to me, almost embarrassed by his emotions, and said, "Next time, make the cut for me for Father's Day." The moment was particularly poignant because it was Father's Day and the U.S. Open historically ended on Father's Day every year. "I promise I will next time, Dad," I assured him, holding my breath and hoping against hope that I would have one more chance. Deep in my heart, I knew it was a long shot.

Despite my retirement from full-time competition the next year, my prayers were answered in 1981. I qualified to play at Merion Golf Club in Ardmore, Pennsylvania, for my second (and last) U.S. Open. Once again, my family joined me to share in this special experience, and I brought along my best friend, Sam Irwin, to caddie for me. My expectations were low, and more than anything I was just hoping to play well and have a great time.

McKay described Merion as a lovely old dowager. It was a traditional course, built in the early 1900s, relatively short by today's Tour standards, but laced with thick rough, deep bunkers and lightning-fast greens. She was a mighty test despite her length. But most intriguing to me was the history of the great course. It had hosted other championships, including the U.S. Amateur Championship where Bobby Jones had defeated Gene Homans to win the final leg of the Grand Slam.

This time I started well, shooting a solid round of 73, despite a triple bogey at the fifth hole and bogies on 17 and 18. My score had placed me in a position to make the cut, yet none of us dared speak about it for fear that it would play too much into my psyche the next day. I had not competed in almost nine months, and my nerves and confidence were just too fragile. Besides, I was having fun for the first time in years, just playing for the pure enjoyment and not to put food on the table!

The second round started well, too. I played the front nine in even par before bogeying 11 and 12. As I came to Merion's brutal finishing holes, I knew that I would be tested like never before. I was hovering near the cut line, and one bad shot could end any hopes of playing the weekend. I managed to par 14 and 15 without difficulty. A good drive and a 6-iron to the green at 16 left me with a monstrous forty-foot putt with more than five feet of break. All I wanted to do was get close enough to two-putt and go to the next hole. To my surprise, my putt wandered and curled its way across the green and into the cup for a birdie! Even a bogey at the difficult seventeenth "Quarry Hole" left me thinking a bogey at the last would afford me the 36-hole cut I wanted so badly.

I played the eighteenth hole—a long 470-yard, dogleg-left par-4—more conservatively than usual. I used a 3-wood off the tee to clear the quarry wall and to better shape the tee shot so that I could easily make the fairway. However, I was left with a very long iron shot to the green, which I left considerably short. My pitch came to rest fifteen excruciating feet from the hole. I only had to get down in two putts now, but the speed of the greens was so fast that I had to be careful—very careful. When I struck the putt, I knew instinctively that it was struck too hard. My heart leapt to my throat as I looked up to see where the ball would finish. To my relief and almost disbelief, it hit the back of the cup and dropped in the hole for a par-4!

I almost danced to the scorers' tent to sign my card. I knew that my score was good enough to make the 36-hole cut, but I didn't think my father knew. He knew that I had played well and that it would be close, but he didn't dare raise his hopes. I had missed too many cuts in the past by one or two shots; it was difficult for anyone in my family to expect good fortune.

After I finished signing my card and shaking my fellow competitors' hands, I walked outside the tent to see my dad standing only a few yards away. As I walked toward him, I could tell he was obviously pleased that I had played well. He said, "Way to go, Punkins," my nickname since childhood. I could hardly contain myself as I hugged my dad tighter than I ever had. All the years of support and encouragement had finally reaped its just reward. "Happy Father's Day, Dad," I said proudly, two days early. I didn't need to say anything more. At that very moment he realized that "we" had made the cut in the U.S. Open.

~Bill Pelham
Chicken Soup for the Golfer's Soul

88

BOYS' DAY OUT

"**M**an Crippled in Fishing Accident, Nowhere Near Water." The headline flashed across my mind as I reached for the practice lure. The orb hung there, just beyond my grasp, like a defiant Day-Glo orange Christmas ornament. I heard a creaking sound. Whether it was the limb I was standing on or my knees, I couldn't be sure. But I knew my nearly forty-something, two-hundred-pound body had no business being there. I shot a quick glance through the branches below. Graham and Anders, my five-year-old twins, stood there shoulder-to-shoulder, squinting up at me in awe and with more than a little amusement.

"Maybe we should come up, too?" Anders asked hopefully.

"No, I think I've almost got it," I lied.

The cast that sent me up a tree occurred minutes into the boys' first fishing lesson.

"Watch this," Graham said, whipping the rod forward and releasing the button on his tiny new reel. We watched the lure arc from his rod tip, rise and disappear into the foliage. Should have bought more lures, I thought. At the same time, I couldn't help but admire the distance.

So there I was, thirty feet off the ground, perched on a magnolia limb no thicker than my wrist. Stretching to the brink of shoulder dislocation, I was finally able to grab the lure and snap the line. I stuffed it into my pocket and climbed back down, trying to make it look easy.

Other than climbing trees to untangle a few dozen monofilament bird nests, the practice session went well. I knew of a small stretch of trout stream about an hour away that would be just right for our first real fishing trip. I promised to take them the following weekend.

The big day began at 5:30 A.M. I put coffee on and crept upstairs to confront the first obstacle I'd face with my new fishing buddies; the boys aren't what you'd call morning people. By the time I'd dressed their somniferous little bodies and strapped them in their booster seats, we were an hour behind schedule. The boys finally woke as I parked on the shoulder of the dirt road that meandered alongside the creek.

I assembled their gear beside the car while they munched bananas and Pop-Tarts. The next order of business was to teach them how to bait live night crawlers. We live in the city, so their experience at handling wild animals of any sort was, shall we say, limited. I assured them that worms were "friendly," but they had absolutely no interest in holding onto the slippery little guys. And the idea of stabbing their new friends to death with a hook was even less appealing, especially over breakfast. I switched them to the default bait, canned yellow corn. We gathered our stuff and headed down the path toward the creek. We'd covered less than twenty yards when I heard a scream behind me.

"Daddeeeeee!"

I whirled and saw Anders, wide-eyed, frozen in place. He was pointing, like a miniature grim reaper, at a fallen tree beside the path.

"Don't move," I said.

As calmly as I could, I walked back to him, fully expecting a water moccasin or a swarm of hornets. I followed Anders's stare down the log until my eyes finally rested on the object of his terror; a millipede was inching its way along the tree trunk. To a child who'd never encountered anything more menacing than a cockroach, it must have looked like some horrible interplanetary creature waiting to pounce with all thousand legs on the next small boy who wandered by.

"It's just a millipede," I said. "It won't bite."

I leaned down and touched its back to show him, then turned

to tell Graham to come over and look. He was already on his way, brandishing a large stone. For some reason, the compassion he felt for earthworms was totally lost on invertebrates with legs.

"Let's kill it," he said.

"Leave it be," I said. "Let's go catch some trout."

Unfortunately, while searching for his antimillipede missile, Graham had left his rod and reel in the woods. I had the boys stay on the path while I kicked through piles of leaves and brambles. In the few minutes it took to locate and extract the rod from a bed of poison ivy, the sky darkened considerably. Then it started to rain. Hard. And with that, our planned assault on the trout population of the creek turned into a full-scale amphibious retreat back to the car.

We piled, soaking, into our seats. "Aren't we going fishing?" they asked in almost perfect unison. Two small chins started to tremble.

"Tell you what," I said. "Let's go for a ride and see if this lets up." For the next two hours, we cruised through the downpour and a maze of gravel U.S. Forest Service roads, taking careful aim at every puddle. As the boys discussed the morning's events and needled each other about misplaced tackle and multilegged beasts, their moods lightened considerably. The rain finally stopped, but I knew the creek would be too high and muddy for fishing.

Just as I was about to point our car back toward the highway and break the news, I saw a sign: "Stocked Pond — Rainbow Trout by the Pound." I pulled in. For the avid fisherman, the "stocked pond" isn't exactly sporting. The pond was about the size of your average backyard pool, and with all of the rippling, flashing and finning, it looked like you could walk straight across it on the backs of all those trout without getting wet. We grabbed our gear and baited up. It took less than ten minutes for each of the boys to hook and land a monster rainbow.

While one brother (with a little help) wrestled his prize into the net, the other slipped and slid on the wet bank, shouting at the top of his lungs, "Reel him faster! Don't let go! You got him!"

The pond's owner weighed and cleaned the trout, then put the pink slabs on ice for us. We loaded up and headed for home. By the time we reached the highway, the twins were asleep, each with an arm draped across the cooler that rested between them.

Not the day I'd planned, but I couldn't have scripted a better ending. A few small adventures, a slight case of poison ivy (mine) and two trophy-sized rainbow trout—much larger than anything I'd ever caught in a stream. The bill was a whopper too, about five times what we'd pay for trout at the market.

Best money I ever spent.

~Robby Russell
Chicken Soup for the Fisherman's Soul

THE LAST RAINBOW

*If people concentrated on the really important things in life,
there'd be a shortage of fishing poles.*
~Doug Larson

The old man was still getting around pretty well. In slow motion, to be sure, with a gingerliness that bespoke the pain of terminal cancer—but getting around nevertheless. I'd taken a few days off from my job and flown to join him at the cabin, the one he'd built with his own hands when my brother Jack and I were barely tall enough to reach his waist.

The cabin. Those two words will evoke a montage of memories for as long as I live. Goldeneyes whistling down the lake, the rowboat, perch in the pan, baby loons riding their mother's back and rainbow trout.

This day was superb for chasing rainbows: a gentle breeze from the west and a cloudy, somber sky, delicious with the aroma of impending rain. A day positively heavy with the promise of good fishing.

I glanced at the rods in the corner of the cabin, wondering if I should suggest it, wondering if the old man still had the strength.

"Might be a good day," he said slowly, grinning slightly, "to try the old bridge at Silver Creek."

We were there in minutes, at a spot to which he'd first brought me thirty years before. In those days, it was a rickety, dangerous-looking crossing fashioned from old timbers. You could look down at the creek between each plank. A rusty sign peppered with bird shot said "Cross at your own risk."

But the bridge was different this day, sadly different. The planks had been replaced with concrete. The sign was gone. The stream, however, was everything it had ever been. Cool and clear and rushing, choked with overhanging branches and moss-covered logs, a stream that sang "Trout!" to anyone with a lick of sense to listen.

We would fish from the little bridge today, as usual, but unlike years gone by, we would not wade downstream in our hip boots, sneaking up on a dozen beautiful holes that always seemed to yield a creel of trout. Because the old man was already tired from the short ride, our fishing would begin and end at the bridge.

And it began just as we had hoped. Dad had no sooner started stripping out line, when a good ten-incher darted from beneath the bank and nailed his night crawler. He played the trout as he had always played them, with a slight, patient smile on his face, the rod held gently at a sixty-degree angle. He tired the fish as it flashed back and forth, then swept it with one easy motion up and into the weeds.

I unhooked the rainbow, placed it in the creel with a bit of grass, and baited his hook again. Not thirty seconds later, he'd enticed another trout from the same dark patch of water.

Dad offered me the rod then, but I declined, because watching him fish was all the fishing I wanted. He had always said that he enjoyed watching my brother or me catch a fish, just as much as he enjoyed catching one himself. That day, I understood what he meant.

The old man had exhausted the downstream hole, but we both knew that the best had been saved for last. Under the bridge—that was where the best rainbows always waited. And it was right there, in fact, that I had caught my very first trout: a fat twelve-incher.

I watched the tip of the old man's rod as he floated a fresh crawler toward the hole neither of us had ever really seen but had fished a hundred times.

He stopped feeding line just when I thought he should.

Instinctively, we both knew the bait was precisely where it ought to be. We waited. Five seconds, maybe ten. Then it happened.

The tip of the rod twitched, twitched again, and then bent double as the trout bit down and held on, and the old man began easing the fighting fish out of the hole.

"It's a good one," he said. For that moment, at least, he forgot he was dying, forgot that this stream and all the streams he loved so deeply would soon be flowing past without him.

"It's a good one," he said again, and my eyes traveled up the rod to his face. The slight, patient smile was a little wider than usual.

It was good. Before it was over, the old man was breathing heavily and tiring as fast as the fish. But he worked the trout out of the bridge's shadow and into the upstream light. It wasn't any record. Maybe fifteen inches, but fat and thick and feisty. As good as any we'd ever taken from under the bridge at old Silver Creek.

"It was a great fishing trip," I said, putting my arm around him as we walked slowly to the car.

"Yes," he replied. "We'll do it again sometime. Sometime soon."

Several months later, I traveled back home once more, this time for his funeral. I walked into his bedroom and found his fishing rod in the corner rigged with a brand-new Eagle Claw and two tiny split shot.

My mother came in and saw me holding it. "He had it all ready for another trip," she said. "He thought maybe the two of you could go fishing together one more time."

We will, old man. We will.

~Jim Berlin
Chicken Soup for the Father's Soul

A SIMPLE PLAN

When you look at your life, the greatest happinesses are family happinesses.
~Dr. Joyce Brothers

I found my great love for fishing while growing up on the San Carlos Apache reservation in Arizona. Whenever my uncles or neighbors went fishing, I grabbed my tackle box and fishing pole and jumped in the back of their pickup truck. My dad never understood why I enjoyed fishing so much, but because he knew his three sons liked to fish, he bought us fishing rods and tackle. He even helped us look for worms, but never showed any interest in the sport.

One day my two younger brothers—ten-year-old Carl and nine-year-old Boy—and I somehow talked our dad into taking us to nearby San Carlos Lake. As we began to cast out, Dad remained in the truck, reading his paper.

All of a sudden I had an idea! What if I talked Dad into fishing just this once? What if he somehow caught the biggest fish today? Then he'd have to fall in love with fishing, too! Then he'd want to take us fishing ALL the time. What a great plan!

I shared my amazing plan with my younger brothers. We coaxed Dad out of the truck, and to our surprise, he walked down and joined us at the shoreline. But he ignored the fishing poles and simply opened his lawn chair and continued reading his paper. My brothers and I looked at one another, dumbfounded. Now what do we do?

Then, a possible answer—a large fish jumped not far from us. Quickly I put on the biggest worm in our can, cranked back as far as a twelve-year-old could, then let the line fly. I hit the spot almost dead-on where the big fish had jumped.

Propping my rod next to Dad and his newspaper, I walked over to my brothers and pretended to untangle their lines. Every now and then I would glance at the bobber on my line. After what seemed hours, the bobber moved! Then it moved again!

"Dad! Grab my line! I can't get over there," I yelled. "Carl's line is all tangled up!"

"You boys come pull it in before it eats your worm," he countered.

All four of us watched the bobber dance on the water. Then Dad scooted to the edge of his chair and dropped his newspaper on the ground. Suddenly, the bobber disappeared.

In unison, my brothers and I yelled, "Pull the line, pull the line!"

Dad jumped up, grabbed the rod and pulled the line tight. "Something big's on here, boys!" he shouted. "Get over here and help me!"

We ran over and stood by him as the line moved slowly through the water.

"Don't lose him, Dad!" I yelled.

"Don't give him any slack," my brother yelled.

"Start turning the handle; reel him in!" screamed my other brother as we watched a grown man holding tight to a fishing rod, straining as it bent from the weight of something big.

"Turn the handle now, Dad, pull that fish in, Dad. You got him, Dad!" I yelled again. It was funny to see three little boys, jumping up and down and yelling orders at their dad as he tried to land his first fish.

Finally Dad, all excited about the fish he was about to catch, braced himself.

"Okay, Dad, we'll get him when you drag him out," my brothers and I said. One last pull and out came the...

"It's a turtle, a big turtle!" we yelled.

"Turtle!" Dad gasped as he instantly jumped back. "See? See?

You boys know turtles are not to be touched by Apaches—they are taboo!" he said, as the turtle wiggled on its back. "This is why I never wanted to fish!" He dropped my pole and stormed back to the truck.

My brothers and I stared down at the turtle wiggling at our feet.

"You take it off!" my brothers said.

"No, you take it off!" I answered.

"No, no, it was your idea," they reminded me.

Many years later, I can still hear my brothers' words, and I smile, remembering that day long ago when we tried to get our dad to fall in love with fishing. I really don't recall who took the hook out of the turtle that afternoon. But one thing I do remember. Although Dad never did develop an interest in fishing, he did help us dig for worms many more times, and he still took us on many more fishing trips during our childhood—and he did it simply because he was our dad.

~Kenny Duncan, Sr.
Chicken Soup for the Fisherman's Soul

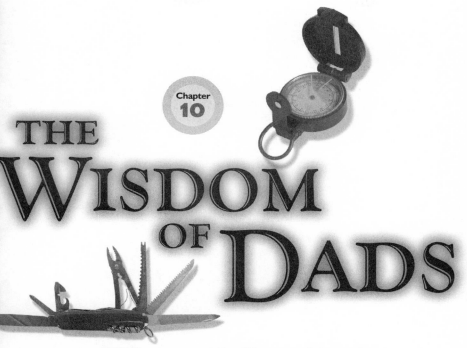

THE WISDOM OF DADS

Gifts and Gratitude

*The manner of the giving shows the character of the giver more than
the gift itself.*
~John Casper Lavater

91

THE BEST SEAT
IN THE HOUSE

The doctors said they found a grapefruit-sized tumor in his lungs. I guess I shouldn't have been surprised. My dad, John Mathew Morris, had been a two-pack-a-day guy for the better part of forty years. He loved his "cancer sticks," and maybe now he was paying the price.

It was April of the 1987 baseball season when I received the bad news. Instantly, I wanted to be transported home, but I was one thousand miles away, and there was little I could do for him. So I continued doing what I could: I played baseball to the best of my ability so Dad could feel proud of his son.

Since I was single and totally devoted to my baseball career, my teammates and coach were my support system. I spent almost all of my time with them.

Our team, the St. Louis Cardinals, was serving notice to the rest of the National League that we were legitimate pennant contenders. As the season progressed, we built a ten-game lead heading into the All-Star break. Following the break, we came to New York to play the Mets. Before each game, I drove the Long Island Expressway to visit Dad at the Suffolk County hospice facility.

While Dad and I were together, our conversations centered on baseball and the Cardinals. Dad loved baseball. It was his one true passion in life. As a matter of fact, he had been quite a player himself back in the 1920s, when he played first base for a semi-pro team.

The series gave Dad and me some quality time together. I felt good knowing I was bringing some joy into a life that was now full of pain and struggle. He was a proud father who, given the fact that his youngest son was playing major league baseball, liked to show me off to all the nurses and doctors when I visited. He loved telling them that his son was a major leaguer. As embarrassed as it made me, I played along, letting him enjoy the attention, all the while hiding my own pain. My whole life away from Dad was playing baseball with my teammates. How could baseball ease my grief?

Two months later, in September, my team returned to Shea Stadium to play the Mets again. Our lead over the Mets had been reduced to one game. During the series, there was a great deal going on in my head—Dad's failing health, the pressure of the pennant race and our lead slipping away. For the first time in my life, I began to use baseball to bring some sense of joy to a sad situation. I played each day with the hope that it would allow Dad to think of something other than his illness.

I visited with Dad all three days while we were in New York playing. Dad was in a helpless state. He weighed about one hundred pounds and was unable to walk or talk. Seeing him in that condition was almost too much to handle. Every day before I left the hospital to go to the stadium, Dad would communicate one thing to me. Scribbling on a note pad, he'd write that he'd be watching our game on TV. My fellow players knew about Dad's faithful support, but they couldn't know my pain.

The series proved to be a battle between two long-standing rivals. Fortunately, we won two of the three games. Meanwhile, back on Long Island, Dad was watching. He spent whatever energy he had left in his shrunken body watching our games. But they were to be his last games. Three days later, we were in Pittsburgh to play the Pirates when manager Whitey Herzog knocked at my hotel door in the early morning hours. Right then, I knew Dad was gone.

I flew home that Wednesday afternoon for Dad's wake and burial. I'd known this day was coming for some time, but the knowledge in no way eased the hurt.

The Sunday morning after the funeral began with a scheduled 6:30 flight to St. Louis, but the flight was canceled, and I was left unsure if I could make it to St. Louis for the start of the afternoon game against the Chicago Cubs. But somebody was on my side that day. A seat opened up on a later flight, allowing me to arrive in St. Louis at 11:30.

Entering the clubhouse, I was greeted warmly by my teammates. Their genuine concern touched and calmed me. Then Dave Ricketts, our bullpen coach, walked over to me. "Johnny, Whitey wants to see you." I walked into the skipper's office, not knowing what to expect. I noticed that the lineup card was missing from its usual spot on the wall adjacent to his office.

When I turned the corner, Whitey rose from behind his desk. "Hey, kid! It's nice to have ya back." He paused for a moment, as if he was trying to gather his thoughts.

"Look, I know there's nothing more trying than a funeral and that you've been through a lot the past few days," Whitey continued. He grabbed two cards from the top of his desk. "Johnny, I'm gonna leave it up to you. I've made out two lineup cards. One has you starting, and the other has you on the bench in case you're not ready yet. Whatever you decide is fine with me."

A string of questions exploded in my head. Was Whitey actually waiting for me before he was going to post the lineup? Was I dreaming? Managers just didn't do this; was he serious with this unusual offer? It dawned on me that Whitey was offering me more than a choice: He was offering a challenge.

I responded: "I just flew one thousand miles to get here. I'd love to play today." Whitey smiled with approval. "Great! You're in there," he said. His face softened. "Now, go get a few hits for your dad."

In the first inning, I came to bat with the bases loaded. Greg Maddux hung me a slider, and I drove in the first two runs with a single to center field. In the third inning, my grounder to the shortstop scored another run. In the eighth inning I drove in another run with a single up the middle. Our lead was now seven to two.

Though I could have no idea that these four RBIs were a career high, I did know I had just done something special. The fans knew about my loss, and the crowd of 46,681 stood to acknowledge my performance and to lend their support in my time of grief. While I stood on first base and listened to their applause, the ovation seemed to last forever. A lump formed in my throat as a mixture of joy and sorrow swelled inside me.

I realized I had just paid Dad the greatest tribute I could have given him, and I realized that I had never been alone in my pain. With both feet planted on top of first base, my eyes glistened as tears ran freely down my cheeks. I glanced upward, and seeing the gorgeous blue skies, I suddenly had an image of Dad smiling down on me with approval and pride, content in the fact that his youngest son was winning the game he loved. Dad was indeed watching over me that day, and his vantage point provided him with the best seat in the house.

Days later, the Cardinals clinched the division title, and a week later, we became National League champions. We were off to the World Series to play the Minnesota Twins. The season was complete, and so was my relationship with Dad—all because Whitey Herzog and my enormous extended baseball family gave me the chance to say a special farewell to my biggest fan.

~John Morris
Chicken Soup for the Single's Soul

92

SOME SERVICE

He didn't tell me how to live; he lived, and let me watch him do it.
~Clarence Budington Kelland

My father was the hardest-working man, and he loved to give orders: what to eat, how long to stay up, even when to shower. After a long day's work, he always stretched out in his throne-like recliner, making us take off his socks and shoes. "Give me some service," he would say.

When I was sixteen, he brought me to the restaurant where he waited tables. It was Thanksgiving Day, and he didn't even bother to tell me where we were going. He just told me to slap on a pair of black slacks and a white dress shirt and get in the car. When we got to the restaurant he handed me a jacket and bow tie, telling me — not asking me — that today I would start to work.

All the waiters were surprised to see me come in wearing a busboy's outfit. I mean, they had seen me in the booths as a kid, eating dishes of ice cream. They swirled all around, plates stacked along their arms. The customers all looked wealthy and important, the men dressed in suits, the women wearing mink coats and tons of makeup. Each table was clothed in a sparkling white tablecloth. I just knew I was gonna spill things on all these people's laps.

An old, gruff Chinese man, the head busboy, showed me the layout of the kitchen and the dishwashing section, a flat metal table stacked with dirty plates. He flung the dirty utensils, forks and knives, with fury into this gray murky basin of water. Some of the utensils first ricocheted off the wall. There was no way I was going to copy his style.

I cleared dirty dishes from the tables into a bus box of my own, learning to balance it and not to set the box on the floor. I barely knew the menu, but toward late evening my father made me go over to a table of customers — "a party" — and take their order. "Does the lasagna have any onions in it?" the lady asked, frowning into the menu. "I'm very allergic to onions." Allergic to onions? I didn't know there could be such a thing. My father overheard, and he told the woman, "Yes, it has onions. Take the ziti instead." I managed with the rest of the order and served the food — ziti for the woman and broiled salmon for her husband.

Soon I was working part-time as a waiter. My protective father made me suspicious of everyone, the other waiters, even the customers. "Pick up the money the second you see it, before someone else puts it in his pocket." Most of the other waiters were over seventy years old. Roy had tattoos on his forearms from his days in the Navy. Mad Diego used to work as a shoe-shiner in Panama. And Walter, the slowest waiter, was still hoping to be an actor, performing poetry for strangers in the subway.

With his broad smile, my father was the customers' flat-out favorite. They were demanding, but he knew how to take care of them, and they kept on coming back, lining up at the door even when the other waiters had open tables. My father would introduce me to them: this one's a dentist, a lawyer, a wheeler and dealer in real estate. I was never really sure if he was telling me that one day I would have such a job, or if he wanted me to recognize them in case someday he couldn't be there to take their orders.

His shift went from 2 P.M. to midnight. After 8 P.M. the other waiters went home, and he worked alone, covering the entire restaurant. On many nights over the years, even while I was in college, he would call me for help if it got too busy. I'd drop everything, grab my stuff and race to the restaurant. "Hey, the bull pen made it on time!" the cashier always joked as I rushed through the door.

Maybe it was all those long hours and being around so much

food, but my father's health got worse. He gained weight, had trouble sleeping and was often on antibiotics.

One day, when I was off from college, my father called me from work. I groaned, knowing my free day would be ruined. "Can you come to the restaurant fast, and bring me a fresh white shirt? Size seventeen." He hung up. I went there quickly. But when I got there I found him in the shadows of the back room of the restaurant, pale and ashen.

"Why'd you need a white shirt?" I asked him, "Yours got dirty?" And then I saw his shirtfront and stopped; it had a dark red blotch spread across the front of it. "Are you all right?" I asked. He just shook his head softly. I told him to go home. "I won't let you work like this." I went into the locker room and put on the shirt myself, gathering his pencils, waiter jacket and checkbook. Worried that I would not be able to handle the station alone, my father wouldn't leave until my mother finally came with the station wagon to take him home.

Somehow I managed by myself with my father's customers. I found out later that he did not go to the hospital until nighttime, when he woke up coughing blood. Even then he insisted that he was just vomiting some beets he'd eaten. My mother had to practically drag him to the ambulance.

Those doctors saved his life. It turned out that a growth was putting pressure on his esophagus. Hooked to an IV in intensive care, he was too weak to sit up or sip water or even have family come see him. I couldn't believe this man, who had taught me to swim in the waters of Coney Island, would ever be anything other than invincible. After all, he was the strongest man in the world.

I visited him at night after work, the bow tie stuffed into my back pocket, my white shirt and black pants smelling of the restaurant. I went upstairs through the maze of corridors and florescent lights. My mother had arranged it with the staff so that I could see him after hours. After a bunch of false starts, when I thought this person lying down, white and weak, must surely be my father, I arrived at his bed. His appearance was so abrupt and sudden. There he was.

He opened his eyes immediately. He shook his head a little, as if to make some sort of comment on the situation like, "Me in bed, can you believe it?"

And then I leaned over. I leaned over and kissed him on the cheek, my ribs pressing into the metal rails of the bed, because I knew I loved him, and because he was still alive, and he would get better. We would all make him better, my family and the doctors and everyone. And I kissed him because I never kissed him enough; I probably hadn't kissed him in years. "I love you. I took care of all your customers," I whispered to him, and kissed him again. And then I heard a beep and then another. The beeps were coming from the machine he was hooked up to, its monitor showing the lines rising higher and higher to the point of a mountain. The sounds of his pulse.

~Eli Shoshani
Chicken Soup for the Teenage Soul IV

MY FAVORITE FATHER'S DAY

Oh, my friend, it's not what they take away from you that counts. It's what you do with what you have left.
~Hubert Humphrey

The summer after my son Kotter's freshman year of high school, with the exception of senior league baseball, was spent home alone. He wasn't happy.

Without any malice on Kotter's part, he made a typical adolescent freshman mistake that caused the loss of his closest friends. Afterward, he called them on the phone, but they were always too busy to talk. He biked over to their houses, but they were always gone. He often walked with his head down or stared out the window at nothing. I watched the hurt overflow in Kotter and bled for him as well.

I decided to give up what I too often considered my own precious activities to become Kotter's summer companion and help him through this stormy, confusing period in his life. In earlier years, Kotter would often call me his best friend, and now I would work to earn that privileged title.

So I became Kotter's buddy during the summer ball season. I biked with Kotter to and from the games. I took him camping. We went to movies. I cheered Kotter's accomplishments and comforted him in his failures. In short, I became the father that I always should have been.

Little by little, as the senior league season moved deeper into summer, I saw signs that the ice curtain of lost friendship was starting to melt. First, it was his teammates' handclasps after a good play, and then it was the shouts of encouragement from the dugout. I pointed these signs out to Kotter and encouraged him to hang in there. Kotter and I, each in our own way, used these proclamations as our banners of hope.

During the latter part of June, a senior league tournament was held on Father's Day weekend, and Kotter's team earned the right to play in the championship game, which was held on Father's Day. The evenly matched teams took turns taking the lead. Near the end of the game, Kotter's team was behind by one run with a man on base and Kotter at bat. Kotter walked up to the batter's box as tension filled the air. He would not be denied encouragement from his friends at that moment. "You can do it, Kotter" and "Come on, big boy" rang out from the dugout. Kotter fed on this affection as he stepped into the box. I cheered as well. I cheered to encourage Kotter, and I cheered inside for the affection I saw coming from the dugout.

CRACK! — The soft spot of the bat connected perfectly with the ball and sent it screaming out into left field! This ball was tagged. I gripped the edge of my seat and held my breath in disbelief. The left fielder stopped running, turned around and watched the ball sail over the fence! The home run sealed the victory for Kotter's team.

Pandemonium broke out in the crowd. Every spectator was standing up and celebrating, except for one. I remained seated, trying to control my emotions. The home run no doubt made me happy, but the scene I witnessed at home plate overwhelmed me. My son, whose heart bled so profusely those past months, was now being hugged by his teammates as they marched triumphantly back to the dugout.

Once I composed myself, I hurried to the fence near the dugout to celebrate the home run with Kotter and to celebrate something even deeper — to celebrate the resurrection of human spirit that was occurring within him.

When I got to the fence, I saw something else that tugged at my emotions. I saw an old friend and teammate hand Kotter the home-run ball that he had retrieved from outside the park. The gesture brought back memories of these same two boys riding their bikes together the previous summer. I turned from the crowd so my lips could quiver more freely.

After the victory celebration, I went for a long walk to collect my thoughts about the game. I thought about the home run that fulfilled, for my son, a dream that all senior leaguers have. I thought about the crisis that helped strengthen the relationship I had with him. Most of all I thought about the human spirit's ability to revive itself after letdown. This was truly the best Father's Day that I had ever experienced.

Yet the warmest moment was yet to come. When I got home that day, I spotted a baseball sitting on the table with writing on it. I picked up the ball, read the inscription and started to cry. The ball I held was my son's home-run ball, and the inscription read: "Happy Father's Day, Dad! Love, Kotter."

~Jerry Harpt
A 6th Bowl of Chicken Soup for the Soul

94

MY FAVORITE BASEBALL CARD

I had been an avid baseball-card collector as a youth, often collecting and selling drink bottles to pay for my packs. I remember sitting on the floor and arranging the cards for hours, putting the players in position on an imaginary field, stacking them in numerical order or by teams. As with many joys of youth, I set the hobby aside when it came time for college and jobs.

In 1990, I started reading about how the hobby was hot again, almost to the point of becoming a national fever. I was at a gas station in town when I noticed a box of baseball cards by the cash register. I remembered how hard I had to work to buy my cards twenty years before. Now all I had to do was reach into my pocket and pull out some spare change. I bought a couple of packs and took them home.

The cards I bought, Topps, still included a piece of gum, unlike many of the newer brands. The smell of the gum, the cardboard, the ink and the wax paper brought the baseball memories of my youth rushing back as surely as did that first whiff of mown grass in the spring. I flipped through the cards, recognized a few of the players' names and then put them away.

The next time I was at the store, I bought a few more packs. I gave some of the cards to my eight-year-old son, who was also a baseball fan. We often played out in the yard, hitting a Nerf ball with an oversized plastic bat. Now we had an indoor "sport" that we could share as well.

I kept buying packs, and soon I was trying to put together a complete set of 792 cards. I gradually escalated to buying a box of cards at a time. My son and I would sit on the floor and separate the cards, going over the checklists to see which players we needed to finish the set. My son began his own collection with the doubles, the cards I already had.

Since the cards were randomly seeded within the packs, it was easy to get duplicates of certain players while others remained elusive. I must have had a half dozen Ozzie Smiths, and probably ten Steve Bedrosians. But I was unsuccessful in getting a Ken Griffey Jr. card. Griffey was far and away the most popular card among collectors that year.

I could have gone to the local card shop and bought one for the set by spending a couple of dollars, but I was determined to pull one out of a pack. Making my bad luck even worse was the fact that a replica of Griffey's card was on the box, advertising the Topps brand and the card design. It's almost as if that Griffey on the box was taunting me, daring me to buy another hundred packs.

The next time my son and I opened packs, I explained to him how badly I wanted a Ken Griffey Jr. His face set with determination, my son carefully opened pack after pack, almost apologetic when he failed to find one. Now my complete set was only lacking a few cards, Griffey being the most notable of them.

We opened the last of the packs I'd purchased that day, with no Griffey showing up. I sorted the cards, gave my son a stack of duplicates, and put the rest of my cards in a box. Then I forgot about them and became wrapped up in other pursuits.

Later that evening my son came up to me, his hand behind his back. "I have something for you, Daddy," he said.

He handed me a Griffey Jr. card. He'd taken a pair of scissors and cut one of the Griffey replicas off the box. "Now you don't have to look anymore," he said.

The hug I gave him was the best price I ever paid for a card.

I continued collecting and eventually ended up with some old and valuable cards. But there's one card I would never trade, not even for a Mickey Mantle rookie card. I still have that Ken Griffey Jr., the one with the uneven borders and the ragged corners, the one that has only plain gray pasteboard on the back instead of statistics.

That card, to me, is what baseball is all about. It's also what love is all about.

~Scott Nicholson
Chicken Soup for the Sports Fan's Soul

95

HE TAUGHT ME TO FLY

There's something like a line of gold thread running through a man's words when he talks to his daughter, and gradually over the years it gets to be long enough for you to pick up in your hands and weave into a cloth that feels like love itself.

~John Gregory Brown, Decorations in a Ruined Cemetery, 1994

My dad grew up not far from the Cabrini Green housing project in Chicago. The projects were built long after Dad moved out, but the tough, teeming neighborhood of his youth is not so very different from the neighborhood of today. It's still a place for people trying to find a way out of poverty and danger. To finally see that apartment house was to finally know the deepest part of my father. It was to finally understand why we spent so much time at odds.

Dad and I were always passionate about our feelings—we're Italian, after all—and when I reached my teen years, our arguments really heated up. I can't remember a meal from those years that we didn't argue through. Politics, feminism, the war in Vietnam. Our biggest fight, however, was an ongoing one. It was about my chosen profession.

"People like us aren't writers!" Dad would shout.

"Maybe people like you aren't writers," I would shoot back, "but people like me are!"

What I said was truer than I knew.

I grew up in a nice house with a lawn, a dog and lots of room to stretch out in. My only responsibilities were to get good grades and stay out of major trouble. Dad spent his youth squeezed into a tenement, taking care of a widowed mother who spoke no English, helping to parent two younger siblings — and earning enough money in whatever way he could to keep the family going.

Dad's dream was to move up and out of the old neighborhood, and after he married, he did. He drew a curtain over his past, never speaking of his growing-up days. Not to anyone. Ever. It was a point of pride with him that he allowed no one to know what he had suffered through. But by not knowing Dad's past, I could never really know him, or what drove him to want so much security for me.

As I persisted in my career, despite all the rejections, Mom told me Dad read and re-read everything I got published, although he never mentioned my work to me. Instead, he continually tried to steer me into a career he considered far safer — nursing or teaching or secretarial.

But in the last week of his life, as I sat by his bed, Dad opened up. It was as if he suddenly realized that soon it would be too late to let anyone know the truth. That's when he had me dig out a box of pictures he'd buried deep in the garage; that's when I finally saw what he and his brother and sister had looked like as children, and where they had lived. It was when I came face to face not only with Dad's old home, but with my father himself.

In those last days, Dad talked about everything. How it felt to carry buckets of coal up four flights of stairs and share one bathroom with five other families. He told me that he was always worried that his brother and sister wouldn't have enough to eat or that they wouldn't have enough warm clothes for winter, or that someone in the family would get sick and there wouldn't be enough money for medicine or doctors. He told me about the Saturdays he spent on a country club golf course, how wonderful the grass looked to him, and how he tried to get the men to use him as a caddie. After eighteen holes, if he was lucky, they'd toss him a quarter.

Dad told me how he'd wanted to protect me from poverty and want, so I'd never have to go through what he had. He told me how important it was to him that I have something to fall back on. And I told Dad that what I'd fallen back on all these years was him. I told him my hopes and dreams had been built on his strong shoulders. I told him the roots he'd given me ran deep, and when he apologized for trying to clip my wings, I told him that he was the one who'd given me the chance to fly. Dad smiled at that and tried to nod, but I wasn't sure if he'd really understood what I'd meant.

But on the afternoon of the last day of his life, as Mom and I sat holding his hands, he beckoned the two hospice volunteers close. "You know my daughter," he whispered with great effort. "Well, I just want you to know—she's a writer."

It was the proudest moment of my life.

~Cynthia Mercati
A Second Chicken Soup for the Woman's Soul

96

BASHUR, THE IRAQI DOG

My son, Mike—Major Mike Fenzel of the 173rd Airborne Brigade—parachuted into northern Iraq on March 27, 2003. After two weeks on the ground, Mike and the three thousand others in his unit began their mission to capture the city of Kirkuk.

During the first hours of the mission, they made a brief stop to refuel by the side of the road. The unit's intelligence officer noticed something moving in the grass. Looking closer, she saw it was a tiny puppy, no bigger than a dollar bill. The puppy was alone and in bad shape; the officer knew it would die if she left it there. So she scooped the pup into her arms and took it with her into Kirkuk.

When they finally reached Kirkuk, the puppy was brought to headquarters, washed off and fed. There was a vet on hand whose primary responsibility was to check food for the troops, and he gave the puppy a distemper shot. After that, they released the tiny dog on the airfield to roam with the hundreds of other wild dogs who lived on the base. Over the next few weeks, the little puppy made an impression on the soldiers living on the base, including Mike. The men in the unit made sure the little female pup—whom Mike had named Bashur after the airfield they had parachuted into—had enough food, giving her leftovers from the mess hall and from their MREs (Meals Ready to Eat).

Bashur survived being hit by a Humvee in her first weeks on the airfield. After recovering from a badly bruised hip, Bashur grew strong and healthy. Although she had the run of the base, she mainly stuck around the headquarters building, where she received food as well as lots of attention from the men going in and out on their round-the-clock missions.

Bashur stood out from the other dogs on the airfield. Not only was her coloring distinct and beautiful—she had a caramel-colored head with a well-defined white blaze and the soulful amber eyes of a hound—but she was determined to be with the soldiers. She bounded up happily to everyone who passed, tail wagging, eyes sparkling, ready for a game or a cuddle, a comforting sight after the stress of the soldiers' missions. She was a one-dog welcoming committee and the soldiers loved her for it.

But an army camp is a busy and sometimes dangerous place, and one day a pickup truck speeding across the camp ran over Bashur's paw, crushing it. By then, Mike had become very fond of Bashur, and when he heard she had been hit, he ran to find her.

After carrying her to his room, he brought in his medics to give her attention. Mike decided to keep Bashur with him while her paw healed and then possibly until they left Iraq, to prevent her from becoming another casualty. Soon Bashur recovered fully, and Mike began taking her to the battalion headquarters where he worked each day. There he tied her up outside so that she couldn't run free and be hurt again. The men provided her with a special red collar with an "Airborne" patch on it to identify her as their mascot.

Over the next six months, though Bashur remained the unit's mascot, Mike and Bashur developed a special bond. Mike told me that caring for Bashur kept his mind in a positive place. Every morning they jogged together and every evening they relaxed together. Mike marveled at the power of her companionship to lift his spirits.

Living with Bashur had other benefits as well. Once when I was on the phone with Mike, Bashur began to bark wildly. Mike said, "Must be incoming, Dad. Gotta go." It turned out that Bashur could detect mortars and artillery rockets long before human ears could register the sound. When she would look up, startled, Mike knew another enemy artillery strike was on the way.

In February 2004, Mike realized he would be leaving Iraq soon.

He knew he couldn't leave Bashur behind, so when he called home he asked me if we would take Bashur if he could manage to get her to us. My wife and I knew what Bashur had come to mean to him and I told him we would.

At first, Mike thought he would be able to ship her through the country of Jordan with the help of an official at the Baghdad zoo. But nothing is certain in a country at war. First, Jordan stopped allowing dogs to transit through their country and then his contact at the zoo left, taking with her Bashur's best chance of leaving Iraq.

Time was running out, but Mike kept trying. Finally, he found an international veterinary hospital in Kuwait that would be able to ship Bashur to the states. The next hurdle was getting her to Kuwait. As it happened, Mike was the executive officer of a battalion that was preparing to redeploy to Vicenza, Italy—through a port in Kuwait City. He would take Bashur with him when they left.

On the day that his battalion left Kirkuk for Kuwait with their 140 vehicles, Mike loaded Bashur in his Humvee, and they made the 600-mile journey to Kuwait City together. Bashur already had her required shots but had to spend a week in quarantine at the International Veterinary Hospital. Luckily, the hospital was located right next door to the port site, so Mike was able to visit her every day.

The last obstacle Mike faced was finding a crate large enough to ship Bashur home in—she had grown a lot since the day she had been found on the side of the road. There were none available in Kuwait City, so the veterinary hospital built an immense wooden box to meet airline requirements. The refrigerator-sized container had a steel grate in front so that Bashur could breathe and see out.

At last, Bashur, snug in her specially made crate, was loaded onto a KLM plane headed to Amsterdam. From Amsterdam, she would make the final leg of her journey to O'Hare Airport in Chicago.

At the appointed time, I drove to O'Hare to meet Bashur. The KLM freight employees needed a forklift to get the big wooden container onto the terminal floor. When the door was opened, there were probably nine men—including me—clustered around Bashur's crate.

Bashur was cautious, not sure what to expect. She stuck her head out and looked both ways. When I said, "Bashur, how's our baby?" she looked up quickly, recognizing her name.

I had heard she was a big dog, but I really wasn't prepared for her size. When she started to walk out of the crate, one man in the group exclaimed, "My God, when is she going to stop coming out of that crate?" Bashur just kept coming until all forty inches of her emerged.

I dropped to one knee and took her collar. I immediately recognized the "Airborne" patch. Putting the side of my face to hers, I gave her a big hug and then attached her new leash.

We walked outside into the early March sunshine and crossed the parking lot to my waiting van. I had spread a thick blanket behind the front seat, and Bashur stretched out on it like the Queen of Sheba — but not for long! As soon as we began to move, she jumped into the passenger seat, plopped her rear end on the seat, front paws on the floor and chin on the dash, to take in the passing scenery. I shouldn't have been surprised she was good in the car, as she'd had lots of experience in army vehicles for most of her life.

When we got to the house, Bashur jumped out and made a beeline for my wife, Muriel, who took one look at the big dog and immediately melted. Bashur can do that to you. She has a huge tail that is always wagging and eyes so full of love that no one can resist her.

Bashur was officially home.

Now each morning Bashur and I leave the house at six and head to my office — a car dealership northwest of Chicago. Everyone at work loves her. The floor of my office is strewn with her toys and chew bones. Being raised by a battalion of soldiers, she prefers men, and her favorite type of play is wrestling and roughhousing.

When the newspaper printed a story about her, she received countless baskets of goodies from well-wishers — so many that we began to donate them to the local animal shelter — and two women came to take pictures of Bashur to send to their sons overseas. Their sons, soldiers who had known Bashur in Iraq, wanted to make sure that she was okay.

At noon, Bashur and I take our daily walk in the fields around the office. It is a special time for both of us. I love watching her bound joyfully along, gazing with fascination at birds or becoming enthralled by a smell her large hound nose has unearthed. She seems amazed by all the wonderful things in her new life.

Bashur has certainly found her way into my heart as she has done with so many others. Sometimes when she sleeps, she rolls over and sighs, content, and I am happy. We owe this dog, and we want her to have the best life we can give her. There is really no way to repay her for the comfort she brought our son and so many others like him. But we can try....

~John Fenzel, Jr.
Chicken Soup for the Dog Lover's Soul

97

A New Coat

Today I bent the truth to be kind, and I have no regret,
for I am far surer of what is kind than I am of what is true.
~Robert Brault

I f there is one thing that growing up in the Midwest instilled in
me, besides my insatiable craving for red meat, it is a love for
football. I was born and raised in Cleveland, Ohio, and spent
most of my impressionable childhood years rooting for the Cleveland
Browns during the '80s. In those years, the Browns were referred to
as the "Cardiac Kids," seemingly destined to always come one drive,
fumble or interception away from a championship victory. Thousands
of fans would travel over an hour through inclement weather to
arrive at the dingy yet beloved Municipal Stadium and root for their
heroes. I was one of them. Back then, my room—like so many of my
friends'—was a shrine to Browns football. The walls were plastered
with banners and posters of Ozzie Newsome, Bernie Kosar and my
favorite player, Webster Slaughter.

Late in the 1987 season, I went with my dad to the nearby mall
so he could buy a new coat. We didn't have a lot of money, but my
mom convinced my dad to replace his old coat, which had some
pretty sizable holes it. I was only eleven, but my memory of that day
remains vivid. It was lightly snowing when we arrived at the mall.
The parking lot was plowed, but the lines were still buried under
the snow. My dad did an extremely crooked parking job next to an
uneven row of crooked cars. The minute the car came to a resting
stop, I was out of the door and racing up to the mall entrance, leaving

my dad trailing behind. As I approached the familiar tinted glass doors, one of them swung open and a huge figure came through it. The man was wearing a black jacket and sunglasses instead of a brown jersey with the number 84 printed on it, but I immediately recognized him. It was Webster Slaughter.

My heart began pounding, and I felt my ears go flush. I could barely contain my excitement as the man approached me. I looked up at my hero towering in front of me, and in a shaky voice said, "You're Webster Slaughter, right?" He stopped in midstride just as he was passing and glanced back. "Yeah. Are you a Browns fan?" he replied. I think I startled him as I began to rattle off at the mouth at a hundred words a second. I proceeded to tell him I was a huge Browns fan and that he was my favorite player. He smiled but began to walk away saying something about being in a big hurry, which I didn't hear because I hadn't stopped talking. Desperately, I yelled to his back for an autograph, but he made no sign that he heard me and briskly kept going. As fast as he had emerged, he was gone.

I felt a hand on my shoulder and looked up to see my dad. I wondered how long he had been there. "Who was that?" he asked. When I told him, he looked back up and squinted his eyes at the parking lot, but I knew Webster was already gone. I could feel my dad looking at me, probably for some details of the chance encounter, but I said nothing. As we approached the men's department, he finally asked me what had happened. "Nothing really. He was in a hurry. I just told him he was cool," I blurted back.

My dad gave me a concerned look, usually reserved for times he suspected I was about to do something to embarrass him. He dug into his pocket, pulled at a crumpled bunch of bills and handed me a few dollars. He told me to go play at the arcade while he picked out a coat. I grabbed the money and wandered off. About a half an hour later, my dad came for me and we headed home. Once there he opened the shopping bag in his hand. He told me he had a surprise and reached into it. "After you left, guess who I ran into?" he said with a smile on his face. I just stared blankly. "Webster Slaughter came into the store and said he saw me with you. He asked where you were and I said you were at the arcade. He said he went back to his car to get this for you, but you were gone." He pulled his hand out of the bag and in it was a glossy photo of Webster Slaughter signed, "To my greatest fan." I was so overjoyed I almost cried. I grabbed the picture and bolted up the stairs to my room.

Proudly, I placed the signed photo on my dresser. I just sat on my bed almost in tears and stared. It's hard to describe what I was feeling. Then I noticed something on the side. I looked closely at it and saw it was a small tag labeled $30. My first emotion was anger that I had been tricked. I stomped downstairs and yelled for my dad. There was no answer. Then I heard the sound of the shovel out front and went to the window. I stared out of the frosted pane at my dad, shoveling the walkway. He was wearing the same old coat with holes in the sleeves and back.

I thank my dad for the unacknowledged sacrifices he made for my siblings and me. I still have the picture of Webster Slaughter, but now on my dresser sits a picture of my dad and me.

~Peter Lim
Chicken Soup for the Teenage Soul II

98

BEING THERE

I can no other answer make, but, thanks, and thanks.
~*William Shakespeare*

The ninth hole at Caledonia Golf Course is a par-3 nestled in the mountains of south-central Pennsylvania. The tee is perched about seventy-five feet above a tiny green that is surrounded by a raised berm, with trees leaving only the narrowest of openings to the flagstick below: a donut in the middle of a forest clearing, 140 yards away, daring visitors to bite. I remember it well.

The last time I saw this hole was the first time I played golf with my father. I was fourteen. He swung a 9-iron, sailing the ball onto the rear edge of the green. The ball went into reverse and backed itself to within inches of the cup.

I stood amazed at the skill and power of my dad, hoping beyond hope that I could be just like him.

He handed me a 5-wood and said, "Okay, Don, just like that. Keep your head down and take a nice easy swing."

I obeyed his command but the ball did not obey mine. It flew with a wicked hook into the woods. Dad didn't say a word and tossed me another ball. Then another, and another and... six Wilsons later, I finally managed to dribble the ball down the hill and bounced it next to the mounded barrier protecting the green.

We walked down the mountain together and all I could do was stare at the man for whom I had found yet another reason to worship. He was the best golfer I had ever seen. Better than Palmer or even that new guy on the tour, Jack Something-or-other.

I can't tell you how many strokes it took to finally sink that ball on No. 9 at Caledonia. I do remember, however, what my father said when it was finally over: "You're getting there, son, keep up the good work." He gave me assurance, not ridicule, and I loved him even more.

That was thirty years ago. Dad died six years later. We played many rounds of golf together in those six years, but I could never achieve his greatness. My mind was too occupied with girls, war protests, school dramas and more girls. Dad, though, was a patient and willing teacher who allowed my dalliance and led me to the links and through the passages of adolescence.

It was that hole at Caledonia, though, that burned a vision in my soul. I have often described that particular par-3 to others, without regard to a reciprocated interest. It was not only the memory of a perfect golf hole I described, but a perfect day, a perfect shot and a perfect dad.

Today, the first time in thirty years, I stood at that same tee box on the same mountain. Not much had changed. It was the same trees, the same hill, the same green below, but a different me. I thought not about people, politics or work. I thought only of Dad and how a hole-in-one would sanctify and honor his memory. I reached into my bag and withdrew the 9-iron.

His mentoring filled my ears as it had not done in many years. Head down... feet shoulder-length apart... slow backswing... eye on the ball... follow through...!

With his instructions, I teed the ball up and prayed for redemption. My life has not turned out the equal of my, or most likely his, expectations. The trees, the hazards, the traps along the way got the better of me so many times. I have survived though, and I'm happy to report that my life has found the fairway again. But with this shot, with this ball, with his memory, I could atone for my sins.

I drew the club back slowly and reached for the heavens above, begging salvation and guidance. Head down, eye on the ball, follow-through. The club struck squarely and the ball soared into the crisp mountain air. I could swear there was a halo around it.

"You da man!" my partner screamed as the ball headed for the flag that was waving down below. I smiled and kept my eyes peeled on the tiny white dot as it moved away into the distance.

The mountain breezes and early morning mists play tricks, not only with the flight of golf balls, but on the eyes as well. What had looked to be a perfect shot suddenly turned bad. I screamed, "Go baby! Go! Turn! Get there!" The ball, which was out of earshot, did not heed my pleas. It landed short and plugged itself in the right-hand berm. It never had a chance.

Instead of agonizing over a shot of improbable proportions, I laughed at myself as I recalled Dad's most important lesson. "It's the little things in life that matter the most, Son."

Just being there was enough. I didn't need a hole-in-one or even to land the ball on the dance floor to obtain the peace and redemption I sought. He already gave that to me. He gave me the fortitude, the perseverance and the will to overcome difficulties many years ago. When I needed him most he was always there. He still is.

Thanks, Dad.

~Don Didio
Chicken Soup for the Golfer's Soul

His Father's Son

Good fathers make good sons.
~Author Unknown

I could feel the emotion in the air, as thick and heavy as a Florida summer night. I was part of the tens of thousands of NASCAR fans who were returning to Daytona for the Pepsi 400, only five months since the tragic death of the sport's hero, Dale Earnhardt, at the same track.

The stage was set for what would be an opportunity for all of us, in fact the entire NASCAR world, to mourn the loss of the man who epitomized the sport's image. This would be the chance for a mass catharsis that all too clearly underscores the high-speed drama of auto racing. Perhaps this is why the sport is so beloved by race fans, because NASCAR by its very nature is a metaphor for life.

Prior to the race, large crowds had gathered outside turn 4 where Earnhardt's car had crashed into the wall on the final lap of the Daytona 500. The Intimidator was in third place at the time, holding off all pursuers while protecting the first-place finish of teammates Michael Waltrip and the second-place finish of his son, Dale Earnhardt Jr.

Against this somber backdrop an unbelievable sporting event was unfolding at the Pepsi 400. Dale Earnhardt Jr. clearly had the best car all night. He led an incredible 116 of 160 laps, but the most dramatic twist came in the final minutes of the race. As anyone who has ever been to a NASCAR race knows, the final minutes of a NASCAR race are never spent sitting down, and Dale Earnhardt Jr. would give us all good reason to spring to our feet in excitement.

Earnhardt Jr. had been pushed back to seventh place for the restart after a late yellow flag. There were only nine laps left in the race, and many people all but conceded Junior's fate as a gallant effort. Then with only four and a half laps left, Dale Earnhardt Jr. seemed to summon up the same courage that won his father so many victories and endeared him to millions. On this night Dale Earnhardt Jr. would not be denied. He darted through the heavy traffic and overtook the first position only to be followed by an equally aggressive Michael Waltrip who would return the favor Junior's father had given him five months ago.

I do not remember shedding a tear at a sporting event since I played Little League baseball, yet the tears flowed from the eyes of what seemed like every fan in attendance, including myself.

Dale Earnhardt Jr. roared across the finish line as the champion in a performance that was as much a credit to his skills and crew as it was a tribute to his namesake.

Nothing can replace the loss of The Intimidator, the sport's fallen hero, but on this night we all were treated to a view of the strength and courage of a true NASCAR champion.

Like father, like son.

~Matthew E. Adams
Chicken Soup for the NASCAR Soul

MY SUNSHINE

Music, once admitted to the soul, becomes a sort of spirit, and never dies.
~Edward George Bulwer-Lytton

I looked out the window of the plane thinking, is this it? Will Dad be okay again or will this heart attack make me face the inevitable? When I arrived, I went straight to the Intensive Care Unit. Dad was hooked up to numerous tubes and machines. He smiled when he saw me and I took his hand. The look on his face said more than his words. This was going to be a tough one.

The next day the doctor met with Mom, my sister and me outside Dad's room. "I have good news and bad news. The good news is we got his heart started again. The bad news... his kidneys are failing." He paused a moment as we tried to figure out what it all meant. "We could put him on dialysis, however, he'd need surgery to implant a shunt in his arm for the treatments. I'm not sure his heart would make it through that surgery. He's eighty-one and has lived a good life. I suggest you unhook the machines and let him go."

The doctor's words floated off into space like clouds passing over. All I could hear was, "Let him go." I thought, I'm not making that decision. My sister can. My mother can.

But Mom didn't want to. Neither did my sister. They turned to me. I said, "I'm NOT going to make the decision. Dad should. He's coherent and after all it is his life."

I went to Dad.

There was a mutual admiration between Dad and me that formed in infancy and strengthened me in adulthood. He was my advisor, my counselor, my father, but more importantly my friend. I knew the love I had for him and he for me would get us through the experiences ahead.

I walked into his ICU room. "Dad, the doctor says they got your heart started again, but there is scar tissue and it's pretty damaged. And your kidneys are failing. You could go through dialysis to try to keep them going, but the doctor doesn't feel your heart is in any shape to handle even the initial procedure."

I stopped talking and waited. I saw him grow still and speculative. He looked up at me and said, "If I do this dialysis thing, will I ever get out of the hospital?"

"I don't know Dad."

"Will I be dependent on a machine for the rest of my life?"

"Yes."

My throat ached during the long pause that followed and I swallowed back tears. His eyes met mine and there was a slight smile on his face. He said pointing to the machines. "Then, unhook 'em."

We informed the doctor of his decision. Dad was disconnected from all the life-saving devices and moved to a private room. The doctor told us Dad would last twenty-four to forty-eight hours. Bracing ourselves for the inevitable as best we could, we spent the next two days by his side, falling into bed at night in total emotional exhaustion. The third day, Dad was still hanging on.

Day after day, I drove Mom to the hospital. Fifteen days passed. I was really stressed. I'd been away from home three weeks now. I was worried about my family, my business, my life. Dad had been in and out of a coma for days and seemed oblivious to my presence. As I drove into the parking lot, I talked to the higher power above trying to negotiate a deal. Tears streamed down my face as I pulled into the parking space. I had to tell Dad I needed to go home to my family and work.

I walked into his room to find him sleeping with his arms folded across his chest. I looked down at his loving face and hands. This was the man who had supported me in everything I endeavored. This was the man who never missed a concert, athletic event, graduation, or birth of a baby. This was the man who had been there for me every day of my life. How could I even think about going home? He had walked through forty-four years with me, the least I could do was walk the last mile with him.

I held his hand and started humming. My Dad loved music and had a beautiful tenor voice. He always sang to me as a child. He'd bounce into my room every morning to wake me. Enthusiastic and happy, he sang in his most operatic tenor voice to the tune of "Oh My Papa" these lyrics: "Oh my Suzanne, to me you are so wonderful!" He made sure it reached a decibel that not only woke me but half the neighborhood. I would usually put my pillow over my head and beg for mercy. What an awesome message he gave every morning before I went off to school and work. What a positive reinforcement his songs were.

Now it was my turn. I began humming "You Are My Sunshine" as it was a favorite of ours often sung around the family piano. When I finished, Dad didn't budge. His eyes remained shut. He didn't hear a thing. I started to cry.

Dad opened his eyes, "Oh Suzi, I'll never take your sunshine away." He closed his eyes and went back into that familiar deep sleep.

Five hours later, he died.

My Dad was the sunshine in my life and continues to be so in spirit. There have been dark moments and days since he died, but I always look up and say, "Okay, Dad, send me some sunshine."

Without fail, the sun always comes out.

~Suzanne Vaughan
Chicken Soup for the Caregiver's Soul

HOME RUN

I was ten. Life that summer was softball, climbing trees, pollywog hunting and bike riding, in that order.

Our city street was made for softball. A well-hit grounder could skip for a mile down that paved "field." There was, thankfully, very little traffic to disrupt our practice and games. Whenever a car would approach, we simply ambled off to the curbsides, waving to the driver as he or she passed.

Amazingly, I remember not a single accident, mishap or problem with this arrangement... except one. Just one.

The instant that softball shot off from my bat, I knew I had messed up. Big time. In a neighborhood graced with houses lining both sides of the street, room for error was limited. Hours upon hours of practice greatly improved our odds of keeping the ball between curbs and thereby avoiding houses, lawns and cars parked in driveways. Any ball hit beyond either curb was, by necessity, a foul.

Immediately following the earsplitting shatter of that enormous square of glass, my teammates split to parts unknown. This was indeed a grave situation and not the time to contemplate the obvious fact that I had a flock of chickens for friends.

Now, the Hansons were not trolls. Well, at least as long as no one was trip-trap-trip-trapping over their lawn. Up to this point, they had never, as far as I knew, killed any neighbor child. But, this was a serious offense.

Being one of eight kids and the daughter of a milkman, I was aware that, mostly, money was for essential things — not to be taken lightly. I also knew, instinctively, that my dad would replace that window. I was a minor child. My dad was my dad and responsible for me — for better or worse. He would pay for the window because I broke it. Simple as that. The Hansons had a giant jagged gaping hole in the front of their house, and I had put it there.

I finally set my bat down, not wanting to carry a smoking gun with me on this particular journey. Suddenly, each leg weighed about a hundred pounds, as I trudged up the walkway to the porch of the House of Horrors.

No need to knock. Mrs. Hanson wasted no time greeting me, with the door wide open, and escorted me inside to this new vantage point of the crime scene. Like a stoic wooden judge, her grandson's highchair stood starkly in that very room. Mrs. Hanson was saying, "What if he had been sitting there?" Even though the baby was not in the house, the highchair was several yards from the window, and the window screen was still intact, I absolutely felt as if I had killed the baby.

About a year later, I was released and walked down the sidewalk, toward home. I wondered if it were possible to feel any worse. Now, I had to face my dad with what I had done.

I was surprised to see Mr. Terryberry leaving my house. He was an across-the-street neighbor and had never come over before. His son and daughter were on my street softball team — part of the chicken clutch.

I wondered briefly if perhaps his kids had told him what I did. Or, maybe he was an eyewitness, and he had come over to squeal to my dad.

I knew I was not going to get hit. I knew I wouldn't even get yelled at. But, my dad would no doubt say, "Man!" in an agitated manner, and he might grumble for a few seconds, before walking next door to apologize and measure the hole where the window belonged. Then he would drive off to buy the replacement.

He would be disappointed. And, it was my fault.

When I walked in the door and stepped into our living room,

my dad was right there to meet me. I avoided looking right at him, but plainly heard what he said: "I am proud of you."

Oh great. There was some kind of enormous misunderstanding. Anxious to enlighten him and get the truth out, I blurted, "I was the one who hit the ball!"

"I know," my dad said. He had kind eyes. "Mr. Terryberry saw the whole thing."

I was still confused. I was missing something here. My dad, Mr. Character, was proud of me?

He told me Mr. Terryberry had seen his son pitch the ball to me, saw me belt it, saw the window shatter, and could hardly believe his eyes when his kids and the others hightailed it and left me standing to face the music alone. He thought that I would surely drop that bat and follow the others. He said that he was pleasantly surprised to see me walk up, instead, to face Mrs. Hanson.

Mr. Terryberry told my dad, "I am as proud of your kid as I am ashamed of my own."

And, it was Mr. Terryberry who bought the replacement window—and would not accept any argument.

My dad was proud of me and I was on Cloud Nine... until he said no more batting in the street—only ball and gloves.

But, Cloud Eight didn't feel too shabby.

~Alison Peters
Chicken Soup for the Grandparent's Soul

Share with Us

We would like to know how these stories affected you and which ones were your favorites. Please e-mail us and let us know.

We also would like to share your stories with future readers. You may be able to help another reader, and become a published author at the same time. Please send us your own stories and poems for our future books. Some of our past contributors have launched writing and speaking careers from the publication of their stories in our books!

Your stories have the best chance of being used if you submit them through our web site, at:

www.chickensoup.com

If you do not have access to the Internet, you may submit your stories by mail or by facsimile. Please do not send us any book manuscripts, unless through a literary agent, as these will be automatically discarded.

Chicken Soup for the Soul
P.O. Box 700
Cos Cob, CT 06807-0700
Fax 203-861-7194

Chicken Soup for the Soul®

More Chicken Soup
About the Authors
Acknowledgments

Inside Basketball

Chicken Soup has a slam dunk with its first sports book in years, and its first on basketball, with the Orlando Magic's very own Pat Williams, well-known author and motivational speaker. Pat has drawn on his basketball industry connections to compile great stories from on and off the court. Fans will be inspired, surprised, and amused by inside stories from well-known coaches and players, fascinating looks behind the scenes, and anecdotes from the fans.

Tales of Golf & Sport

Golfers are a special breed. They endure bad weather, early wake up calls, great expense, and "interesting" clothing to engage in their favorite sport. This book contains Chicken Soup's 101 best stories about golfers, golfing, and other sports. Chicken Soup's approach to sports books has always been unique — professional and amateur athletes contribute stories from the heart, yielding a book about the human side of golf and other sports, not a how-to book.

The Golf Book

Chicken Soup and Golf Digest magazine's Max Adler and team have put together a great collection of personal stories that will inspire, amuse, and surprise golfers. Celebrity golfers, weekend golfers, beginners, and pros all share the best stories they've told at the 19th hole about good times on and off the course. Chicken Soup's golf books have always been very successful — with the addition of Golf Digest's industry connections, this book should hit a hole in one.

MORE BOOKS FOR MEN!

Dads & Daughters

Whether she is ten years old or fifty – she will always be his little girl. And daughters take care of their dads too, whether it is a tea party for two at age five or loving care fifty years later. This wide-ranging exploration of the relationship between fathers and daughters provides an entirely new reading experience for Chicken Soup fans, with selections from forty past Chicken Soup books. Stories were written by fathers about their daughters and by daughters about their fathers, celebrating the special bond between fathers and daughters.

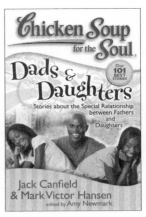

On Being a Parent

Parenting is the hardest and most rewarding job in the world. This upbeat and compelling new book includes the best selections on parenting from Chicken Soup's rich history, with 101 stories carefully selected to appeal to both mothers and fathers. This is a great book for couples to share, whether they are just embarking on their new adventure as parents or reflecting on their lifetime experience.

Moms & Sons

There is a special bond between mothers and their sons and it never goes away. This new book contains the 101 best stories and poems from Chicken Soup's library honoring that lifelong relationship between mothers and their male offspring. These heartfelt and loving stories written by mothers, grandmothers, and sons, about each other, span generations and show how the mother-son bond transcends time.

MORE
BOOKS FOR FAMILIES!

More books for Men

Chicken Soup for the Veteran's Soul 1-55874-937-3
Chicken Soup for the Baseball Fan's Soul 1-55874-965-9
Chicken Soup for the Gardener's Soul 1-55874-966-7
Chicken Soup for the Fisherman's Soul 0-7573-0145-2
Chicken Soup for the Golfer's Soul 1-55874-658-7
Chicken Soup for the Golfer's Soul,
The Second Round 1-55874-982-9
Chicken Soup for the NASCAR Soul 0-7573-0100-2
Chicken Soup for the Father's Soul 1-55874-894-6
Chicken Soup for the Grandparent's Soul 1-55874-974-8
Chicken Soup for the Father & Daughter Soul 0-7573-0252-1
Chicken Soup for the Single Parent's Soul 0-7573-0241-6

Books for Teens

Chicken Soup for the Soul: Preteens Talk
Inspiration and Support for Preteens from Kids Just Like Them
978-1-935096-00-9

Chicken Soup for the Soul: Teens Talk Growing Up
Stories about Growing Up, Meeting Challenges, and
Learning from Life 978-1-935096-01-6

Chicken Soup for the Soul: Teens Talk Tough Times
Stories about the Hardest Parts of Being a Teenager
978-1-935096-03-0

Chicken Soup for the Soul: Teens Talk Relationships
Stories about Family, Friends, and Love
978-1-935096-06-1

Chicken Soup for the Soul: Christian Teen Talk
Christian Teens Share Their Stories of Support, Inspiration and Growing Up
978-1-935096-12-2

Chicken Soup for the Soul: Christian Kids
Stories to Inspire, Amuse, and Warm the Hearts of Christian Kids and Their
Parents
978-1-935096-13-9

Books for Families

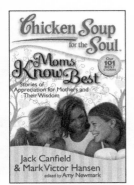

Moms Know Best
Stories of Appreciation for Mothers
and Their Wisdom
978-1-935096-02-3

"Mom will know where it is... what to say... how to fix it." This is the first Chicken Soup book to focus on the pervasive wisdom of mothers everywhere. It includes the 101 best stories from Chicken Soup's library on our perceptive, understanding, and insightful mothers. These stories celebrate the special bond between mothers and children, our mothers' unerring wisdom about everything from the mundane to the life-changing, and the hard work that goes into being a mother.

Grand and Great
Grandparents and Grandchildren Share Their
Stories of Love and Wisdom
978-1-935096-09-2

A parent becomes a new person the day the first grandchild is born. Formerly serious and responsible adults go on shopping sprees for toys and baby clothing, smile incessantly, pull out photo albums that they "just happen to have" with them, and proudly display baby seats in their cars. Grandparents dote on their grandchildren, and grandchildren love them back with all their hearts. This new book includes the best stories on being a grandparent from 33 past Chicken Soup books, representing a new reading experience for even the most devoted Chicken Soup fan.

Chicken Soup for the Soul

Who Is
Jack Canfield?

J ack Canfield is the co-creator and editor of the *Chicken Soup for the Soul* series, which *Time* magazine has called "the publishing phenomenon of the decade." Jack is also the co-author of eight other bestselling books including *The Success Principles™: How to Get from Where You Are to Where You Want to Be, Dare to Win, The Aladdin Factor, You've Got to Read This Book,* and *The Power of Focus: How to Hit Your Business and Personal and Financial Targets with Absolute Certainty.*

Jack has recently developed a telephone coaching program and an online coaching program based on his most recent book *The Success Principles.* He also offers a seven-day *Breakthrough to Success* seminar every summer, which attracts 400 people from fifteen countries around the world.

Jack is the CEO of the Canfield Training Group in Santa Barbara, California, and founder of the Foundation for Self-Esteem in Culver City, California. He has conducted intensive personal and professional development seminars on the principles of success for over a million people in twenty-three countries. Jack is a dynamic keynote speaker and he has spoken to hundreds of thousands of others at more than 1,000 corporations, universities, professional conferences and conventions, and has been seen by millions more on national television shows such as *The Today Show, Fox and Friends, Inside Edition, Hard Copy, CNN's Talk Back Live, 20/20, Eye to Eye,* and the *NBC Nightly News* and the *CBS Evening News.*

Jack is the recipient of many awards and honors, including three honorary doctorates and a *Guinness World Records Certificate* for having seven books from the *Chicken Soup for the Soul* series appearing on the *New York Times* bestseller list on May 24, 1998.

To write to Jack or for inquiries about Jack as a speaker, his coaching programs, trainings or seminars, use the following contact information:

Jack Canfield
The Canfield Companies
P.O. Box 30880 • Santa Barbara, CA 93130
phone: 805-563-2935 • fax: 805-563-2945
E-mail: info@jackcanfield.com
www.jackcanfield.com

Who Is
Mark Victor Hansen?

Mark Victor Hansen is the co-founder of *Chicken Soup for the Soul*, along with Jack Canfield. He is also a sought-after keynote speaker, bestselling author, and marketing maven.

For more than thirty years, Mark has focused solely on helping people from all walks of life reshape their personal vision of what's possible. His powerful messages of possibility, opportunity, and action have created powerful change in thousands of organizations and millions of individuals worldwide.

Mark's credentials include a lifetime of entrepreneurial success. He is a prolific writer with many bestselling books, such as *The One Minute Millionaire*, *Cracking the Millionaire Code*, How to Make the Rest of Your Life the Best of Your Life, *The Power of Focus*, *The Aladdin Factor*, and *Dare to Win*, in addition to the *Chicken Soup for the Soul* series. Mark has had a profound influence in the field of human potential through his library of audios, videos, and articles in the areas of big thinking, sales achievement, wealth building, publishing success, and personal and professional development.

Mark is the founder of the *MEGA Seminar Series*. *MEGA Book Marketing University* and *Building Your MEGA Speaking Empire* are annual conferences where Mark coaches and teaches new and aspiring authors, speakers, and experts on building lucrative publishing and speaking careers. Other MEGA events include *MEGA Info-Marketing* and *My MEGA Life*.

He has appeared on *Oprah*, *CNN*, and *The Today Show*. He has been quoted in *Time*, *U.S. News & World Report*, *USA Today*, *New York Times*, and *Entrepreneur* and has had countless radio interviews, assuring our planet's people that "You can easily create the life you deserve."

As a philanthropist and humanitarian, Mark works tirelessly for organizations such as Habitat for Humanity, American Red Cross, March of Dimes, Childhelp USA, and many others. He is the recipient of numerous awards that honor his entrepreneurial spirit, philanthropic heart, and business acumen. He is a lifetime member of the Horatio Alger Association of Distinguished Americans, an organization that honored Mark with the prestigious Horatio Alger Award for his extraordinary life achievements.

Mark Victor Hansen is an enthusiastic crusader of what's possible and is driven to make the world a better place.

Mark Victor Hansen & Associates, Inc.
P.O. Box 7665 • Newport Beach, CA 92658
phone: 949-764-2640 • fax: 949-722-6912
www.markvictorhansen.com

Who Is
Amy Newmark?

Amy Newmark was recently named publisher of Chicken Soup for the Soul, after a thirty-year career as a writer, speaker, financial analyst, and business executive in the worlds of finance and telecommunications.

Amy is a graduate of Harvard College, where she majored in Portuguese, minored in French, and traveled extensively. She is also the mother of two children in college and has two grown stepchildren.

After a long career writing books on telecommunications, voluminous financial reports, business plans, and corporate press releases, Chicken Soup for the Soul is a breath of fresh air for Amy. She has fallen in love with Chicken Soup for the Soul and its life-changing books, and found it a true pleasure to conceptualize, compile, and edit the "101 Best Stories" books for our readers.

The best way to contact Chicken Soup for the Soul is through our web site, at www.chickensoup.com. This will always get the fastest attention.

If you do not have access to the Internet, please contact us by mail or by facsimile.

Chicken Soup for the Soul
P.O. Box 700
Cos Cob, CT 06807-0700
Fax 203-861-7194

Chicken Soup for the Soul

Thank You!

Our first thanks go to our loyal readers who have inspired the entire Chicken Soup team for the past fifteen years. Your appreciative letters and e-mails have reminded us why we work so hard on these books.

We owe huge thanks to all of our contributors as well. We know that you pour your hearts and souls into the stories and poems that you share with us, and ultimately with each other. We appreciate your willingness to open up your lives to other Chicken Soup readers.

We can only publish a small percentage of the stories that are submitted, but we read every single one and even the ones that do not appear in a book have an influence on us and on the final manuscripts.

As always, we would like to thank the entire staff of Chicken Soup for the Soul for their help on this project and the 101 Best series in general.

Among our California staff, we would especially like to single out the following people:

- D'ette Corona, who is the heart and soul of the Chicken Soup publishing operation, and who put together the first draft of this manuscript

- Barbara LoMonaco for invaluable assistance in obtaining the fabulous quotations that add depth and meaning to this book

- Patty Hansen for her extra special help with the permissions for these fabulous stories and for her amazing knowledge of the Chicken Soup library and Patti Clement for her help with permissions and other organizational matters.

In our Connecticut office, we would like to thank our able editorial assistants, Valerie Howlett and Madeline Clapps, for their assistance in setting up our new offices, editing, and helping us put together the best possible books.

We would also like to thank our master of design, Creative Director and book producer Brian Taylor at Pneuma Books, LLC, for his brilliant vision for our covers and interiors.

Finally, none of this would be possible without the business and creative leadership of our CEO, Bill Rouhana, and our president, Bob Jacobs.

Chicken Soup

www.chickensoup.com

for the Soul